THEY CAME FROM EVERYWHERE

Twelve Who Helped Mold Modern Israel

BOOKS BY ROBERT ST. JOHN

They Came from Everywhere

The Man Who Played God

Israel: World Library

Builder of Israel

The Boss

Ben-Gurion

Foreign Correspondent

Through Malan's Africa

This Was My World

Tongue of the Prophets

Shalom Means Peace

The Silent People Speak

It's Always Tomorrow

From the Land of Silent People

Robert St. John

THEY CAME
FROM EVERYWHERE

Twelve Who Helped Mold

Modern Israel

COWARD-McCANN, Inc.   *New York*

Contents

A section of illustrations follows page 130

Author's Preface

For 1,878 years (starting with the destruction of the Second Temple) a persecuted and scattered people dreamed of a return some day to the land God had promised to Abraham, Isaac, and Jacob, and in which, during the time of David and Solomon, they had had their brief Golden Age. While the majority contented themselves with hoping and praying, a handful, coming from the various lands of the Dispersal, worked in divers ways to fulfill prophecy and bring the ancient dream to bright realization. It is a story of long struggle, heartbreaking handicaps, opposition that was often overwhelming, assistance that sometimes came from surprising sources. It is one of the great epics of human history.

This book is that story, told in the form of the biographies of 12 individuals who played vital roles. They were not the only architects and builders of the new Israel. They were not, necessarily, the 12 most important. But each is representative of a group, a force, or a concept that helped make the reconstruction possible. Each chapter is a brief biographical novel, complete in itself, yet, read chronologically, they tell the story of the only rebirth of a nation that has ever taken place.

During the years that *They Came from Everywhere* was in preparation, the author consulted at least a hundred men and women, on three continents—from ambassadors to nurses in Hadassah Hospital; from a man on a tractor at Degania to a man behind a great desk in Washington. From them came as many combinations and permutations of names as the number of people consulted. The final choice was entirely the author's. He apologizes to the friends, relatives, descendants, and partisans of those noble and important characters not selected. This is not a definitive history book. It aims only at portraying 12 vibrant personalities from 12 different points of the compass—a girl with a Sten gun and a man with a hoe, a rebel and a humanitarian, a philologist and a chemist, a labor organizer and a playwright, a rabbi and a soldier, a French baron and a shy young girl from Yemen. Except for the subjects of Chapters 10 and 12, no living persons are included. The length of the chapters has no significance; later chapters are shorter only because by then the reader knows all the historical details. The order in which the 12 are presented is not in the order of importance, but is an attempt to make a chronological story. Herzl had to be first, Zivia last. The stories in between overlap. They were intentionally made to overlap, in the manner of telling, so that by the time the reader reaches the last page he will feel he has become intimately acquainted with 12 very diverse personalities, but 12 whose lives were closely entwined, because they had one hope, one dream, one vision.

—ROBERT ST. JOHN

Geneva, Switzerland
July, 1962

THEY CAME FROM EVERYWHERE

Twelve Who Helped Mold Modern Israel

Chapter 1

If you will it,
It is no dream.

—THEODOR HERZL

ONE BRIGHT SUNDAY AFTERNOON in June 1895—it happened to be Pentecost—a tall, square-shouldered man with a mass of black, wavy hair, a bushy mustache, and a black beard so enormous that it hid his entire shirtfront, hired a carriage in Paris to take him to the rue de l'Élysée. The driver could not help but notice his passenger's nervousness. Every few blocks he consulted his watch; frequently he opened a large brown envelope and flicked through the 22 pages of white paper it contained, glancing again and again at the German words in his own fine handwriting that he knew already almost by heart; several times he took off, then put on again, the gloves he had bought especially for the occasion.

After a long drive through streets crowded with Sunday promenaders, the carriage arrived at a great stone palace. A guard at the entrance halted the carriage until the black-bearded man said, "I am expected," and gave his name. Several moments later he was being led by a servant through a foyer and up a grand staircase to the billiard room, where he was asked to wait.

Theodor Herzl was not easily overawed. His own family was well-off and his work as a journalist had frequently taken him

into the homes of the great. But what his observant eyes saw
during his first few minutes in the palace of Baron Maurice de
Hirsch made an impression on him he never forgot. "Riches affect me only in the guise of beauty," he was fond of saying.
Here was beauty whichever way he turned: Gobelin tapestries
in rich, faded colors; marble statues perfect of line and propor-
tion; great oil paintings he realized were all the work of the
Masters. He tried to shake himself loose from the spell the
beauty had put upon him and get his mind back to the purpose
of his visit.

The man he had come to see was one of the great multimil-
lionaires of Europe; his grandfather had been the first Jewish
landowner in Bavaria; from his father he had inherited an immense fortune, which he doubled by marrying a woman of almost equal wealth, and since then had multiplied many times
as a builder of railroads in Russia, Turkey, and the Balkans,
and by the success of his many copper and sugar enterprises. But
it was Baron de Hirsch's reputation as a philanthropist, with an
especial interest in the plight of his fellow Jews, that had
brought Herzl here on this Pentecost Sunday. Four years ago
the Baron had founded the Jewish Colonization Association to
establish agricultural settlements for European Jews in countries abroad, especially in Argentina. Although he was pouring
his wealth into the enterprise at the rate of many millions of
dollars a year, only three thousand ghetto Jews until now had
been transplanted, and they were beset by many troubles. Few
people considered this experiment much of a success.

As Theodor Herzl paced up and down the billiard room
waiting for the Baron he realized he would never be able to explain in a few words—or even in a whole volume of words—the
background of his visit. How to explain to a complete stranger
his own sudden interest in his fellow Jews and their problems?
He could hardly explain it to himself.

In Budapest, where he was born, assimilation had been the
style. Many Jewish families took Magyar names, boasted of
their Magyar background, and tried to lose their uniqueness by
identifying themselves as closely as possible with the culture of
the country. The Herzls did none of these things. Theodor was
brought up to know that he was Jewish and to be proud of it;

Passover and Chanukah were celebrated in the home; the boy learned enough Hebrew to read passages from the Torah; when he was thirteen he became a Bar Mitzvah; on Friday evenings he went with his father to the synagogue next door to the Herzl home. Yet the milieu of his youth was not one of intense Jewishness, at least by Eastern European standards.

One of his earliest boyhood recollections was of being caned by the teacher in a Jewish preparatory school because he did not know the details of the Exodus of the Jews from Egypt.

In 1878 the Herzl family moved to Vienna. Theodor, age eighteen, had already acquired a deep love of the written word and had filled many notebooks with his own poems, short plays, and essays on sometimes inconsequential and often frivolous subjects, but he was persuaded to enter the University of Vienna as a law student.

He was twenty-one and halfway through his law course when he chanced one day upon a copy of a book that had just been published: *The Jewish Question as a Problem of the Racial Damage Inflicted Upon the Existence, Morals, and Culture of the Peoples of the World.* The author was Eugen Karl Dühring, German philosopher and economist, who brazenly advocated an outright racist war against Jews everywhere. The young law student was at first shocked that such blatant anti-Semitism should be given the status of a serious literary work. Then he was inspired to write several essays of his own on "the problem." He had no outlet for his writings, so his denunciation of Dühring gathered dust, but from then on "the question gnawed and tugged at me; it tormented me and rendered me profoundly unhappy."

When he was twenty-three he withdrew from a student fraternity, Albia, when it began to develop anti-Semitic tendencies.

After six years of study he won his degree, but a legal career held no interest for him; he wanted to travel and to write, and because his father had become even more successful as a businessman in Vienna than he had been in Budapest, the son was able to indulge his fancy. He roamed over Austria, Germany, Switzerland, Italy, France, and finally Spain.

One night in the German city of Mainz he was leaving a cheap cabaret when someone in the shadows shouted "Hep!

Hep!" at him. (In the Middle Ages anti-Semites would hurl at Jews a strange combination of Greek and Latin words: *Hierosolyma est perdita!*—Jerusalem is lost! Gradually it was reduced to "Hep! Hep!" the first letter of each word.) As young Herzl stopped in his tracks a crowd of ruffians laughed coarsely. It was his first personal encounter with the disease. From then on it seemed impossible to avoid it. "It lurked for me around every turn and corner."

Once in those early days when he was feeling especially bitter he thought he might be able to find happiness if he "slipped over into some corner of the Christian fold." But later he spoke of this whim as "only a faint vagary born of adolescent weakness," and he stated flatly in his own handwriting that he never seriously considered becoming baptized or changing his name, either then or later.

Wherever he went after leaving the university, he kept busy writing his impressions. Each time he returned home he would try to interest Vienna journals in publishing his work. One day the editor of an important paper advised him to adopt a pen name "a little less Jewish-sounding." The young man flatly refused and asked for the return of his manuscript. The editor hesitated, then reluctantly agreed to publish it with a Theodor Herzl by-line.

From time to time the Jewish question, as young Herzl called it, continued to bother him. "I sighed over it and jeered at it; it made me unhappy, but still it never gripped me. . . ." As proof, he wrote in rapid succession a considerable number of popular and rather inconsequential plays that were produced in Germany, Austria, Bohemia, and even in New York. He also sold frequent articles and essays—few of more than passing interest—to papers in Vienna and Berlin. Two collections of his writings were published as books. His talent led to a Vienna paper appointing him its literary editor. His popularity so impressed the daughter of a wealthy Jewish family, Julie Naschauer, that she consented to marry him, apparently with the vision of an eternally gay social life as the wife of so brilliant and witty a writer.

The first of three Herzl children were born during the first year of their marriage, but the incompatability of husband and wife soon compelled the young writer to pack up and leave home, "experimentally," as he explained to friends. Something else was bothering him besides his marital troubles. That winter a dear friend, Heinrich Kana, committed suicide. His ghost seemed to haunt Herzl.

After taking leave of his wife and child, he went to the Pyrenees and there conceived the idea of writing a novel in which Heinrich Kana would be the main character and in which the central theme would be anti-Semitism. He intended to contrast the plight of the masses of poor Jews who were always the first victims of anti-Semitism, with the relative security of the wealthy, who, he had decided, were the ones "actually and mainly responsible for it." While the plot was taking form in his mind he supported himself by sending a constant stream of articles to the papers of Vienna and Berlin. The excitement of his new surroundings and his freedom inspired him to write so brilliantly that the *Neue Freie Presse,* Vienna's leading daily, offered him a position as its Paris correspondent at 1,200 francs per month (almost $300) plus expenses and an additional 100 francs for each essay printed—an enormous newspaper salary for 1891. His acceptance led to a reconciliation with his "beloved Julie," as he called her, to whom his new post meant not only an opportunity to live in the most dazzling capital of the world, but also a chance to escape from the matriarchal influence of her mother-in-law, whom she blamed for almost wrecking the marriage by her idolatry of Theodor.

By the time Herzl arrived in Paris he had written twenty plays, most of them comedies, as well as hundreds of miscellaneous articles.

In the French capital he became as brilliant a reporter as he already was an essayist. He wrote of current history in terms of the people involved; the great, the near-great, and the obscure. He studied the foibles and the machinations of statesmen and exposed them. He wrote of election frauds, parliamentary intrigue, and unemployment riots. He sat in the press gallery of the Chamber of Deputies through many momentous debates. In the excitement of his new life he put aside the notes for his novel of Heinrich Kana. Because of his failure to extirpate the ghost of his deceased friend, it continued to haunt him and probably had a subconscious effect on him for years.

Five years before Herzl arrived in Paris, Edouard Drumont, an influential French journalist and author, had published a two-volume work, *La France Juive,* purporting to prove that France was in the clutches of evil Jewish forces. Now he started an anti-Semitic newspaper, *The Free World,* which concentrated on questioning the loyalty of the handful of Jewish officers—less than 500—in the French Army. One of the court trials Herzl covered during his first year as a Paris correspondent was a libel action against Drumont which came to a climax when the editor leaped to his feet and shouted, "Down with the German Jews! France for Frenchmen!" The cry was taken up by Drumont's friends, who had crowded the courtroom. It was another scene that imprinted itself deeply on the subconscious of Theodor Herzl.

He reported how a bill to disbar all Jews from public office won 160 votes in the Chamber of Deputies. He wrote about a series of duels between Jews and anti-Semites who had publicly insulted them. When a young French-Jewish army officer was fatally stabbed and disorders broke out at the funeral among the forty or fifty thousand sympathizers in attendance, Herzl's article expressed a hope that France's traditional "justice and fraternity" would shine forth through the clouds of the tragedy. He reviewed plays in which the Jewish theme was dominant, and wrote critiques of books that dealt with the problem. More and more the question gnawed and tugged.

One of the front-page stories Herzl covered during his early Paris days was the arrest, trial, and public degrading of a French army officer, Alfred Dreyfus, who was found guilty of high treason for selling military secrets to Germany. Years later Herzl himself encouraged the myth that the Dreyfus Affair, as it came to be known, had influenced him in writing his celebrated pamphlet on the establishment of a Jewish homeland. Actually, he reported the trial for his newspaper as that of a French officer who just happened to be a Jew. Some of his critics even gained the impression that he believed Dreyfus guilty. It was not until after publication of his history-making pamphlet that the anti-

Semitic ramifications of the Dreyfus Affair began to come to light.

After he had been in Paris for about two years, Herzl conceived what he momentarily thought was a brilliant idea. He wanted to obtain an audience with the Pope and say to him, "If you will help us Jews combat anti-Semitism, in return I will lead a great movement for the conversion of Jews to Christianity." With his flare for the dramatic, Herzl imagined a scene that would live for ages in Judaic-Christian history. The setting would be St. Stephen's Cathedral in Vienna. (He intended to try out the solution first in Austria.) At exactly twelve o'clock noon on a Sunday there would be a great noise of church bells and toward the Cathedral would come a solemn parade of thousands of Jewish converts, "not with shame or sorrow, as individuals have hitherto gone over, but with a proud gesture." In his scheme the leaders, himself included, would remain within the Jewish faith and would be the "final generation," but all their children would become converts "before they reached the age of independent decision, after which conversion looks like an act of cowardice or calculation."

Herzl was so serious about it that he even tried to persuade his newspaper to sponsor the idea, but one of the editors told him, "For a hundred generations your race has clung to Judaism. You are proposing now to set yourself up as the man to end this stand. This you cannot do and have no right to do." Besides, he added pragmatically, Herzl would never be able to get an audience with the Pope.

It was only a short time later that this idea was supplanted in Herzl's mind by another. He had gone to visit the Austrian-Jewish literary and music critic Ludwig Speidel, one of the most brilliant minds in contemporary Vienna. While walking across the countryside, they began trying to analyze anti-Semitism. Herzl, in his sensational manner of expression, advanced the theory that "anti-Semitism will do us Jews no harm, for I hold it to be a movement useful for the development of Jewish character . . . we are educated only through hard knocks . . . a sort of Darwinian mimicry will set in . . . Jews will adapt themselves."

An hour later, on his way in to town, two young men, one in

a cadet uniform, stared at his great black beard and at what Herzl himself used to call his "Jewish nose" and shouted "*Saujud!*" at him. It was a vile and insulting word, the most polite translation possible being "dirty Jew."

Herzl's first impulse was to stop his cab and give chase, then the irony of the situation amused him. So short a time ago he had been so philosophical!

Two or three months later, while posing in the studio of the sculptor Samuel Beer, who was doing a bust of him, Herzl began expounding the idea that it was impossible for European Jews to escape from the ghetto. The more he talked the more animated he became and on his way home he conceived the idea of writing a play he would call *The New Ghetto,* based on the theme that the modern Jew, even though he escaped all legal restrictions and emancipated himself from Jewish tradition, still lived in a spiritual ghetto; that he must free himself from this self-enslavement.

The next morning he set to work in a frenzy. For the next three weeks he wrote at white heat. The longer he worked the more he convinced himself that he owed it to his fellow Jews to apply his talents to finding some solution of their problem. For the first time in years he went to a synagogue. To his surprise he found the service solemn and impressive. This was his first contact with any large number of French Jews. He studied the faces and decided they looked no different than the faces he remembered in the synagogue he and his father had attended in Budapest when he was a boy. "Bold, curved noses; furtive and cunning eyes." Yet the thought kept recurring to him, these are human beings whom men slander without taking the trouble to know.

Now an inner turmoil began to obsess him. He was unable to explain it even to himself. An eruption seemed to be taking place inside his mind and his soul. He pushed the unfinished play aside and decided to write, instead, a book he would call *The Situation of the Jews.* As he was debating what form it should take he went to see Alphonse Daudet to ask the great French novelist to write a story for the *Neue Freie Presse.* During their conversation the Jewish question was mentioned and Daudet, although confessing himself to be an anti-Semite, gave Herzl a piece of advice: "If you want to write something about the problem that will live, make it a novel. Remember *Uncle Tom's Cabin!*"

Herzl took the idea home with him, but he was too restless to sit down patiently and try to plot a novel. He felt it was a time for action. He was annoyed with intellectuals who, while anti-Semitism was on the march, did nothing but talk of preserving Jewish culture. He was contemptuous of wealthy Jews whose desire to protect their own comfortable life kept them from going to the aid of their brothers in distress. He was overwhelmed with the need for explosive self-expression. He was impatient with God.

Suddenly he conceived the idea of seeking an interview with Baron de Hirsch. In his letter asking for an appointment for a "Jewish-political conversation" he suggested it might be of such importance that it would have an effect on the future, long after they were both dead. The Baron replied that Herzl should put anything he wanted to say in writing and send it by the post. Indignantly Herzl wrote back that he knew such a communication would never be read, then added that the Baron thus far in life had distinguished himself principally as a philanthropist, "but I want to show you the way to become something more." Back came an appointment for Pentecost Sunday. This greatly increased his feverish agitation. He skipped meals as he covered more and more pieces of paper with more and more thousands of words of notes. He wrote an outline of what he wanted to say, when he should have been composing articles for his paper. He scribbled as he walked down the street, as he waited for the curtain to go up in the theater, as he lay in bed too excited to sleep.

And now here he was, in the great man's billiard room, clutching his new pair of gloves in one hand and the twenty-two pages of his outline in the other. It was divided into three sections:

> Introduction
> Uplifting of the Jewish Race
> Immigration

Finally the Baron appeared and escorted him into his study. Herzl was trembling with nervousness, but he blurted out, "Can you give me an hour? If not, I would rather not begin at all."

The Baron smiled and quietly replied, "Begin."

Five minutes later the telephone rang. Herzl was convinced it had been prearranged; a way to bring the interview to an end with an excuse of imaginary business. But the Baron said over the phone that he was not at home to anyone and turned back to his guest. This gave the young journalist courage to plunge into his introduction again.

"During our two thousand years of dispersion we have been without united political leadership. This has been our chief misfortune. It has done us more harm than the persecutions. It has rotted and ruined us from within. . . . If we had a united political leadership . . . we could proceed to a solution of the Jewish problem."

Then he introduced his idea of emigration. "It will take a long time before we can reach the promised land. Moses needed forty years. We will require perhaps twenty or thirty."

Growing bolder, he spoke out about what he thought of the Baron's avocation. "The principle of philanthropy I hold to be altogether mistaken. You breed beggars. . . . Philanthropy debases the character of our people."

To Herzl's surprise the Baron quietly interjected, "You are quite right."

Then the young visitor began a detailed criticism of the Baron's experiment in Argentina, contending that the Jewish people were not yet ready to become colonists. "They must first be made strong, as for war, and they must be taught the joy of work and the exercise of virtue."

The Baron astounded Herzl by saying, "I don't want to raise the general level. All our misfortunes come from the fact that Jews try to climb too high. We have too much brains. My intention is to restrain Jews from pushing ahead. They should not make so much progress. All the hatred against them stems from this." Next he criticized his young guest for having "such visionary notions."

At that Herzl jumped to his feet, his eyes blazing. "You do

not know what a visionary really means! Only from the heights can one understand the vital instincts of man."

Hirsch raised his voice, too, at which Herzl began to scream, "I will go to the German Kaiser. *He* will understand, for he has been trained to think of big things!"

The French Baron blinked.

Herzl went on shouting about how he would buy from the Kaiser the right for Jews to leave Europe.

"Where will you get the money?" Hirsch demanded.

Herzl blurted out that he would raise a Jewish national loan of ten million marks.

"The rich Jews will give you nothing," Hirsch said. "The rich ones are worthless and care nothing for the sufferings of the poor."

"You are talking like a Socialist!" Herzl retorted, to hide his own surprise.

"I am one!" the Baron snapped back. "I am perfectly willing to hand over everything, provided the others do likewise."

On that note the conversation ended. It had been stimulating, but on the way home Herzl realized he had covered only six pages of his outline. The next day he wrote a long letter to Hirsch telling him that if he and other men of wealth failed to support him, he would turn directly to the Jewish masses. He said that what divided them most was that "you are a great money-Jew; I am the Jew of the spirit." He wrote that in the days of Moses, water and food were the problem; today it was money, money, money, for transportation and all the other vast expenses of emigration. He even wrote about such small matters as a flag. "Men live and die for a flag; it is indeed the only thing for which they are willing to die in masses, provided one educates them to it."

He told Hirsch that what the Jewish people at this moment in their history needed most was revitalized vision. "Consider if you will what the Jews have withstood throughout two thousand years for the sake of a vision. Visions alone grip the souls of men. And whoever does not know how to deal in visions may be an excellent, worthy, and practical-minded person, even a benefactor in a big way, but he will never be a leader of men, and no trace of him will remain." Then he gave the Baron a short lesson on the importance of "imponderables that float high in thin air."

For the first time he referred specifically to an "exodus to the Promised Land." He said to move the Jews of the Diaspora to Palestine would present a transportation problem "unparalleled in the modern world." He tried to excite Hirsch with the enormity of the project that was now obsessing him. He wrote in military terms of forming a General Staff of members of the educated Jewish proletariat who would lead "the cadres of the army which will seek, discover, and take over the land." He offered to make Hirsch Commander in Chief of this new army if he would obligate himself to contribute fifty million marks as soon as one hundred million had been raised from other sources. He mentioned an ultimate goal of ten billion, although he said one billion might do for a start. "With it we shall build houses, palaces, workingmen's homes, schools, theaters, museums, government buildings, prisons, hospitals, asylums, in short, cities, and make the land so fertile it will have earned its title of the Promised Land."

He wrote, angrily, that "mints of Jewish money are available for a Chinese loan, for Negro railroads in Africa, for the remotest undertakings—and would none be found for the deepest, most pressing and bitterest need of the Jews themselves?"

Herzl did not sit with folded hands waiting for a reply from the Baron. The obsession was upon him now. He was in a frenzy of excitement over the possibilities of the dream. Of course, Zionism was not his invention. When Herzl was two years old Moses Hess had written a book, *Rome and Jerusalem,* urging Jews to set about rebuilding the Jewish state. When Herzl was twenty, Dr. Leon Pinsker in an historic pamphlet, *Auto Emancipation,* advocated the re-establishment of the Jewish state as the only self-respecting course for the Jewish people to take. But somehow Herzl had missed both of them. He was aflame not with anything he had discovered in a book, but with the excitement of his own wild imaginings. He wrote and talked as if he had conceived a totally unique idea.

Sitting at a bare wooden table in his room in the Hôtel de Castille on the rue Cambon in Paris, he covered thousands of small pieces of paper with the ideas that churned through his mind. Then he began keeping a diary into which he transcribed this torrent of thought. By the time of his death nine years later, it filled sixteen large copybooks—hundreds of thousands of words. His decision to keep this "log-book of the Mayflower," as a friend called it, was motivated partly by his certainty that he was embarking on a historically important voyage and that posterity would be interested in all the details. But the diary turned out to be more than a day-by-day account of the storms and crises of the trip. It is a document as personal as a looking glass. In it the author is seen sometimes with a fanatic's expression on his face, sometimes arrogantly self-assured, occasionally annoyingly pompous, often humble, discouraged, and tragically self-analytical. Many of the entries illuminate the conflicts and inner turmoil he faced. His foibles are as clearly revealed as the vigor of his idealism. Yet always he is the visionary, dreaming of how it might be, if men in power would only listen to him. No detail of life in a Utopian state was too minescule to be worthy of an entry. ("The first man ashore carries a cheap plain flag. It will later be preserved in the National Museum. For the future legend: provide distinctive headgear, à la Stanley. All these people are to receive a little yellow ribbon.")

Into the diary went instructions, as if he were an emperor. ("To the architects: Typical designs of workshops for shoe-makers, tailors, carpenters, etc., to be reproduced and distributed abroad in countless numbers . . . an advertisement to attract immigrants.")

Sometimes he made small personal confessions. ("I could not permit myself to be tied down to sober fact. Intoxication was necessary.")

Entry after entry recorded details of Utopia. His people had waited so long. If finally they were to have a land of their own, why not make it at least an approximation of perfection?

> Breathing space between the towns. Each town to be like a large house planted in its own garden, the area between the towns to be given over to nothing but agriculture and woods. Thereby I prevent overgrown cities. . . .
> A crop of professional politicians must be prevented at all costs. . . .

We must become a people of inventors, warriors, artists, scholars, honest merchants, upstanding workers.

Although he had not as yet a single supporter, he worried about strangely remote problems. ("Should the dowries of wealthy girls be taxed? The proceeds could be used to take care of impoverished old maids. . . .")

Some of his thoughts were rhapsodic. ("The Promised Land, where we can have hooked noses, black or red beards, and bandy-legs, without being despised for it . . . where we shall live at peace with all the world . . . and the derisive cry of 'Jew' may become an honest appellation like German, Englishman, Frenchman. . . .")

Now and then in his own blunt way he expressed his belief in the divine mission of the Jews. ("For God would not have kept us alive so long if there were not left for us a role to play in this history of mankind.")

With his genius as a phrasemaker, he sprinkled his notebooks with aphorisms that would be repeated and reprinted long after his death: "A man grows as his aim in life becomes higher." "Nothing turns out as one fears or hopes." "I find the great just as small as I am." "Whoever wishes to change men must change the conditions under which men live." (He called that his chief tenet of life.) "So build your state that the stranger will feel contented among you."

The autointoxication of his own ideas was so great that several times he was frightened that he might literally be going mad, "so wildly the streams of thought raced through my soul." He took up bicycle riding, hoping the physical exertion would arrest his thinking, but he discovered that the faster he pedaled, the faster his thoughts poured forth.

Not having heard from Hirsch he wrote again, this time in what may have been a spirit of studied despondency.

"We shall have to sink still lower," he wrote; "we shall have to be more widely insulted, spat upon, mocked, beaten, robbed, and slain before we are ripe for the idea." It was one of many sentences he wrote in those days that turned out to be precisely prophetic.

This time Hirsch replied, saying he would be delighted to

see Herzl when he, Hirsch, returned to Paris from London, but no specific time was set. Nine months later the Baron died on his Hungarian estate without a second meeting having taken place. But Herzl fortunately was never one to put all his eggs into a single basket. Meanwhile he had written a long letter to Bismarck, outlining his plan for a Jewish state and asking the former German Chancellor if he thought it feasible. To his diary Herzl confided this comment:

"Bismarck is great enough to understand me, or to cure me."

No reply arrived, so Herzl made up his mind to turn to the Rothschilds. Instead of trying to deal with the French, Austrian German, and British branches one by one, he decided to call them all together in a "Rothschild Family Council." First he set to work, with his letters to Hirsch and Bismarck and his diary as source material, writing a twenty-thousand-word address he intended delivering to the Rothschilds. It started out:

"You are accustomed to making worldwide deals, so perhaps you will understand me." Then he explained that he was going to ask "our protector, the Prince of Wales," to introduce him to the Russian Czar, whom he would persuade to give permission for the exodus of all Russian Jews. Then he would negotiate with the German Kaiser. Then with Austria. Then France. Then, "as need dictates." He intended to tell the Rothschilds that he brought them an opportunity to perform a great historical mission. He even included this bait in his prepared address:

> To the Rothschild Family Council: Your older men will stand by us with advice as to finances, banking, railroads, and politics, and will enter our diplomatic service. Your sons, and I hope you will have as many as possible, will play their part in the army, diplomatic corps, etc., according to their capacities—but strictly according to their capacities—and will govern provinces, etc. We will reward your daughters with our best officers, finest artists, and most brilliant officials. Or marry them off in Europe, as the Americans do, and which I believe to be very useful. The main thing is that your money be scattered far and wide.

While he worked on the address he kept wondering why he had not heard from Bismarck. Perhaps, he told himself, he had not been explicit enough for the great German statesman to understand. ("Napoleon failed to understand the steamboat and he was younger—that is, more susceptible to new ideas.")

To arrange a gathering of the Rothschilds, Herzl needed help, so he appealed to the Chief Rabbi of Vienna, Dr. Moritz Güdemann, who was well acquainted with the family. In the private dining room of a little German tavern in Munich one hot summer day in 1895, Herzl sat across the table from Güdemann for hours reading him excerpts from "My Address to the Rothschild Family Council." The declamation went on until late afternoon. It was resumed at 6 P.M. in Herzl's hotel room. It was finally concluded late at night over dinner in a Munich restaurant. The Chief Rabbi's advice was that the Rothschilds would not be interested; that Herzl should publish the address in the form of a pamphlet.

In Vienna about this time (September 1895) a new Prime Minister, Count Casimir Badeni, decided to revive a long-defunct daily newspaper and Herzl was offered the editorship. He decided that this might be the hand of fate assisting him with his dream. The paper could be used as an organ for propagandizing Zionism, and at the same time it would give him an opportunity to win over his first world statesman, the Prime Minister of Austria.

After meeting Count Badeni, Herzl wrote him down as a demagogue. ("I don't like the man!") Although he decided to refuse the editorship, the offer at least gave him a club over the *Neue Freie Presse*. If he turned down Count Badeni and remained with the *Neue Freie Presse*, he asked the owners, would they open their columns to his Zionist ideas? They refused, declaring that his proposal of a Jewish state was like a powerful machine gun that at any moment might go off backwards. In reply Herzl angrily predicted that he would ultimately succeed and they would be forced to publicize his scheme, to which one of the proprietors said, "Remember, after twenty years we have still not mentioned the Socialist movement!"

But a compromise was finally reached. Herzl would be given a leave of absence from the paper to go to Paris and London and create a committee to study his ideas and decide on their worth. If nothing came of this, he could publish a pamphlet, which the NFP would then discuss in its columns. This was the second time the idea of a pamphlet had been suggested.

Herzl agreed and rushed off to Paris, but he ran into discouragement every way he turned. He decided the hostility of French Jews was because "things go too well with them to admit any thought of change." Yet it was in Paris that he made his first important convert.

Max Nordau was born in Hungary, but he had lived most of his life in Paris. He was a man of brilliance and versatility—a physician, a playwright, a philosopher, and a publicist. He was eleven years Herzl's senior and was already an author of worldwide repute. His most popular book to date was *Conventional Lies of Our Civilization,* which blamed the individual and social restlessness of the 1890's on the hypocrisy of the current European civilization. It had been denounced by the Vatican, banned in Russia and Austria, but had established Nordau's reputation as a fearless thinker.

Herzl and Nordau had much in common. Both wrote for German language papers. Both were now using their pens to help the harassed Jews of Europe. The houses in which they were born were only a stone's throw from each other in the Pest half of Budapest. Herzl described himself as a freethinker; Nordau, son of a rabbi, did not subscribe to all the Jewish religious dogma. Yet they both believed in the historic mission of their own people.

One day after they had spent hours over glasses of beer in a bistro in Paris, Herzl wrote in his diary, "Never before were we in such perfect accord. Each spoke with what was on the lips of the other. I never felt so plainly that we belonged together." Nordau agreed that the tragedy of the Jews was that "this most conservative people, which yearns to root itself in the soil, has had no home for the last two thousand years," but he was certain that anti-Semitism would force them to give up their dream of a fatherland.

After returning from Vienna, Herzl decided to concentrate on Nordau. For days they talked, Herzl completely hypnotizing the more mature physician-philosopher, until Nordau became not only a convert to his ideas, but a prisoner of his enthusiasm.

"You may be mad," Nordau told him, "but if you are, I am mad, too."

In his diary Herzl wrote, "Nordau, it seems, is completely won to the cause." In his practical way, Herzl even made a note to himself that Nordau would be very good as Minister of Education in the new Jewish state. Their only point of disagreement was a mathematical one. Herzl predicted to Nordau that they ought to be able to get their Jewish state established within thirty years, whereas the older man questioned whether Jews were "anthropologically fit for nationhood," and suggested that the plan would need three hundred years for realization. When Herzl waved aside such pessimism, Nordau suggested he ought to go to London and try to set up a committee there and gave him letters of introduction to many British intellectuals, among them members of the Maccabeans, an organization dedicated to fostering an interest in Jewish culture.

In London, Herzl saw Israel Zangwill, the eminent novelist and playwright, who in stumbling French indicated his agreement with the idea of "territorial independence" and offered to help with additional introductions. Then he called on the Chief Rabbi of London, who, after listening to his plan, dryly remarked that nineteen years earlier George Eliot had written *Daniel Deronda,* a brilliant novel, on the same subject. Herzl had never read it, so he quickly interjected, "I do not claim the idea is new. It is two thousand years old. The only novelty lies in the methods whereby I launch the idea and then organize the Society, and finally the State."

Later Herzl had lunch in a home of English elegance as the guest of Sir Samuel Montagu, a Jewish banker, Member of Parliament, and a leader of the Liberal Party, who twenty years earlier had visited Palestine and just three years ago had presented the Turkish Sultan with a petition for Jewish colonization of a quarter of a million acres of Transjordan. Herzl called Sir Samuel "the best Jew I have met so far" and was impressed that the meal consisted of kosher food served by three liveried footmen. Over coffee in the smoking room, Herzl expounded his ideas and was delighted with his host's agreement to join the Committee as soon as one of the Great Powers reacted seriously to the idea. He also was encouraged by Sir Samuel's statement that he would be willing to settle with his entire family in Palestine when the time came.

Herzl's appearance before a dinner meeting of the Maccabeans was not so successful. He spoke partly in French, partly in German, which few members understood so that there had to be a translation into English. The Maccabeans had innumerable objections, principally that they were all patriotic Englishmen and intended to remain so. Herzl left aware that he had made no great conquest; that he had better return to Paris and start turning the Address to the Rothschild Family into a pamphlet, as his friends had suggested. He arrived back in the French capital with what Dr. Nordau diagnosed as a bad case of bronchial catarrh.

"A prophet must have healthy lungs!" he told his patient.

Herzl, although in pain, smiled back and said, "With a winter coat a man can't be a prophet."

Despite his condition he went to work, packing his days with a frenzy of megalomaniacal literary activity. Under the narcotic of his self-generated excitement he worked long hours without interruption, sifting his material, rewriting passages of the Rothschild address that dissatisfied him, arranging, expanding, editing. At night he tossed on his bed, thinking of revisions that ought to be made, omissions, errors. At times he engaged in bitter self-criticism; at other times he indulged in rhapsodic dreams of what life would be like in the Utopian state he was creating on paper.

By mid-January 1896, he decided his manuscript was ready for the printer. An excerpt had already been published in the *Jewish Chronicle* in London under the title: "The Solution of the Jewish Question," but at the last minute Herzl decided to call the pamphlet, "The Jewish State: an Attempt at a Modern Solution of the Jewish Question." When he delivered the manuscript to his Vienna publisher, Herzl made him sit and listen while he read him long passages. That night in his diary he recorded the publisher's enthusiasm, but several weeks later, he was indignant to learn that a first printing of only three thousand copies was planned. Not a very bold display of faith, he decided. Then a Jewish publisher in Berlin to whom he had

sent a copy of the manuscript returned it with a letter saying he
found Herzl's ideas distasteful and therefore refused to put out
a German edition. "I consoled myself," Herzl wrote, "when I
noticed from the envelope of his letter that he publishes a
hairdressers' journal and the like."

The owners of his own newspaper gave him more trouble.
When they saw proofs of the pamphlet they indignantly told
him he had no right to "take upon himself the tremendous
moral responsibility of setting this avalanche in motion"; that
the time was not ripe; that he was endangering the future of
the paper, because one of its greatest assets was his literary
reputation, which he was now about to destroy. They told him
that talk of emigrating to a Jewish fatherland would be seized
upon by the anti-Semites as an admission by Jews that they were
incapable of assimilating in the countries of their present residence, a claim the anti-Semites themselves had always made
and Jews had denied. They begged him to stop publication of the
pamphlet or at least to take his name off it. Herzl rejected both
suggestions.

One of his fellow journalists told him, "If I were a Rothschild
I would offer you five million to suppress the pamphlet, or I
would assassinate you, for you will do the Jews a frightful injury."

The Jewish State was published on February 14, 1896, an
86-page, paper-covered pamphlet, six by nine inches. It was
the outline Herzl had made for Baron de Hirsch, expanded
into the Address to the Rothschild Family Council, augmented
by many entries from the diary, into what was to become a
history-making pamphlet. In its final form it advocated that the
Jewish problem be treated as a world political question; that
it be dealt with by European governments; that immediate
plans be made for an orderly exodus of Europe's Jews to a
land of their own in which they would govern themselves. Although later generations of critics would agree that *The Jewish
State* had a more profound effect on the history of the Jewish
people than any other secular book ever written, its immediate
reception on publication was so adverse that Herzl wrote in his
diary, "At this juncture, my good father is my only standby."
Then he added, aphoristically, "Whoever wishes to be proved

right within thirty years must needs be considered crazy for the first two weeks."

In dispatching a copy of *The Jewish State* to Prime Minister Badeni, Herzl wrote, "The pamphlet will probably evoke a certain amount of excitement, laughter, outcries, wails, abuse, misunderstanding, stupidities, and baseness. I anticipate these reactions with the utmost composure. *Les chiens aboient; la caravane passe.* [The dogs bark, the caravan moves on.]" Then not too subtly, he added, "Through the door I am trying to push open for the masses of Jews, a Christian statesman who rightly seizes the idea will step forth into world history." Prime Minister Badeni did not seize the idea, and his place in world history, therefore, remained inconsequential.

Herzl's prediction about the reaction to his pamphlet was not far off. He was accused in print of being out for personal financial gain; a Vienna paper called his Zionist ideas "the madness of despair"; a writer of humorous articles for the *Neue Freie Presse* jeered, "The Jewish Jules Verne." German journalists were so antagonistic that Herzl accused them of "yelping like the Berlin theater hyenas [dramatic critics] when they are out to ruin the opening of a new play." To his embarrassment, about the only journalistic support came from an anti-Semitic paper in Pressburg, Hungary, that "bombards me with flattering editorials and sends me two copies of each issue."

The mixture of emotions that possessed Herzl in these days was compounded by his doctor's announcement that "the powerful excitement" to which he had recently been subjected had caused a weakness of his heart.

In his diary about this time appeared one of the frankest confessions an author ever made:

> Read today Pinsker's pamphlet, *Auto-Emancipation.* . . .
> A pity I had not read it before my own pamphlet was printed.
> Still, it is a good thing I knew nothing of it, or perhaps I might
> have abandoned my own undertaking.

While the professional and amateur critics were attacking him ("niggling about this and naggling about that") Herzl received a glowing letter from Nordau that filled him with pride. It called *The Jewish State* "a great deed" and a "revelation."

Herzl was equally pleased a few days later when he received a call from the Reverend William H. Hechler, chaplain to the British Embassy in Vienna, whom Herzl frequently called the most extraordinary character he had ever encountered. The Reverend Mr. Hechler had been a Protestant missionary in South Africa. Thirteen years ago he had published a book, *The Restoration of the Jews to Palestine According to the Prophets.* Although only fifty, he had a long gray beard which oddly contrasted with the bushy black beard of the younger man. He said that as soon as he finished reading *The Jewish State* he rushed to inform the British Ambassador that prophecy was about to be fulfilled. From his own Biblical calculations he figured that Palestine would be restored to the Jews in either 1897 or 1898. What he then said interested Herzl even more. He had once been tutor to Prince Ludwig, son of the Grand Duke of Baden, and in this way had become acquainted with the Prince's cousin, Wilhelm, now the German Kaiser.

"We must get your book into the hands of the Kaiser as well as the Grand Duke," he told Herzl. He even suggested that he might be able to arrange an audience for Herzl with the German monarch. Before they separated, the two bearded men, one a deeply religious Christian, the other a Jewish freethinker, had cemented a friendship that would endure during the rest of Herzl's life.

Now began a new era in the career of Theodor Herzl. The playwright, essayist, journalist, and literary critic decided to become a statesman, a diplomat, and—if necessary—a conniving politician. What his scheme needed more than anything else was the support of some powerful state. Why waste his time on little men with small vision? Why try to convince people who, even if they became partisans, still would be able to do little to help bring the dream to fulfillment? What he needed was the support of a king, an emperor, a kaiser, a sultan. With supreme confidence in his own persuasive powers and in the contagion of his ideas, he decided to conduct a one-man campaign on behalf of the eleven million Jews of the world, although as far as he knew not one-tenth of one per cent of them at this point was showing the slightest interest in his ideas.

First he decided to make use of the Reverend Mr. Hechler, so he offered to pay the travel expenses of the impecunious clergy-man to Berlin in return for his help in arranging an interview with Kaiser Wilhelm. While Herzl waited for a message from the minister, he wrote to Nordau asking him to see if the Baron de Hirsch would be willing to advance "a few millions" to be used as baksheesh in Turkey, for he realized that the real cam-paign must center there. After all, it was the Ottoman Empire that owned and occupied Palestine. While the letter was on its way to Nordau, Herzl learned of the Baron's sudden death. But the bad was balanced by the good; that same day Chaplain Hechler sent a message for Herzl to take the first train for Karls-ruhe, Germany. The Grand Duke of Baden awaited him.

Two days later the Christian with the white beard and the Jew with the black beard drove side by side in a carriage up a long ramp to the castle of the man who exactly a quarter of a century ago, when the German Empire was formally established in ceremonies at Versailles, was chosen to proclaim Wilhelm I as Emperor. They waited in a great rococo salon hung with red damask draperies, the walls covered with immense oil portraits. Finally they were received in his private study by the Grand Duke, a robust man for all of his seventy years. The conference lasted two and a half hours, with Herzl doing most of the talking. At first he spoke with restraint. ("I thought it best to lower my voice and thus escape the usual self-intoxica-tion of speech.")

After Herzl had explained his scheme in detail, the Grand Duke said his chief worry was that if he supported the cause, people might think he wanted to get rid of the Jews and so would accuse him of anti-Semitism.

Herzl quickly replied that only Jews who wanted to go would emigrate.

The Duke spoke in praise of Jews in general, saying, "I have yet to see a drunken Jew. They are sober and thrifty and they always know how to shift for themselves."

Herzl said it was essential for his scheme that he receive recognition from the Great Powers. The Grand Duke replied that Germany did not have an excessive number of Jews and that their departure would not be welcomed by German econo-mists.

Herzl, after answering all his host's arguments one by one, finally said, "If an experienced prince—one who had helped in the creation of the German Empire, a statesman to whom the Kaiser turns for counsel—were to endorse this new enterprise, it would make a profound impression."

The Grand Duke finally gave permission for the use of his name. As they separated, the old man, with a benign expression on his face, said softly, "I would like to see it come about. I believe it will be a blessing for many human beings."

On the way to their hotel, Herzl, joyful over having made his first convert among world statesmen, turned to his companion and exclaimed, "My, what a wonderful man!"

In the following months Herzl became more and more obsessed. He transformed himself into a one-man diplomatic corps of a state that so far existed only on paper and sent a stream of communications to everyone of importance he thought might possibly be sympathetic. He wrote to Baron Edmond de Rothschild, to Zangwill, to the Maccabeans he had met in London, to the Papel Nuncio, and to hundreds of others.

He fumed at what he considered the stupidity or the maliciousness of his opposition. The first time his own newspaper mentioned his pamphlet was in an article about Count Tolstoy expressing opposition to the idea of a Jewish state, but Herzl's name was not even mentioned. ("This silent treatment is fast becoming ridiculous.")

He had an audience with the Papal Nuncio ("tall, slender, well-bred, and formal, exactly as I had envisioned a Papal diplomatist"). He promised the Vatican representative that if Palestine was obtained as a national Jewish home, Christian holy places would be safe, because Jerusalem, Nazareth and Bethlehem would be given extraterritorial status. But that night in his diary he wrote, "I believe Rome will be against us. . . ."

At a special gathering in Vienna he met Philip Michael Nevlinski, descendant of a long line of Polish counts, who had had a brief but brilliant career in the Austrian diplomatic service, and now was publisher of a daily newspaper specializing in Balkan affairs. The Count boasted that he was on friendly terms with the Sultan and for a "nominal fee" might consider helping Herzl procure Palestine as a Jewish homeland.

Four months later, after many preliminaries, the two men took the Orient Express for Constantinople. At Nevlinski's suggestion Herzl had brought along a package containing one bunch of asparagus, six peaches, several bunches of grapes, and some strawberries, all imported from France. They would be welcome gifts at court, Nevlinski explained with a wink. Herzl made a note that they cost him the considerable sum of seventy florin (about $35).

On the train, Nevlinski explained the Ottoman Empire's financial troubles. France and England controlled the Commission of the Public Debt, which, in return for consolidating Turkey's half-billion-dollar indebtedness, had been given many monopolies, including those on salt and tobacco, and even had the right to impose certain taxes. Turkey was smarting under the humiliation of this impairment of her sovereign rights. This situation, said the Polish count to the Viennese journalist, ought to suggest to him a way to win the Sultan's friendship. Herzl, who was trying to turn himself into a statesman, now found himself forced to grapple with international high finance, whether he liked it, or understood it, but with typical boldness, as soon as Nevlinski finished he started expounding a plan: Among the millionaire Jewish bankers of Europe he would raise twenty million pounds sterling. He would give two million to Turkey in exchange for Palestine, and with the remaining eighteen million would free Turkey from control of the Debt Commission.

En route across Bulgaria, Herzl had his first taste of being a popular public figure. Until now his dream had won him more ridicule than anything else, but as the Orient Express pulled in to the depot at Sofia the platform was thronged with Sephardic and Ashkenazi Jews: men who came to cheer the fearless-looking character with the immense black beard standing on the steps of his railroad car; women who wanted to kiss his hand; children who presented him with flowers. One of the crowd made a speech in which he called Herzl "our great leader." As the train began to move a shout went up: "*Leshanah habah bi-Jerushalayim!* [Next year in Jerusalem!]"

Constantinople delighted Herzl, with its brilliant sunshine, picturesque poverty, and dilapidated buildings. But the trip proved to be a waste of three thousand francs and ten days of time. Nevlinski saw the Sultan, who sent word to Herzl that he would not under any circumstances sell a single square meter of his land, which was fertilized with Turkish blood, "and we will cover it once more with our blood before we allow it to be torn from us." Then he made a statement as strangely prophetic as many of Herzl's own words: "The Jews may spare their millions. When my Empire is divided up, perhaps they will get Palestine for nothing. But only our corpse can be divided. I will never consent to vivisection."

That night in his diary Herzl wrote, "I was touched and moved by the truly lofty words of the Sultan, although for the time they put an end to my hopes."

Nevlinski and Herzl left Constantinople a few days later with nothing to show for the trip except a medal, the Commander's Cross of the Medjidié Order, a gift from the Sultan. It pleased Herzl until he discovered it was a Class III medal.

Next, London, where he was greeted by news that the British edition of *The Jewish State* to date had sold 160 copies. He permitted himself to be persuaded to address the Maccabeans again, this time in English, with many of the words written out phonetically between the lines of his script to help him with the pronunciation. After he finished his presentation, such a puerile debate broke out that he wrote in his diary the experience "only strengthened my antipathy to piddling about with societies."

Another day he had lunch with the banker Montagu, who now imposed three conditions as the price for his support: that Herzl obtain the approval of the Great Powers; that the Hirsch Fund put ten million pounds into the project; and that Edmond de Rothschild join the Committee. They were conditions that might have caused a less dedicated man great discouragement, but instead Herzl simply warned that while he did not want a demagogic movement, if "the gentry prove too genteel" he would "set the masses in motion."

The next night every seat in the East End Working Men's Club was taken and the aisles were packed. It was a hot mid-July evening and not a breath of air was stirring, but no one left, although the man with the great black beard spoke for more than an hour. Those who followed on the program compared him to Moses and Christopher Columbus. After the meeting there was a demonstration for Herzl that had a profound influence on him. He preferred to enlist the help of the Rothschilds, even at the price of his own withdrawal from leadership of the movement, but if this failed, he was now aware that he could become a mass leader.

Several days later, while on the way back to Paris with the experience of the mass meeting still sharp in his mind, he wrote in his diary:

> As I sat on the platform . . . I underwent a curious experience: I saw and heard my legend being made. The people are sentimental; the masses do not see clearly . . . a faint mist is beginning to rise and envelop me . . . and may perhaps become the cloud on which I shall walk. But even if they no longer see my faults distinctly, still they sense that I truly mean well by them and that I am the little people's man. Probably, as a matter of fact, they would lavish the same affection on some clever seducer and impostor as they do on me, in whom, however, they are not deceived.

Six days later, in a wood-paneled reception room of the Rothschild bank on the rue Laffitte in Paris, Herzl had his long-awaited conference with the French baron. The multimillionaire banker was nervous and impatient. He listened to Herzl at first with annoyance, later with some interest, and occasionally with astonishment. But he was voluble with objections. He didn't believe in Turkish promises. It would be impossible to control the flood of immigrants. Thousands of beggars would pour in, perhaps as many as 150,000 at the start. They would have to be fed. There would be tragic accidents and unfortunate incidents.

"Isn't anti-Semitism an unfortunate incident?" Herzl asked angrily. "Doesn't it bring loss of honor, life, and property?"

The interview lasted two hours. Finally Herzl picked up his umbrella and prepared to leave, saying, "You are the keynote to my whole plan. If you refuse to help . . . I shall be obliged to proceed in a different manner. I shall begin a widespread agitation. Then it will be even more difficult to keep the

masses in order." He repeated that if Rothschild were willing
to accept the leadership, he, Herzl, would eliminate himself
and return to being just a writer, but Rothschild refused to
commit himself.

They separated on good terms, even though their views were
so diametrically opposed. Each swore he had been delighted to
meet the other. In his diary that night Herzl recorded his real
impressions of Rothschild: a decent, good-natured, fainthearted
man. "I believe he is now disgusted that he ever began with
Palestine and he'll perhaps run to Alphonse and say, 'You're
right, I should have gone in for racing horses rather than
wandering Jews'. And the fate of millions of persons hangs on
such men!"

Herzl was bitterly depressed by Rothschild's attitude and by
the complete lack of support from any other influential quarters. He told his intimates that he had reached the point of
being "demoralized." In Germany he was certain he had nothing but opponents. In London the Maccabeans seemed merely
"Pickwickian." Russian Jews in general were sympathetic but
were doing nothing to help him. Those in Austria who were
active seemed to him to be merely trying to further their
personal careers. In bitterness he wrote, "I am beginning to
have the right to become the world's worst anti-Semite." But
it was characteristic that each new depressing report or experience goaded him into a greater frenzy of activity. He appealed to the Chief Rabbi of Paris to try to wheedle Baron
Rothschild. ("Perhaps I was too clumsy, too impatient.") He
sounded out King Milan of Serbia. He urged Prince Ferdinand
of Bulgaria to try to interest the Czar. He continued his efforts
to gain the ear of the Pope and the Kaiser. He founded a
weekly newspaper devoted to propagandizing his ideals. Despite
hundreds of prepublication announcements, only two sub-
scriptions came in and the first issue contained only one small
ad, that of a local clothing merchant. But nothing affected his
conviction that he was right or dimmed his enthusiasm. He
continued to write rhapsodically about a Jewish state and to
have dreams that sometimes were astonishingly prophetic. He
imagined great chemical industries established on the shores
of the Dead Sea. (Sixty years after his death, the Dead Sea

mineral project would grow into a fifty-million-dollar industry.)
He predicted that someday Jews would plant a total of ten million trees in Palestine. (Sixty years after his death, trees were
being planted in Israel at the rate of six million each year.)

Although Herzl's heart was now beginning to trouble him
(his doctor called it a result of "tension") he decided to carry
out his threat to organize a mass movement, encouraged by his
East End London experience. He began by urging friends in
countries with a large Jewish population to organize groups
for eventual emigration. Caustically he described the new cleavage as between "a few money-bags with their beggars and
lackeys, and, on our side, all the high-minded, stout-hearted,
intelligent, and educated forces of the Jewish people." Then
he began planning an international meeting at which a program could be formulated.

The first Zionist Congress was to have been held in Munich,
Germany, but when the Jewish community of that city objected, the locale was changed to Basel, Switzerland. Herzl knew
in advance there was danger in bringing together so many of
his followers in one place; it would be a miracle if there were
no jealousies and internecine feuds. Also, he was afraid they
might lose their faith when they saw "with what slender means
I have built up the present structure."

The Congress was called for August 29, 1897. Herzl appeared in Basel a few days in advance and set up headquarters
in an empty tailor shop. Almost immediately the delegates
began to arrive, 197 of them from twelve European countries,
the United States, Algeria, and Palestine. They came caked with
coal dust and sweat, exhausted from their travels, "brimful of
intentions, mostly good; some bad." Some represented long-
established Zionist societies and looked on Herzl as something
of an upstart; others spoke for groups that had only recently
sprung into existence and only because of Herzl. They came
not only from many countries but from every stratum of
society, and with every shade of political opinion. Some were
deeply religious. Others were freethinkers. A few were atheists.
Many were socialists. There was even an anarchist or two. But
they had one thing in common, a deep interest in the creation
of a Jewish state.

Herzl had suggested months ago that petitions be circulated by his followers, and now they were pouring in to Congress headquarters. The one from Rumania contained signatures of fifty thousand people who declared their eagerness to move to a Jewish state. There were hundreds of congratulatory telegrams.

Before the sessions even began Herzl was beseiged by so many people asking questions, giving him advice, arguing over principles and procedures, that he felt as if he were being forced to play thirty-two games of chess simultaneously.

To give the proceedings the air of dignity and solemnity he felt they deserved, Herzl had made it obligatory for every delegate to attend the opening session in swallow-tails and white tie. The only one who caused trouble was his close friend Nordau, who appeared in a frock coat. It took a quarter hour of arguing before he could be persuaded to go to his hotel room and change.

The deliberations were held in a concert hall, in the Basel Casino. In addition to the delegates, many distinguished non-Jews attended, among them Jean Henri Dunant, founder of the Red Cross. Some delegates, seeing on display in the hall a white flag with blue stripes and the Star of David, assumed that the flag of ancient Israel had been revived. Actually it was the invention of David Wolffsohn, one of Herzl's colleagues who would succeed him as Zionist leader after his death. He had chosen the colors of the *tallit*, or prayer shawl.

There were problems from the very start, major and minor. A doctor from Rumania who was supposed to talk ten minutes was still rambling on at the end of half an hour, although Herzl sent four requests to him to stop. Several important delegates were offended because they received no committee assignments. A delegate from London, claiming that he, not Herzl, was the founder of modern Zionism, began a campaign for the post of secretary-general, with salary.

But despite the confusion, the schisms, and the conflicts, when Herzl arose to deliver his opening address the delegates clapped, shouted, whistled, and waved handkerchiefs for fifteen minutes. One reporter wrote, "It was as if the Messiah had confronted us." Another observer said he appeared as "a scion of the House of David, risen from the dead, clothed in legend and fantasy and beauty." It was Herzl's golden hour—he knew it; the others sensed it.

With deep emotion he declared to the 197 delegates, "We wish at this first Congress to lay the foundation stone of the house that is to shelter the Jewish nation."

As he talked, Zangwill wrote in his notebook:

> A majestic, Oriental figure . . . dominating the assembly with eyes that brood and glow . . . you would say one of the Assyrian Kings. . . . In a congress of impassioned rhetoricians he remains serene, moderate, his voice for the most part subdued; in its most emotional abandonments there is a dry undertone, almost harsh. . . . And yet beneath all this statesmanlike prose, touched with the special dryness of the jurist, lurk the romance of the poet, the purposeful vagueness of the modern revolutionary, the fantasy of the Hungarian, the dramatic self-consciousness of the literary artist, the heart of the Jew.

Herzl was elected president by acclamation. Nordau, not accustomed to play an inferior role, ever, was piqued and showed it. But when his turn at the rostrum came, he delivered such a moving address that at its conclusion Herzl rushed over to him, declaring, "A monument more lasting than bronze!"

Although *The Jewish State* had not been so specific, the official program of the Zionist movement drawn up at Basel stated: "Zionism seeks to obtain for the Jewish people a publicly recognized, legally secured homeland in Palestine."

Before adjourning, the Congress agreed on a constitution for the World Zionist Organization, approved the idea of a bank and a national fund for the purchase of land in Palestine, and decided that expenses would be met in small part by annual dues of one shekel for each member of each organization sending delegates. They used the ancient Hebrew word, but in practice it would mean one German mark, one French franc, one Russian ruble, or one American quarter.

Only a few days before the Congress opened, Herzl in a burst of pessimism had written, "The fact is that I have only an army of *schnorrers*. I stand at the head of a mass of youths, beggars, and jackasses." But back in Vienna after it was all over, he wrote in his diary, for no one but himself to read, "At Basel I founded the Jewish state!" He knew that if he made this boast publicly he would be laughed at by Jews and non-Jews alike, but he was sure, he wrote, that in fifty years the dream would become reality. That prediction was dated September 3, 1897. Fifty years and eight months later, on May 14, 1948, the State of Israel was proclaimed.

Between the First and Second Congresses, Herzl had the task of trying to organize the bank authorized by the Basel meeting. He consulted British, German, French, Austrian, and even Polish bankers. He finally decided that the trouble with bankers was that they loaned money only to the rich—to those who really had no great need of it. In despair he said, "We are like the soldiers of the French Revolution who had to take to the field without shoes or stockings."

The Second Congress, also at Basel, formally established the Jewish Colonial Trust, but it was still up to Herzl to obtain money for its operation. After the Congress adjourned, he and his Protestant clergyman friend, the Reverend Mr. Hechler, went to an island in Lake Constance to pay another call on the Grand Duke of Baden, who told them, to their great delight, that he had submitted a detailed report on Herzl's ideas to the Kaiser, who seemed not unfavorably disposed to them. He also told them that in a few weeks the Kaiser was going to Palestine by way of Constantinople, ostensibly to dedicate a German-built church in Jerusalem, but he added that the visit was inspired by politics as well as piety. It was no diplomatic secret that Germany was eager to try to penetrate the Middle East.

All this news set Herzl's mind to dancing. If he could meet the Kaiser before he left on this trip, perhaps he might be able to persuade him to discuss the Zionist program with the Sultan. The Grand Duke dropped the information that the Kaiser had ordered a report on the Zionist movement from his Ambassador to Vienna, Count Philip de Eulenburg, a Prussian courtier, poet, and literary dilettante, who was an intimate adviser to Wilhelm II. That gave Herzl an opening. He rushed back to Vienna. By odd coincidence, an anarchist in Geneva, Switzerland, had just assassinated Empress Elizabeth of Austria, and the Kaiser was going to attend her funeral in Vienna. Herzl thought that if luck was with him, he might be able to speak with the German Emperor while he was in the Austrian capital. But that same day the Prince Regent of Bavaria had a stroke, adding further complications. However, Herzl did manage to see Count Eulenburg. He won his complete sympathy by saying, "Our movement exists. I anticipate that one or another of the Great Powers will espouse it. Originally I had thought it would be England. . . . But I would be even better pleased if it were Germany. The majority of Jews today are part of the German cultural world. I am not saying this because I am sitting in the German Embassy, but because it is true. Proof: German has been the language of our two Basel conferences."

The Ambassador said the Kaiser was under a great emotional strain. Besides, he was in Vienna for only eight hours. Undaunted, Herzl suggested that he might join the Kaiser's train and talk to him en route. The Ambassador said he would see what could be arranged. Meanwhile, Herzl was given an audience with Count Bernhard Von Bülow, German Foreign Minister. During a long discussion of socialism vs. individualism, Von Bülow spoke of "egalitarian louts" and said he was sure Jews would never "put up with this equality business." Herzl agreed, explaining that Egypt before the days of Moses had been a socialist state, but that the Ten Commandments created an individualistic society, and in his opinion Jews would remain individualists and would never become socialists.

Herzl brought up his intense desire to talk to the Kaiser, saying he would hold himself in readiness in a baggage car of the Kaiser's train if necessary. Von Bülow said neither yes nor no, but Herzl left his presence so full of optimism that he immediately bought a pair of black gloves and put a black band around his hat so that if he were summoned, suddenly, to accompany the Kaiser, he at least would appear in proper mourning. But no summons came.

From Paris a few days later the undiscourageable Herzl wrote Count Eulenburg again urging an interview with the Kaiser and pointing out that the monarch's trip to the Holy Land could become something more than just an ordinary pilgrimage —that it could make history—if it were to sponsor the return of the Jews. No reply came, so the father of modern Zionism continued his trek from one European capital to another seeking backing for the Jewish Colonial Trust. In Paris, he decided the wealthy French Jews could not be counted on. In London, he failed to raise any formidable support, but ten thousand people attended a mass meeting in the East End and cheered him wildly when he predicted "the homeland will soon be a reality." Nordau dampened his spirits. He was not optimistic about Herzl's chance of seeing the Kaiser. He said Von Bülow had received him "merely because he wanted to chat with an interesting person whom people were talking about." While in Amsterdam he received a telegram from Count Eulenburg that the Kaiser would be disappointed if he did not see Mr. Herzl in Jerusalem. The message upset him so much that he took a bicycle and pedaled furiously up one street and down another, trying to decide what to do. He had been on leave from his newspaper, but the leave was about to expire. If he went to Palestine instead of back to work in Paris, it might cost him his lucrative and professionally important position. He thought of himself as a locomotive pulling a long string of cars at full speed, without much choice of the route he ought to follow, now that he was underway. Before he went to sleep that night, he decided to go to Palestine regardless of the cost.

In Berlin, Count Eulenburg informed him that the Kaiser had become enthusiastic about the idea of a Jewish state under German protection and he thought the German monarch would be able to persuade the Sultan of the wisdom of such an idea. Herzl was delighted. He knew that there were many who would disapprove, but his own feeling was that to live under the protection of a "strong, great, moral, splendidly governed and thoroughly organized Germany is certain to have the most salutary effects upon the national character of the Jews," and he expressed this thought to Eulenburg.

While in Berlin he had another audience with the Grand Duke of Baden, who treated him with such kindness that Herzl decided he had "never in my life met a man so noble in every fiber of his being." Then he saw Von Bülow, for whom he had little respect, and asked him if it wouldn't be possible for the Kaiser to receive him in Constantinople rather than Jerusalem. The Foreign Minister, late for a dinner party, rushed off without giving a definite answer, so Herzl returned to Vienna to prepare for a trip. The ultimate destination was in doubt, but he had no uncertainty about the historical importance of the journey. He was engaging in high-level statecraft that was going to affect the lives of millions of his people, so he chose as members of a strategy board to go along with him the four most prominent Zionists who were willing to undertake the adventure, each of a different profession: David Wolffson, a merchant, who eventually would succeed him as president of the Zionist Organization; Max Bodenheimer, a lawyer; Joseph Seidner, an engineer; and Dr. Moses Schnirer, a physician. They served him well, not only as diplomatic advisers but when the occasion demanded it, even as valets and messenger boys.

On arrival in Constantinople, Herzl sent Bodenheimer to the German Embassy to make diplomatic approaches. The lawyer returned crestfallen. The German Ambassador said he had never heard of Herzl. Wolffson was then dispatched to the palace in which the Kaiser and his entourage were being housed as guests of the Sultan. He carried with him one letter addressed to the Imperial Chamberlain asking for an audience for Herzl with the Kaiser before he left Constantinople; a second letter to the Emperor himself, proposing the establishment of a Jewish land company under German protection; and a third letter to Count Von Bülow. Herzl was so confident of success that while Wolffson was gone he dressed in his frock coat, to be ready at a moment's notice. He ate lightly "in order to feel trim and brisk."

Wolffson finally returned with a report that the Imperial Chamberlain had promised to hand the letter to the Kaiser at once. Von Bülow, however, had not been pleasant.

Herzl tried to take a nap, but his mind was churning at such a speed that it was impossible to sleep, so he summoned his strategy board. While he was discussing the situation with them a hotel porter appeared, trembling with the news that there was someone in the lobby with a message from "His Majesty." Herzl slipped on his frock coat, his advisers retired, and the messenger was sent for. He bore a slip of paper reading:

THEODOR HERZL TO REPORT AT 4:30 TO HIS MAJESTY

The advisers were as excited as their president. One straightened his necktie. Another gave his shoes a dusting. Schnirer the physician felt his pulse, and when he found it was 108, suggested a little bromine. Wolffson, who had been chosen to accompany Herzl, slipped a clothes brush into his pocket. Herzl put on a pair of delicate gray gloves he had bought for the occasion and they left, with a dragoman on the coach box described by Herzl as "a sly-faced Jew who looked as though he had police connections."

The interview was much longer than Herzl had even hoped for. He found the Kaiser to be exactly his own height. Apparently he was constantly embarrassed because of a stunted left arm. His large sea-blue eyes, Herzl decided, mirrored "a remarkable soul."

The Kaiser took immediate command of the conversation, explaining at once why he was attracted to the Zionist movement. He was certain Herzl and his followers would be able to raise enough money to colonize Palestine. He led the talk from subject to subject: the Dreyfus Affair, Russian prestige, the possibility of a *coup d'état* in Paris, French corruption, and finally back to Zionism again, asking what specifically Herzl wanted him to ask of the Sultan.

"A chartered company under German protection!" Herzl quickly replied.

The answer apparently pleased the Kaiser, and when Herzl asked about an audience with him again in Palestine at which he could deliver a formal outline of his Zionist plan, the Emperor told him to prepare the address at once and submit it to Von Bülow for approval. Then he gave Herzl a smile, shook his hand vigorously, and strode from the room.

Back in his hotel, Herzl made a report to his excited advisers and then started work on the address. Shortly before midnight, too tired to write any more, he went to bed, after drinking a large bottle of Bavarian beer to induce sleep. But at 4 A.M., unable to sleep, he lit all twelve candles in his room and went to work again.

That afternoon they left by ship for Palestine. Days later they landed at Jaffa, which they found to be a place of bright colors, but depressing because of its poverty and misery. Palestine at

this time was thinly populated, with less than half a million inhabitants, only fifty thousand of them Jews, of whom fewer than
five thousand lived on the land. Less than ten per cent of Palestine was being cultivated. It was against the law for Jews to buy
land or erect buildings, but eighteen settlements had been established after recourse to extensive bribery.

There was little in this place of his ancestors that impressed
Herzl. He found nothing idyllic about the settlements they
visited. When he first saw Jerusalem in the moonlight he decided there was a peculiar and special magnificence to it, but the
next morning he wrote, "When I remember thee, in the days
to come, oh Jerusalem, it will not be with delight. The musty
deposits of two thousand years of inhumanity, intolerance and
foulness lie in your reeking alleys." He was especially disturbed, when he visited the Wailing Wall, by "the hideous,
miserable, scrambling beggary pervading the place," and by the
superstition and fanaticism he encountered.

But then Herzl the Dreamer took over from Herzl the Realist.
If a Jewish state could be established here, he was certain Jerusalem could be converted into one of the most beautiful cities
in the world. ("On the ring of encircling hillsides, which our
labor would clothe with greenery, there would gradually rise a
glorious New Jerusalem. . . . Loving care can turn Jerusalem
into a jewel.") In his practical way he decided the first thing to
be done when Jerusalem became Jewish again would be to clear
out everything that was not sacred, tear down all the tene-
ments (he called them "filthy rat-holes"), burn all the non-sacred
ruins, move the bazaars, and build a brand-new city of comfortable, modern buildings.

Everywhere he went in Palestine the magnificence of the
dream was increased rather than diminished by the imperfec-
tion of the reality.

On the day that the German Emperor went from Jaffa to
Jerusalem, a holiday was declared in all the towns and villages
through which he was to pass. At Mikveh Israel, the oldest agricultural school in the country, bunting had been draped over
the gateway, a display of all the farm machinery stood along the
roadside, the students and teachers were dressed in holiday
clothes, and a children's choir stood ready to burst into song at

their leader's signal. The German entourage was preceded by a Turkish cavalry unit, then the advance guards of the Emperor. Finally, Wilhelm II himself, astride an immense white horse. As he passed the school entrance, bowing formally to left and to right, he suddenly reined in his horse, for his alert eyes had spotted, standing at the side of the road next to a plow, a tall man with an immense black beard whom he recognized. Herzl took off his cork helmet, smiled, then bowed low. The Emperor motioned for him to come closer. For the next few minutes, while the choir leader waited to give the signal for the singing to begin, the two men exchanged pleasantries.

Herzl asked the Kaiser how he found Palestine.

"Very hot, but the country has a future." Bending down, he added in a lower voice, "But it needs water. Much water!" Then he straightened up and repeated, "It is a land with a future!"

Almost a week later, the delegation of five Zionists was received by the Kaiser in his private quarters, an immense tent in the center of the German encampment in Jerusalem. Herzl read his prepared address, the text of which had been drastically censored in advance by one of the Emperor's aides. When he finished, the Kaiser thanked him and said he felt the matter certainly called for further study. Then he spoke in technical terms of irrigation, agriculture, and forestry. He said the German and Jewish settlements he had seen demonstrated what could be done with the country. "There is room for everyone. Only provide water and trees." Then, fixing Herzl with his sea-blue eyes, he said, "Your movement is based on a sound, healthy idea."

After the historic interview was over and they were on a ship homeward bound, Herzl and his advisers realized that they actually had gained nothing. When the reached Naples they saw in the newspapers the text of a dispatch the German officials had authorized. (They themselves had been forbidden to publicize the interview.) Kaiser Wilhelm II had received a Jewish deputation. (No names were mentioned.) They had presented him with an album of pictures of Jewish settlements. In his speech of thanks the Kaiser had said his "benevolent interest could be relied upon in all efforts aimed at a furthering of the welfare of the Turkish Empire, through the improvement of agriculture in Palestine, with complete respect for the sovereignty of the Sultan." This was a long way from what they had hoped for: German support of free Jewish colonization of Palestine, under German protection.

Herzl tried to buoy up the spirits of his advisers. A German protectorate would have been an exciting immediate gain, but in the end they might have had to pay usurious interest. Other ways would be found.

In the months that followed, as it became evident that the Kaiser had no intention of aiding the Zionist movement, Herzl himself grew discouraged. The tempo of activity was slowing down. His followers were weary of slogans without results. He was having more and more difficulty raising money for the bank and organizing the land company authorized at Basel. If only he could have an audience with the Sultan it might produce something to revive the drooping spirits. For this purpose he decided to use his friend Nevlinski. With difficulty he raised the money to send him off to Constantinople. Three days after his departure, a telegram arrived saying he had died in the Turkish capital of a heart attack.

Herzl's next approach to the Sultan was through the most bizarre character he had ever met, Arminus Vámbéry, a seventy-year-old Hungarian adventurer, explorer, scholar, and amateur diplomat. Born of Orthodox Jewish parents, Vámbéry went as a young man to Constantinople and became both a Moslem and a Turk, traveled for three years on foot through Armenia, Persia and Turkestan, returned to his native Hungary late in life, became a Protestant, and now was professor of Oriental languages at the University of Budapest. Herzl heard that he had expressed an interest in Zionism, so he traveled for fourteen hours by express train to meet him in the Tyrol, taking along his Protestant minister friend, the Reverend Mr. Hechler, to make the introductions.

But it turned out that no intermediary was needed. The two Hungarian Jews got along so well together that Herzl was soon calling the older man Uncle Vámbéry, and when they separated they embraced and kissed as if they were lifelong friends. Uncle Vámbéry, Herzl discovered, spoke twelve languages, was more Turk or English than Hungarian, wrote books in German, had professed five different religions during his life, in two of which he had served as a priest, and now was an atheist.

When he found out Uncle Vámbéry was working on his auto-biography, Herzl suggested that the last chapter be entitled: "How I Helped Prepare the Homecoming of My People, the Jews." And since Uncle Vámbéry knew the Sultan well, Herzl asked him to write the Sultan in support of Zionism. When the professor protested that it would be difficult to accomplish anything by letter, Herzl replied with the words of Disraeli to a young Jew: "You and I belong to a race which can do everything but fail." Then he added, "We *can* really do everything but we must be willing. Will it, Uncle Vámbéry!"

Almost a year later Herzl finally had his long-dreamed-of audience with the Sultan, partly through the good offices of Uncle Vámbéry, partly through the assistance of a conniving Turkish official, Nuri Bey, Secretary-General of the Ministry of Foreign Affairs, to whom Herzl had to pay forty thousand francs (about $10,000) in baksheesh before he would permit the meeting to take place.

May 17, 1901, was a day Theodor Herzl never forgot. He awoke at 6 A.M., and while sitting in his hip bath facing a large mirror, he rehearsed, with gestures, all he intended to say to the Sultan. He dressed meticulously, putting into the buttonhole of his frock coat a rosette indicating the third-class decoration he had received five years earlier. On the way to the Sultan's palace he kept the windows of the carriage closed so not a speck of dust would get on his suit.

Before being received in the audience chamber, he was informed that His Majesty had bestowed upon him the Grand Cordon of the Medjidié, which he agreed to accept when he was assured that this one was a first-class medal.

When he was ushered into the Sultan's presence he found the Turkish monarch exactly as he had always pictured him: small, thin, with a great hooked nose, a bushy dyed beard, a weak, quavering voice. He was in full uniform with a cloak over his tunic, his chest covered with diamond-studded decorations. During the two-hour conversation he sat on a divan with a sword between his knees.

For five years Herzl had been rehearsing how he would get to the heart of his business by reminding the Sultan of the story of Androcles and the lion. The Turkish monarch smiled as he said, "His Majesty is the lion; perhaps I am Androcles, and perhaps there is a thorn that needs pulling out." He explained that the thorn, as he saw it, was Turkey's public debt. The Sultan sighed and said that if Herzl had any ideas for extracting the thorn he would be grateful. Most of the conversation that followed concerned Turkey's financial problems and the visitor's idea of enlisting the assistance of international Jewish bankers, in return for some pro-Jewish pronouncement by the Sultan at some future propitious moment.

The Sultan referred to himself as a friend of the Jews and promised they would always receive his protection if they sought sanctuary in his lands.

The interview over, Herzl found that it was more difficult to leave the palace than it had been to enter. He had to hand out to men he had never seen, gold coins as baksheesh until his pockets were empty.

Three days later Herzl asked for another audience with the Sultan to clear up certain questions about unification of the public debt. The imperial blue envelope that finally arrived at his hotel contained not the hour of an appointment but a scarf pin set with a diamond—a token of the Sultan's friendship. Herzl would have been sick with bitterness if he had been able to foresee that this was all he would ever receive from the Ottoman Empire.

Before he left Constantinople, he discussed with the Sultan's confidants his detailed plan for organizing a Jewish company that would receive a grant of land in Palestine from the Sultan and in return would pay taxes, make the land arable, and settle colonists on it.

Several days later, on the ship taking him home, he recorded his considered impression of the man who ruled over such a large area of the Balkans and the Middle East. By this time he had decided that the Sultan was a weak and craven but thoroughly good-natured man, neither clever nor cruel, "an unhappy prisoner in whose name a thieving, infamous, scoundrelly camarilla perpetrates the vilest abominations." He felt that in

Turkey, everything was done for what was in it for someone, and that every government official was a swindler.

However, he was certain he was on the road to obtaining the sort of a charter he wanted. ("It needs only luck, skill, and money to put through everything I have planned.")

For months Herzl sought financial backing in Paris and London. Then, early in 1902, he was summoned to Constantinople and was offered concessions for the exploitation of mines and the establishment of a bank, in return for the right to organize a company that would settle Jewish immigrants on the land, but not in Palestine. A short time later even this unattractive offer was withdrawn, an indication that it had been made only as a maneuver to force the hand of a French financial group.

Shortly after his forty-second birthday, Herzl wrote in his diary that he was now an "aging and celebrated man; the days of my youth, despite their spells of melancholy, were preferable." He had just been invited to testify in London before a Royal Commission appointed by Prime Minister James Balfour to examine the question of immigration into Britain, in the face of demands that a current influx of Jewish refugees from Rumania and Russia be halted by putting an end to Britain's tradition of free asylum. The invitation led Herzl to one of the most curious of his many pieces of introspection. In a burst of modesty and egotism combined he declared that he had become world-famous in a field in which he felt he had displayed only mediocre political skill—that anyone "with a grain of horse-sense could have done as well"—whereas by instinct he potentially was "a great writer" whose creation of important literature had been held down only because he had become "nauseated and discouraged."

One member of the Royal Commission, Lord Nathaniel Rothschild, head of the English banking firm, a director of the Bank of England, and the first English Jew to become a nobleman, had vigorously objected to calling Herzl as a witness. For years Herzl had been unsuccessfully seeking an interview with him. Now, suddenly, Lord Rothschild agreed to see the man he had publicly termed a "demagogue and a windbag."

The sixty-two-year-old banker, who was so hard of hearing that his visitor had to shout at him to be heard, and the volatile man with the black beard were from the first at swords' points. Herzl was disgusted with "the silly stuff he rattled off . . . like a rope-dancer's patter." When Lord Rothschild asked him what he was going to tell the Commission, Herzl replied that he was going to describe the frightful misery of Eastern Jews and say that they must either die or get out; that in Galicia alone there were nearly three-quarters of a million destitute Jews who would soon be forced to leave. Rothschild bluntly declared that Herzl must not testify in this vein, for it would encourage the passage of restrictive legislation. At this Herzl lost his temper and replied that no one was going to tell him how to testify. Then in a roar he made the accusation that Jewish philanthrophy had become a device for stifling Jewish cries of distress.

After lunching with Lord Rothschild and other members of the family, Herzl, calmer now, discussed the aims of Zionism, declaring that he wanted to found a Jewish colony in a British possession and suggesting the Sinai Peninsula, Egyptian Palestine, and Cyprus as possible locations.

"Would you be for that?" he bluntly asked his host.

Lord Rothschild considered for a moment and then with a chuckle replied, "Very much!"

Herzl, feeling he had scored a victory, prepared to leave. Lord Rothschild saw him to the door, while Leopold Rothschild, a brother, pressed on Herzl an invitation to a garden party.

That same day, Herzl received a message that the Sultan wanted him to come to Constantinople as soon as possible.

The next week, Herzl gave the Royal Commission a frank and comprehensive explanation of the Jewish problem and the solution proposed by the Zionists. He finished testifying in time to attend the Rothschild garden party, where he spoke for some time with the sister of King Edward VII, and where he felt he had perhaps served the Zionist cause well by being seen with so many important figures of British Jewry.

In another meeting with Lord Rothschild, Herzl tried to persuade him to organize a Jewish company to establish a colony in one of the three locations he had mentioned, on a strictly business basis, with no philanthropy involved. Lord Rothschild intimated he might be interested in a small project involving not more than 25,000 settlers, to which Herzl explosively replied it must be on an immense scale or not at all. The only satisfaction that came out of this meeting was that Lord Rothschild, who had once called him a demagogue and a windbag, declared as they parted, "In my opinion you are a great man."

During the ensuing months many letters were exchanged by the two men, but nothing concrete ever materialized.

A long visit by Herzl to Constantinople resulted in a summer villa, a steam yacht, and a state carriage being placed at his disposal, and a small bag of gold pieces being presented to him for his expenses, but the trip was fruitless except for the Sultan's vague assurances that he was interested, still, in the plight of the Jews.

Back in London, Herzl interceded with Colonial Secretary Joseph Chamberlain for the right to establish a Jewish colony on Cyprus. Although expressing sympathy with the Zionist cause, Chamberlain said Cyprus was already populated by Greeks and Moslems; that an influx of Jews would cause even greater tensions; but that if Herzl could find a spot somewhere in the British Empire that was not yet inhabited by white settlers, they might work out something. Herzl's answer was that when the Jews began arriving on Cyprus, the Moslems would leave and the Greeks would eagerly sell their land at a good profit and go to Athens or Crete. Then they discussed the El Arish area of Egyptian Palestine. When Chamberlain had to look in an atlas to find out where El Arish was, Herzl decided he was as ignorant of the geography of the British Empire as the owner of some large secondhand store who was not at all sure where to find the articles he had in stock. He was also depressed by the discovery that the Colonial Secretary had as little imagination as a nut-and-bolt manufacturer whose only interest in life was in expanding his business. However, Chamberlain finally arranged an interview for Herzl with Lord Henry Charles Keith Petty-Fitzmaurice Lansdowne, Secretary of State for Foreign Affairs, who promised to take up with the Cabinet the suggestion that a Jewish colony be established in the El Arish area or the Sinai Peninsula.

Back in Vienna, Herzl's heart began "acting up in all sorts of ways," but he was happy in the belief that the result of all this activity in London might be a British charter and, at last, a Jewish state.

Altneuland (Old-New Land), a novel inspired by Herzl's visit to Palestine that he had been working on for the past several years, was published in the autumn of 1902. On the frontispiece was the motto, *If you will it, it is no dream*. (Also sometimes translated, *If you will, it is no fairytale*.) This became the slogan of Zionism, and one of Herzl's biographers called it his most important contribution to the struggle for a Jewish state.

Altneuland is the story of two men, one a Viennese Jew, the other a retired German army officer, a Christian, who live for 20 years on a desert island, out of touch with the world. Then, in 1923, they decide to pay Europe a visit. On their way they stop at Palestine and find that a Jewish state has been created there, so Utopian in every respect that instead of going on to Europe or back to their desert island, they remain and join the New Society, as the state is called.

One of the characters in the book was patterned after Heinrich Kana, the friend of Herzl's youth who had committed suicide and whose ghost he now extirpated by giving a happy ending to the Kana story. More important, into *Altneuland* Herzl put all his dreams. Many who read the book laughed, as he predicted they would, at his Utopianism. Yet just fifty-eight years later, on the centenary of his birth, an edition of *Altneuland* was published in Haifa with an editor's note that said:

> We do not claim that this vision of a Jewish state in Palestine, which Herzl put out in the guise of light fiction in 1902, is an exact and accurate description of the present-day state of Israel. Yet the resemblances between Herzl's ideas and those of the planners of Israel today are so close . . . that they give this essay-in-prophecy an historical importance which is not always realized.

Scattered through the hundred thousand words were these phrases, which might have been written in 1962 instead of 1902:

> A beautiful city had been built at Haifa . . . vessels of all shapes and sizes lay at peace there . . . handsome buildings. . . . You might have thought yourself in some large Italian port. . . . Mount Carmel covered with villas . . . equal rights for

women. . . . Every needy person is efficiently aided. . . . We do
not allow begging. . . . Once Jewish children were weak, pale,
cowed. Look at them today! . . . We brought these children from
dark cellars and slums. . . . There are all kinds of cooperative
societies here . . . both consumers' and producers' cooperatives.
. . . This is the middle way between individualism and collec-
tivism. . . . Workers are insured against accident, sickness, old
age, and death. . . . The swamps are drained. . . . These people
[the Arabs] are far better off than before. . . . They are healthy,
have better food, their children go to school . . . nothing has
been done to interfere with their customs or their faith. . . . The
slopes are terraced, as in ancient times. . . . Numerous flourishing tree nurseries show how expertly horticulture and afforesta-
tion are practiced here. . . . On the ridges of the little hills pines
and cypresses stood against the blue sky. . . . The accumulated
experience of all the advanced nations of the world was used by
the settlers who streamed into the country from every corner of
the globe. . . . Rich pastures where cattle and sheep were graz-
ing. . . . The sun made the steel of great agricultural machines
gleam. . . . A sparkling new town with fine houses and colorful
gardens. . . . Tiberius was a favorite of rich Americans and Europeans. . . . We compete successfully with Tunisian and Algerian
phosphates, not to mention those from Florida. . . . We have
gotten rid of malaria because of our drainage, canalization, and
eucalyptus groves. . . . Soon every day we saw 500 to 2,000 immigrants arriving. . . . Everywhere in the country free enterprise
was building factories. . . . Jerusalem had become full of life.
. . . Parks, boulevards, great educational institutions, emporia,
some splendid public buildings and places of amusement.

Herzl in his *Altneuland* did not foresee the extermination of
six million Jews by Nazi sadism, the rebirth of the Hebrew language, the refusal of the Arabs to accept establishment of a
Jewish state, the disintegration of the Ottoman Empire, or the
part that pioneer-socialism would play in the development of
the new Jewish state, and all his Utopian dreams did not become bright reality after Israel was reborn, for he envisioned a
country in which there would no longer be professional politicians, and a world from which anti-Semitism had disappeared.
Some of his practical ideas were ignored by the rebuilders of
Israel, such as living trees taking the place of lampposts in the

cities; a tunnel under every street containing all the pipes and wires of public utility services so there would never again be the need of digging up a street; a canal from the Mediterranean to the Red Sea with a 394-foot drop, used to generate electricity for the country's entire needs; and a Peace Palace in Jerusalem in which "friends of peace" would hold their international congresses, and world gatherings of scientists and scholars would take place—"for this was the home of the common lot of all mankind: suffering."

But what Herzl *did* foresee in his *Altneuland* proved him a man of great vision. Devout Jews were happy that the last word on the last page was "God." Seven characters were debating what force was responsible for the creation of a Jewish state. After they had guessed "distress," "tolerance," "will power," "knowledge," "self-assurance," and "love and suffering," an old rabbi stood up and said, "God!"

Late in the year the novel was published in Hebrew under the title *Tel Aviv* (hill of spring). This was seven years before the first foundation stone of the city of Tel Aviv was laid.

The review of *Altneuland* in his own paper, the *Neue Freie Presse*, said, "No Moses entered the Promised Land." It may or may not have been intended as a compliment to Herzl, but at least it was accurately prophetic.

In 1903, Herzl was the organizing genius of a British commission sent to El Arish to investigate the possibilities of colonization. He supplied the commission with experts, maps, life insurance policies, and even a "gramophone to amuse the Bedouin." Then he went down to Cairo and offered his own services to the commission. Out of the trip came one more scintillating piece of observation and prophecy. Writing of the Egyptians, he said, "They are the coming rulers of the country and it is a wonder the British don't see this." Then he added, "They [the British] are cleaning up the East, letting air and light into its dens of filth, breaking old tyrannies, and destroying ancient abuses. But together with freedom and progress, they are teaching the fellahin the art of revolt. I believe that the English colonial methods must either destroy England's colonial empire, or lay the foundations for England's world domination, one of the most fascinating alternatives of our age."

Largely because of the opposition of Lord Evelyn Cromer, Viceroy of Egypt, whom Herzl branded "the most disagreeable Englishman I have ever met," an unfavorable report was made to London on the El Arish scheme. It was a blow to Herzl, who had been so optimistic that he had decided not to buy a family vault in the cemetery in Vienna where his father had been provisionally laid to rest. But now, with the collapse of the El Arish scheme, he acquired Vault No. 28.

When Herzl next saw Chamberlain, the Colonial Secretary suggested Uganda, the interior of which, he said, had an excellent climate for Europeans. Herzl did not immediately commit himself.

During the spring of 1903, one of the worst pogroms in European history occurred in Russia: the Kishinev Massacre. For days anti-Semites killed, raped, and tortured. The world was shocked, and the Zionists were spurred into action. Herzl became a tornado of activity. Among his new schemes were attempts to get land in Tripoli from the Italians, part of Mozambique from Portugal, a piece of the Congo from Belgium. Then he conceived the idea that Russia might be persuaded to appease world indignation over Kishinev by helping to obtain a Jewish sanctuary in Palestine. Unable to make contact with the Czar, he accepted the help of a Polish countess. She obtained for him an audience with Russia's most notorious anti-Semite, Minister of the Interior Plehve, who was said to have been the instigator of the Kishinev Massacre and the most influential member of the Cabinet. The meeting took place in St. Petersburg. Herzl later spoke of it as "an immortal game of chess." In barely understandable French the sallow-faced anti-Semite admitted to Herzl that only a limited number of Jews were being given the opportunity for a higher education; that Jews were being widely discriminated against; that most Jews were being forced to live in ghettos. He said Czarist Russia was demanding that all Jews become assimilated.

Herzl finally was afforded a chance to make three demands: that Russia intervene with the Sultan to obtain a charter for Palestinian colonization; that Russia allot money raised by taxing Jews for emigration expenses; that the government assist rather than obstruct the work of the Zionist movement inside

Russia. Plehve agreed to all three points. The meeting ended with Herzl being ordered to submit a written summary of his demands and an outline of what he intended to say about their meeting at the forthcoming Zionist Congress.

Then Herzl had an interview with Count Sergei Witte, Minister of Finance, who professed to be "a friend of the Jews" but treated his visitor to a stream of vile language about them. He said he had told the late Emperor Alexander III, "If it were possible for your Majesty to drown the six or seven million Jews [of Russia] in the Black Sea I should be perfectly satisfied. But if it isn't possible, we must let them live." He quoted this as proof of what a tolerant and intelligent man he was. When Herzl asked for some help in the emigration of Jews, the Minister replied that Russia gave them plenty of encouragement to emigrate—"for one thing a good kicking."

In a second meeting with Plehve, Herzl was told his suggestions had all been submitted to the Czar, that Russia favored the creation of an independent Jewish state capable of absorbing several million Jews, but that she would wish to retain all those of superior intelligence for her own use. "Brains know no distinction of creed or nationality, but we should be glad to part with those of little brains and less means." When Herzl again brought up his request for government assistance to the Zionist movement inside Russia, the Minister said he had been preparing to take exactly the opposite step: to recommend its suppression. The meeting ended with Plehve indicating that whatever Russia decided about his three requests would depend on what happened at the forthcoming Zionist Congress.

At Vilna, on the way home, Herzl was given a welcome by the Jews of the city that made a deep impression on him. His regal appearance encouraged the hope in these distressed people that here was a modern deliverer who would somehow lead them from this place of tears and terror to the land of the promise. At a banquet in his honor a toast was proposed to "King Herzl." Telling about it later, he said, "An absurdity, but it had an uncanny ring in the dark Russian night."

A few days after Herzl's return from Russia, the Sixth Zionist Congress opened in Basel. It was to go down in history as the Uganda Congress. While he had been away, the British Foreign

Office had made a definite offer of six thousand square miles in the Guas Ngishu or Uasin Gishu Plateau of British East Africa on which Jewish immigrants could have local autonomy and their own governor. Although Chamberlain had said "Uganda," the land was not in Uganda at all, but in what is now Kenya. However, in that stubborn way that error has of often overpowering truth, no one ever called it anything but the Uganda Plan.

Herzl, while stressing that Palestine remained the real goal, favored consideration of Uganda as what he and another supporter, Dr. Nordau, called "an overnight resting place." The question was put to the Congress only in the form of a motion authorizing the dispatch of an investigating committee to East Africa, then the Seventh Congress would hear its report and decide. The debate was acrimonious. Tempers mounted to a hysterical pitch. There was bitter name-calling; charges and countercharges. The opposition was composed largely of Russian Zionists. Finally a vote was taken. The motion was approved, 295 to 177. But the opponents, convinced that Zion had been abandoned, marched indignantly from the Congress hall to an empty room where some continued to make speeches, while others sat on the floor weeping. (This caused it to be nicknamed "the Crying Congress.") They were on the verge of denouncing Herzl as a traitor when he stalked into the room. After much effort he persuaded them to return to the hall, but they persisted in their opposition. There were predictions Uganda had split the Zionist movement irreparably. As it turned out, the controversy was a waste of energy and tempers, for a report was received before long that there was no British territory in East Africa either suitable or available for Jewish colonization.

After the Congress finally adjourned, Herzl, accompanied by Zangwill and Nordau, went to a hotel room to review what had happened. Over a bottle of mineral water, he made another of his prophetic remarks. To his two friends he said, "I will tell you the speech I am going to make to the Seventh Congress—that is, if I am alive." He was well aware that the strain he had just undergone was hastening his end.

In December at a Zionist ball in London, Herzl almost lost the first convert to his Zionist dream. A fanatical Russian Zionist fired a revolver at Nordau, but fortunately his aim was bad; neither of his two shots found their mark.

Despite his own physical condition, Herzl continued his frenetic diplomatic activity. He wrote a long letter to the anti-Semite, Plehve, asking him to obtain from the Czar a letter recommending the Zionist plans, which he, Herzl, would deliver in person to the Sultan. He was so optimistic of the effect such a move would have that he told Plehve, "I believe it possible to conclude the entire business in a short time. . . . Emigration could begin within the next few months."

When nothing came of this move, the indefatigable Herzl decided to turn to Italy. In Venice he had another of his providential encounters with a strange character. He had already been helped by a Protestant clergyman who believed in Biblical prophecy, and a man of twelve languages and five religions who had ended up an atheist. Now it was another complete stranger, a Roman Catholic who was a Papal Count and official Vatican artist, B. Lippay. After five minutes of conversation he offered to present Herzl to Pope Pius X. The audience took place on January 25, 1904. Lippay had taken care to advise his newfound friend on Vatican custom and especially cautioned him that when the Pope held out his hand, Herzl was to kiss the fingertips. But when the moment arrived and the Pope did hold out his hand, Herzl ignored it. Later he said he was convinced that this spoiled his chances. However, the audience lasted almost half an hour, with Pope Pius on his throne and Herzl seated by his side. As soon as the black-bearded Jew had outlined his Zionist plan, His Holiness expressed opposition. The Church might not be able the prevent the return of the Jews to Jerusalem but would never sanction it. "The Jews have not recognized Our Lord, therefore we cannot recognize the Jewish people."

Herzl tried to be conciliatory, to talk international politics, but the conversation kept getting back to religion.

"The Jewish faith was the foundation of our own," the Pope declared, "but it has been superseded by the teachings of Christ and we cannot admit that it still enjoys any validity."

Herzl replied that terror and persecution are not the best methods for trying to convert Jews, or anyone else.

"If you come to Palestine and settle your people there," the

Pope said, "we will be ready with churches and priests to baptize you."

Herzl's audience with the Italian King, Victor Emmanuel III, who had succeeded to the throne just three years earlier upon the assassination of his father, was more pleasant. On his way by carriage to the Quirinal, he engaged in his favorite whimsy of odd moments: putting the clothing of reality on his nude dream. He decided that when Palestine finally belonged to the Jews, he would lay out a street in Jerusalem called Diaspora Road and line it with samples of the architecture of all the ages in all the lands in which Jews had lived during the dispersal. Each city block would represent a different period or a different country.

As the doors of the palace reception chamber were thrown open and the King came forward to meet him, Herzl's observant eyes took in every detail. Victor Emmanuel III was a short man with broad shoulders. He wore a general's uniform without a sword. After hoisting himself up on a sofa until his feet swung clear of the floor, he was soon talking of "a thousand things." He told Herzl that Italy was the only European nation to admit Jews into its diplomatic service; that he had been to Palestine several times and considered the land already "very Jewish"; that it "will be yours and must be yours; it is merely a question of time."

He started to say something about "once you have half a million Jews there—" when Herzl interrupted to point out that Jewish immigration was forbidden.

"Nonsense!" the King replied. "Everything can be done with baksheesh." He suggested that Herzl ask the Sultan for the Jordan Valley and promise him fifty per cent of the profit in return. "The only thing that has any effect on him is money."

He said he disliked Jews who were embarrassed that they were Jews and that whenever he encountered such people he talked about nothing but Jews. He was glad Uganda had been given up. He liked the Jewish love of Jerusalem. He rejected Herzl's idea of a Jewish colonization of Tripolitania, and when asked to write a letter to the Sultan he replied he would have to consult his advisers. "I cannot do what I please, you know."

Next, Herzl turned to Count Agenor von Goluchowski, Foreign Minister of Austria-Hungary, with whom he had a long discussion in Vienna, during the course of which the count asked why, with a hundred thousand Jews at the start of the Christian Era, and the number doubling every fifty years, there were not now a billion Jews in the world.

"We have suffered grievous losses in the course of history," Herzl replied.

"But the Christians, too, have been persecuted, especially the early Christians."

Herzl smiled and replied, "The early Christians, sir, were Jews."

The meeting ended with the count suggesting that England was the country that should help to establish the Jewish State.

A few days later, Herzl was turning in another direction, this time toward the United States. He had heard that Jacob B. Schiff, New York banker, was ready to do anything to help oppressed Jews. Herzl by now was seriously ill, so he sent one of his Zionist associates to see Schiff in London. The last entry in Herzl's diary is the start of a letter to Schiff.

In June 1904, Herzl and his wife went to the mountains. His heart was weaker than ever, but his prophetic powers were still good. To a Zionist colleague he said: "To what purpose shall we fool ourselves? I have heard the ringing of the third bell."

To David Wolffsohn he wrote: "Don't do anything silly while I am dead." (There would be much postmortem discussion of why he had used the word "while.")

On his desk he left a paper on which he had written these words in English:

In the midst of life there is death.

His old friend, the Reverend Mr. Hechler, came to see him and found him suffering from bronchial catarrh, his body wracked by violent and bloody coughing, his breathing painful, his heart functioning badly.

"Say that I gave my blood for my people," Herzl whispered. Then he became delirious and pounded the bedclothing with a mythical gavel as he presided at a meeting of the organization he had created to help make his dream come true, the Zionist Congress.

Pneumonia settled in one lung and on July 3, 1904, with his wife, his mother and his children at his bedside, he breathed his last. He was only a few months past the age of forty-four. He left his family penniless. Although he had fired his people with a spirit they had not had since Biblical times, he died under the impression that his life had been a bleak failure. Yet he was a prophet, even in death, for his will provided that he was to be laid to rest in the Jewish cemetery in Vienna beside his father, "to remain there until the Jewish people take my remains to Palestine."

Less than half a century later, on a summer day in 1949, the Jewish people kept their pact with the man who had done more than any other human being, alive or dead, to mold the new Israel. His dust was gathered up and flown to the Jewish State in an Israeli plane named *Herzl*, and the next day was reburied on the highest hill of the Holy City, now renamed Mount Herzl.

It was no longer a dream, partly because he had willed it.

Chapter 2

Why should our lot be
Meaner than that of all others?

—ELIEZER BEN YEHUDA

THE LETTER that arrived in Jerusalem late in September 1897 from Vienna was in a neat but firm handwriting, in coal-black ink. Eliezer Ben Yehuda read it over three or four times before he called his wife and said to her excitedly:

"*Bitti,* it's from Herzl! Theodor Herzl. He writes to tell me that at Basel—at the Zionist Congress—I was elected a member of the executive board."

"Are you going to accept?"

"It's a great honor, *bitti.* A great honor."

"But you are angry with them because they talked about a flag, and a university, and a bank, yet never even mentioned a language for the new Jewish State."

"Yes, but if I were on the board I could convince them that the revival of Hebrew is much more important than some of the things they wasted their time discussing."

"As if you didn't have enough to do!" the young wife sighed. "The paper. The dictionary. Your teaching. Besides, won't this get you into more trouble with the Turkish authorities? Oh Eliezer, you mustn't go to prison again!"

"We shall see," was all he replied, as he turned back to the hundreds of scraps of paper that littered his desk. After his wife left the room, he sat thinking that some of the men who had assembled in Switzerland were probably still just boys when he and Deborah came to Palestine seventeen years ago to commence their lonely campaign for a land and a language. It was strange that it had all started with so sectarian and so un-Jewish a book as *Robinson Crusoe*.

He was Eliezer Perlman in those days, one of the three sons of the *reb* or wise man of the Lithuanian village of Luzhky, and of Feygeh, a gentle woman who had to open a grocery store to support the family because her husband, although brilliant, was such a bad provider. Even with the store's income, the family finances were still so critical that Eliezer was sent to live with an uncle, David Wolffson, and was enrolled in a Yeshivah (rabbinical school) in Polotzk. There he met a local rabbi who changed the course of his life. In the rabbi's library, under the cushion of a chair, was a book he kept hidden from the eyes of more conventional people who would have violently disapproved if they had seen the title: *Robinson Crusoe*, by Daniel Defoe, in Hebrew. Eliezer was fascinated that the tongue of the prophets could be used to tell the story of a shipwrecked sailor, and he often went to the rabbi's home to listen to him read from the book. Finally the rabbi loaned it to him. Although Eliezer read it only when he was alone, someone reported that he was engaging in sacrilegious activities, and his uncle withdrew him from the Yeshivah and took him home with him. One night Uncle David tiptoed up the stairs to the boy's room and caught him reading in bed by candlelight. Eliezer was quick to slip the book under the mattress, but the uncle found it and when he saw the title, *Robinson Crusoe*, he drove the young "infidel" from the house, although it was late at night.

The next morning as Shlomah Naftaly Yonas, a prosperous and pious brewer in the nearby city of Glubokiah, answered the call of the *shammash* to morning prayer, he discovered on the first bench inside the door a small dark figure, dressed in the costume of a rabbinical student, sound asleep. That day Eliezer Perlman, aged fourteen, became virtually the adopted son of Mr. Yonas, who had an immense library, a deep love of Hebrew, and six children of his own. The youngest was Paula, a baby, who stared in wonderment at the two long curls that marked Eliezer as a rabbinical student—and cried when they were finally cut off some days later. The oldest was Deborah, eighteen, who was assigned by her father to teach him French, German and Russian. (He already knew Lithuanian, Yiddish, and Hebrew.)

The impressionable boy never forgot the speech Father Yonas made to him one day when they were walking through the woods. He wrote it down in a notebook that he used years later in compiling his autobiography.

"I hope you will never forget your Hebrew, Eliezer," he said. "It is a language of great beauty. The tragedy is that it is like Latin; today it is fit only for prayer and the preservation of our old Jewish literature. But we must keep Hebrew alive, always. It has a melody of its own, like some of the deep sounds of the forest we have been hearing on our walks together. So promise me, my boy, that you will repay what I am trying to do for you by always keeping Hebrew alive in your mind and your heart."

Eliezer, age fourteen, promised.

Nine years later, Mr. and Mrs. Eliezer Ben Yehuda arrived by ship at Haifa. He had dropped his family name of Perlman for the Hebrew pen name he had been using lately as a journalist in Paris (Ben Yehuda means son of Judea), and Deborah had dropped her family name of Yonas when she married the man for whom she had been waiting so patiently while he prepared himself for a career. After two years with the Yonas family he had gone to Paris as a student. There a doctor had told him he had a serious case of tuberculosis and implied that he had a very short time to live. He wrote Deborah that the news frightened him not because he was afraid to die, but because he had recently become obsessed with the idea that his people— the Jews—should return whence they had come and remake Israel as a nation.

"I work now without sleep," one of his letters said, "to put onto paper the reason it is so important for the Jewish world to become inflamed with the idea of returning to the land of our forefathers and working for the freedom to which we are entitled. I have decided that in order to have our own land and political life, it is necessary that we have a language to hold us together. That language is Hebrew, but not the Hebrew of the rabbis and scholars. We must have a Hebrew language in which we can conduct the business of life. It will not be easy to revive a language that has been sleeping so long a time. The day is short, the work to be done is so great."

His first step, he decided, was to issue an appeal, as he called it, to the Jewish world at large. While he coughed, and spit blood, and worried that his death was imminent, he covered hundreds of pieces of paper with arguments, reasons, and proofs. Finally he sent the article to *Hashahar* (The Dawn), an important politico-literary magazine in Vienna, which published it under the title, "A Worthy Question." It was signed by his new name, Ben Yehuda. The article began:

> If, in truth, each and every nation is entitled to defend its nationality and protect itself from extinction, then logically we, the Hebrews, also must needs have that same right. Why should our lot be meaner than that of all others?

It concluded:

> And now the time has come for us to do something positive. Let us create a society for the purchase of land in Eretz Israel; for the acquisition of everything necessary for agriculture; for the division of the land among Jews already present and those desiring to emigrate there, and for the provision of the funds necessary for those who cannot establish themselves independently.

This was 1880, sixteen years before publication of *The Jewish State*.

One of Herzl's earliest and most enthusiastic supporters was a Protestant minister. Ben Yehuda's first convert was a Catholic whom he met in Paris, an aristocratic Polish journalist named Tshashnikov, who represented a liberal Russian newspaper. Tshashnikov befriended him in many ways. When Eliezer was near death from tuberculosis just after the appeal was published, Tshashnikov went to Baron Rothschild and persuaded him to send the twenty-two-year-old consumptive to Algeria in the hope that the hot dry climate there would benefit him.

After a few months, Tshashnikov went to Algeria to visit

Eliezer and found him improved in health and aflame with the desire to revive the Hebrew language.

Even before the start of the Christian era, he told Tshashnikov, Hebrew had begun to die out as a spoken language. Christ, for example, spoke Aramaic. In one period, Greek was the common language of most Jews. Later, as they scattered around the world, they began to use the languages of the countries in which they found themselves. In the ghettos of Russia and Poland, Jews who had fled from Germany in the Middle Ages continued to speak medieval German, with some Hebrew and Slavic words grafted onto it, and the language came to be called Yiddish. In the same way, medieval Spanish became Ladino.

"I read somewhere," Eliezer told his friend, "that we Jews speak seventy different languages. The dialects of the ghetto have clung to us like leprosy. We can never aspire to be free men as long as we use ghetto languages.

"They argue with me that Hebrew is a bookish language; that it lacks vitality. But they are not referring to the Hebrew that was spoken in the streets two thousand years ago. Then it was a language of the masses.

"I agree that it's equally important to have words for tools and dishes as for philosophical concepts. Hebrew once had those words, but they have become lost. They entered Arabic and Greek and other languages as immigrants and remained as citizens. Now we must find them and bring them home. Someone will have to spend years searching through Hebrew literature and the books of other languages, in libraries all over the world, for words which our people once used but have become lost."

"Yes, Eliezer," his friend said, "you will have to be detective, scholar, magician, and midwife, all combined."

Now Eliezer and Deborah were on their way to Palestine where he intended to begin just such a career. The young husband no longer coughed blood, but he had not been cured and he knew it, so for the rest of his life he lived, worked, and planned as if he expected to come face to face with death around the next corner.

They arrived in Jerusalem with one gold louis as their total cash reserve. The position Eliezer obtained on a weekly newspaper paid him the equivalent of five dollars a month. The owner of an abandoned tenement rented them two rooms and took their gold coin. To reach the building it was necessary to cross seven filthy courtyards ankle-deep in debris, and to get to their rooms they had to climb a rope ladder. There was no furniture, not even a bed or a chair. The two windows looked out on the Wailing Wall, which for centuries had provoked the lachrymose lamentations of pious Jews. Even when the windows were closed they could hear the moaning and sobbing that seemed to infiltrate through cracks in the wall.

Eliezer, though he had become a freethinker, decided to let his beard grow and adopt the dress of a religious Oriental Jew: a long olive-green robe trimmed with the fur of a red fox, a broad girdle, and a tarboosh, or fez. He insisted that Deborah keep her luxuriant crop of reddish-blond hair covered at all times with a scarf, to conform to Orthodox practice.

Some months after their arrival the young wife announced that she was pregnant. Eliezer, with a faraway mystic look in his eyes, made a long speech, saying:

"Deborah, you are going to become the first Hebrew mother in nearly two thousand years. Our child will be the first infant in all those centuries to come into the world hearing nothing but the beauty of our own ancient language. You must take a solemn pledge right now, Deborah, that you will make this dream of mine come true. Never must the child hear any words but Hebrew!

"Until our crusade finds popular favor, we must isolate our young one from the contamination of the languages and dialects of the Diaspora. This is even more important than all the writing and teaching I shall be doing, for by this example we may be able to inflame the Jewish world with our idea."

Deborah called it has "holy stubbornness," but she took the oath.

Meanwhile, the opposition to Ben Yehuda had begun to crystallize. It was made up mostly of religious Jews who felt that he was profaning the holy language by trying to make it fit to be talked in the streets. It was not uncommon for him to be stoned as he walked through Old Jerusalem. Often they shouted at him the word "Heretic!"

Deborah's firstborn was a boy they named Ben Zion. The first word she spoke to him after he had been placed in her arms was "*Yaldi* [My child]!" From that moment on she saw to it that not a word of any language but Hebrew was spoken in the room the child was in.

For years Ben Zion was treated like a prisoner, to keep him from hearing other languages while his mother tried to teach him to speak Hebrew. Long past the age when normal children had started to talk, Ben Zion made only occasional noises with his mouth. Ben Yehuda's fanatical opponents whispered this news with delight from one end of Jerusalem to the other. They said it was God's curse on the man who was trying to profane the holy language. They predicted that the boy would grow up an idiot. When Ben Zion by his second birthday had still not spoken a word, Deborah herself began to grow frightened. But it was only a few months later that the boy finally began to talk and soon he was speaking Hebrew beautifully, "the first He-brew child in two thousand years," the proud father always called him. Never in all those centuries had a child grown up speaking the language of the prophets as his mother tongue.

Meanwhile Eliezer, despite his tuberculosis, was working six-teen to eighteen hours a day. He taught conversational Hebrew to children in schools established by the Alliance Israélite Uni-verselle. He started a weekly paper of his own called *Hatzevi* (The Deer) and not only wrote most of the articles himself, but set them into type, folded the papers by hand, addressed them, affixed the Turkish postage stamps with Deborah's help, and then, while most of Jerusalem slept, took them to the post office. He wrote textbooks in Hebrew, collaborated on a play, and translated novels into the old-new language. He also or-ganized a small group of intellectuals in Jerusalem into what he called "the Army of the Defenders of the Language" and per-suaded them to sign a pact that read:

> The members residing in the land of Israel [Ben Yehuda from the start refused to call it Palestine] will speak to each other in Hebrew, in society, in meeting places, and in the streets and

market places, and shall not be ashamed. They will make it a point to teach their sons and daughters and the rest of their households this language.

The members will watch in the streets and the market places over the Hebrew speech and when they hear adults speaking Russian, French, Yiddish, English, Spanish, Arabic, or any other language, they will not spare a remark even to the eldest amongst them, saying, "Aren't you ashamed of yourselves!"

Ben Yehuda never stopped his intellectual labors before midnight and was always up before the sun. When Deborah would reprove him and say he needed more sleep, he would tell her, "I get the strength I need to carry me through the day by watching the miracle of the sunrise each morning."

One morning he greeted Deborah by saying, "I have just decided that our crying need is for an up-to-date dictionary. Just think, here we are trying to teach people to speak a language and there is no dictionary of that language! There is not even a Hebrew word for dictionary."

Finding the word was one-millionth the task of making the dictionary, for he devoted the rest of his life to this objective and after his death many others took over.

Now he was so busy that he was even unaware of the family's desperate financial situation. Deborah took to eating alone, so he wouldn't see how she cheated herself because there was not enough food to go round.

And all the time he was uncovering more and more long-buried words and adding them to the language, or using Hebrew roots to make entirely new words. At first he launched them merely by publishing them in *The Deer.* He tried to give his readers at least one new word per issue, and so each week Hebrew became more and more a language in which women could do their marketing, children could play games and call each other names, and men could discuss political and scientific developments.

By the time Deborah was thirty-seven she had borne Eliezer five children. Thanks to her consideration of his fanaticism, the three older ones all spoke Hebrew and no other language, while the two babies were being sheltered, as the others had been, from "the contaminating languages." Then one day the "first Hebrew mother in two thousand years" commenced to cough. She had a terror from the start that she had contracted the disease that doctors fifteen years earlier had predicted would take her husband's life almost any day. When she became bedridden, Eliezer had to run the house, play nurse to his dying wife, and take care of five children, the youngest a baby in arms, in addition to running the newspaper, trying to revive a language, making a dictionary, teaching school, and engaging in all his other intellectual labors.

As Deborah's condition grew worse, he decided to send for his mother. There was a Turkish rule at this time against Jewish immigration, but he begged the Pasha of Jerusalem to make an exception, pointing out that Mrs. Perlman was almost seventy, much too old to bear arms or children either, and therefore hardly a danger in any way to the Ottoman Empire. When the Pasha replied with a firm "No!" he sent for her anyway. She was smuggled into the port of Jaffa disguised as a sack of potatoes. After her arrival in Jerusalem, her son made his first exception to the primary rule of the household. Because his mother knew no Hebrew he permitted her to talk to Deborah and the children in Russian, but it was understood that she must never again utter another word of Yiddish.

When Deborah died, Eliezer's grief was intense. It was multiplied several months later by the passing away of three of the five children. The ultrareligious people of Jerusalem were convinced these tragedies were God's punishment for his tampering with the holy language. They believed that they were assisting Divine Providence by placing on a black list not only pupils who insisted on studying Hebrew but their fathers, mothers, brothers, and sisters as well. Schools that encouraged or even permitted the study of Hebrew were banned. Yet the new language continued to make progress. With Ben Yehuda's assistance, a school was established that became the first in two thousand years in which no other tongue but Hebrew was spoken. Here and there Jewish mothers were singing Hebrew lullabies to their children. Ben Yehuda's most startling victory was getting Hebrew introduced into the curriculum of several of the oldest theological schools that were known as citadels of reaction. For years no one but he and those directly involved knew how he had done it—by paying a small weekly bribe to each pupil willing to take lessons, and a similar bribe to each teacher who agreed to conduct Hebrew classes. The poverty of teachers and students alike made them easy victims for his trickery.

One day Eliezer received a letter from Pola, Deborah's younger sister, who had cried when he cut off the curls that had marked him as a Yeshivah student. She was now a student in the University of Moscow, specializing in natural sciences, but was discouraged about pursuing a scientific career because of the difficulties put in the way of a woman. She wrote that she wanted to change her name to one more Hebrew-sounding; would her brother-in-law please suggest a good one? Eliezer sent back a list of twenty, with a translation of each. In a burst of sentimentality she chose Hemda because it meant, he said, "my cherished one." After a short correspondence, Eliezer proposed that she also change her last name. She wasted no time in debate with herself. She knew that this was the career she wanted most and had always wanted.

There was a danger now that the Ben Yehuda household would lose its Hebrew character. Mrs. Perlman spoke Yiddish and Russian, while Hemda spoke French and Russian. Eliezer's colleagues chided him and asked why he had not taken a "Hebrew wife!" His enemies rejoiced. Obviously the structure was crumbling. Eliezer met the crisis drastically by moving the printing equipment into his house. This added four printers to the menage. All four had been given their jobs with the understanding that they would never speak anything but Hebrew. As they worked they sang Hebrew songs, which Hemda and the children were also soon singing. (She often said that they sang more than they worked.)

Although Hemda had had little trouble mastering European languages, she found Hebrew grammar impossible. "Never," she said, "will the Semitic spirit be able to vanquish the Slav in me." But six months to the day after her arrival in Palestine, on the Feast of Succoth, she walked into her husband's study and made a speech in almost perfect Hebrew, declaring, "I know you have waited patiently for what I now say. From this moment on I shall speak exclusively Hebrew, not only with you but with everyone we meet."

With tears in his eyes he replied, *"Bitti,* you are like a beautiful flame, giving both light and warmth."

One day some weeks later he said to her, *"Bitti,* the language needs a feminine touch. You can help give it the softness it lacks, the flexibility, the delicacy, the subtle nuances."

So Hemda began writing for *The Deer,* first "Letters from Jerusalem," then a fashion column, to the disgust of Orthodox Jerusalemites, who saw this as the extreme in the sacrilegious use of the holy language. With her husband's help she even created a Hebrew word, *ofnah,* for "fashion," from a Hebrew base meaning style or manner. This was one word the women of Jerusalem fought against using for years, preferring *modah* because it sounds more like the word Paris uses.

Hemda also sold advertising for *The Deer,* set up a bookkeeping system, wrote letters to important personages around the world soliciting money for the dictionary, copied philological material, and even helped search in musty volumes for lost Hebrew words. Hemda tried to reconcile herself to being the wife of a fanatic. She never forgot a story her sister had told her, of how once, while walking in the woods, she and her husband sat romantically side by side on a log. Suddenly Deborah saw a scorpion and jumping up shouted in Hebrew, "Help, Eliezer, a scorpion!"

Instead of coming to her rescue, her pedantic husband replied, "Deborah, how many times have I told you that the word is *akrab,* not *akreb!"*

The Ben Yehuda financial situation gradually improved. He now received a subsidy of ten napoleons a month from Baron Rothschild, the paper was making a slight weekly profit, and a Russian publisher had paid him a thousand rubles in advance for a small Hebrew dictionary. During this period, Eliezer was spending most of his time reading through Spanish, Egyptian and Italian literature for traces of lost Hebrew words.

When Hemda was twenty-two, she began bearing Ben Yehuda children. Her first (his sixth) was a girl, so they named her Deborah, after the first Mrs. Ben Yehuda. Four days after

the birth a special Chanukah edition of *The Deer* appeared
containing an editorial praising the courage of the ancient
Maccabeans and exhorting Jews to follow in the footsteps of
their illustrious ancestors. Like the Maccabeans, "we must collect our forces and march forward," the article said.

A few hours later the walls of Jerusalem buildings were suddenly plastered up with posters, signed by the chief Ashkenazi
rabbi, denouncing Ben Yehuda for using his paper to stir up
armed revolt against the Turks. The poster quoted the phrase
"collect our forces and march forward," contending that this
obviously meant *armed* forces.

Two days later a policeman appeared at the Ben Yehuda
home and Eliezer was taken off to prison. His arrest had been
ordered by the Sultan himself, after the Orthodox religious
leaders had taken a translation of the article to Turkish officials,
disavowing any responsibility for the "diabolical suggestion."

Ben Yehuda's friends sent a cable to the Chief Rabbi of
France imploring him to intercede with Baron Rothschild. A
fund of a thousand gold francs was raised to bribe prison
officials in order to obtain permission for Ben Yehuda's family
and friends to visit him. Hundreds flocked to his cell to pay
their respects. One day on the way home from the prison,
Hemda found Ben Zion, then eleven, surrounded by a crowd of
boys who were taunting him in Hebrew (knowing that he
understood no other language): "Your father, the Heretic, is
in prison. He's behind bars with murderers where he belongs."
Ben Zion cried for hours that evening, but then finally
brightened up and said, "Father will be happy to know that
every word they shouted at me was in Hebrew!"

Telegrams by the hundreds poured in from all parts of
Europe. Many progressive Arabs, angered by the Turkish action, openly supported Ben Yehuda. Offers of help also came
from Christians, some of them diplomats, some Catholic priests.
A group of Free Masons sent a resolution of support. Most
encouraging, the arrest brought a degree of solidarity among
those Jews who were not actually in the camp of the opposition.

After eight days of imprisonment, part of the time in a cell
with fifteen assassins, the emaciated, consumptive editor-philologist was taken to the Palace of Justice to stand trial for

treason. His defense counsel was a Dominican monk, one of his best friends in Jerusalem. The judges were a Sephardic Jew and two Arabs. The trial hinged on a translation of an old Hebrew expression that had been used in the article, *laassot hayil,* which figuratively means "to progress, to go ahead," but litterally means "to form an army." It had, of course, been used in the metaphoric sense.

The case was prejudiced, just before the trial started, by the arrival in Jerusalem from Constantinople of a cable from the religious leader of the entire Jewish community of Turkey, proclaiming against Ben Yehuda a ban or *herem,* which was as serious as the excommunication of a Catholic by an order from Rome. By custom, no one but members of the immediate family could have any contact with a person under such a ban. It amounted to a business and professional boycott. Following Jewish religious procedure, the herem was carried out in the principal synagogues of Jerusalem by the blowing of the *shofar* (ram's horn) and the burning of black candles.

The judges were in a difficult situation. Ben Yehuda's own people had already condemned him, for it was no secret that the herem had been arranged by the rabbis of Jerusalem. The Jewish judge was afraid to compromise himself and so held out for a verdict of guilty. The two Arabs had been bribed by both sides.

The compromise verdict they finally reached was a one-year prison sentence, with Ben Yehuda permitted to go free on bail while he appealed to a higher court. Meanwhile, he was forbidden to publish his paper.

Ben Yehuda's friends knew that the one person who could save him was Baron Rothschild, so they deluged him with appeals. Finally the Orthodox rabbis received a brief cable from Paris:

EXERCEZ VOS PRIERES
BARON ROTHSCHILD

The admonition to "look to your prayers" obviously meant that the French philanthropist felt they had gone outside their province when they interfered in judicial matters. The cable led to an immediate lifting of the *herem.*

Some weeks later, Baron Rothschild's chief representative in Palestine received a cable that read:

ACQUITTEZ BEN YEHUDA COUTE QUE COUTE

The last three words were a French idiom meaning "regardless of cost." With the message came a check for ten thousand francs, five thousand of which went to the prosecutor as a bribe, the rest being used for minor baksheesh. The higher court sitting in Beirut voted unanimously for acquittal.

With that crisis in his life over, Ben Yehuda became so absorbed in his language-revival that he turned the editing of the weekly newspaper over to Hemda, who became editor in fact if not in title, even though she was pregnant with her second child (Eliezer's seventh.) While she put out *The Deer,* he covered thousands of pieces of paper with his fine aesthetic handwriting. They overflowed from his desk and tables onto the floor. It was a sacred rule in the Ben Yehuda household that no one was ever to throw away a scrap of paper, no matter where it was found or how unimportant the words written on it might seem. They all knew that on the back of an envelope might be notes for the creation of a word that someday would be used by millions of people as part of their everyday speech. Once a piece of paper no larger than a postage stamp was lost. The house was turned upside down for hours while everyone hunted for it. Eventually it was found in the cuff of Eliezer's trousers. President Solomon Schechter, who later became president of the Jewish Theological Seminary of America, advised Ben Yehuda to put his notes on small cards and inaugurate a filing system. Two young theological students were hired at ten francs a month to work half-days copying his notes onto the cards.

When Theodor Herzl's *The Jewish State* was published, Eliezer turned away from his work on the language long enough to read every page of the pamphlet many times over and to contribute several articles to *The Deer* supporting Herzl's ideas.

When the convening of the first Zionist Congress at Basel was announced, he was as excited as a small boy. Men from all over the world would be there discussing ideas that had been his obsession since his student days in Paris—ideas he had been working so unceasingly to popularize. He was eager to go to Basel, but the state of the family finances and the ban against traveling that the Turkish government had placed on him made it impossible. To his wife he said, *"Bitti,* wouldn't it be wonderful if these men were to declare for all the world to hear that Jews should return to their own land and make it into a place where they could live as free men?"

When reports of what had happened at Basel arrived in Jerusalem, he realized that delegates to the Congress had gone farther than he had imagined in his dreams they might go. He was delighted that they had created a permanent World Zionist Organization and had talked of a Hebrew University, and a Jewish world bank, and a Jewish national fund, but why, oh why, he asked Hemda rhetorically, had they not had the courage and vision to call for a revival of Hebrew. It would be possible to have a Jewish state without a flag, or an anthem, or even a university, but how could they revive Israel without a language?

When the letter came from Herzl inviting him to serve on the executive board, friends in Turkish government circles advised him to turn it down quickly—he must remember that he was still not out of the shadow of prison bars. Even though he followed the advice, he still suffered from repercussions of the Basel Congress. One day the Turkish censor summoned him and gave him an order that not a word about Zionism was henceforth to be printed in *The Deer,* and the expression *"Eretz Israel"* must never be used. "Remember," the censor warned him, "that you Jews do not have a country, and never shall!"

Despite this warning he wrote what he termed his "Second Appeal" in which, without mentioning the verboten word "Zionism," he called on Jews everywhere to turn their faces toward the Promised Land and prepare for The Return. This movement, he wrote, was not exclusively for those who had deeply religious reasons for coming to Jerusalem. It must include assimilated Jews and even those who had embraced Christianity. Then he issued a warning: when the dream finally did become reality, Israel must not be re-created as a theocratic state.

Hemda's second child lived only a year. Her third (Eliezer's eighth) was a healthy boy, but the young mother was now weak from malaria and rheumatism, and so her husband borrowed money and took her to Europe. In Paris they met Max Nordau, spent an evening with Israel Zangwill, went to the opera, saw Baron Rothschild long enough to thank him for his generosity, and had an interview with the great Georges Clemenceau, who spoke of Palestine as a country from which three religions had issued, all three of which he disliked in equal measure. He considered Zionism a retrogressive movement and concluded the interview by saying:

"*Voulez-vous la Palestine, Monsieur Ben Yehuda? Prenez-la! Elle ne nous intéresse pas.*" (Mr. Ben Yehuda, you wish Palestine? Then take it! It does not interest us.)

Then to London, where Eliezer worked for two months in the British Museum library, in a philologist's seventh heaven as he found traces of many lost words. Then back to Paris, where he worked another month in the National Library checking his London discoveries and adding hundreds of additional words to the language.

Preparations were being made now for the Second Zionist Congress. While it would be dangerous for Eliezer to attend, Dr. Nordau convinced him that there was no reason he could not go to Basel before the sessions began and talk with Herzl, but when he and his wife arrived in the Swiss city they were told Herzl had just been called to Vienna. They counted their remaining money and took a train to Vienna. There Madame Herzl told them her husband had gone to Ischl to try to interview Emperor Francis Joseph. Again they counted their money and again bought railroad tickets. At Ischl they missed him once more; he had just taken a train back to Basel via Vienna. Ben Yehuda's funds were too depleted to continue the chase, so they went, instead, to Constantinople to argue with Turkish officials about an official announcement that their permit to publish *The Deer* had expired and would not be renewed. In the Turkish capital Eliezer began having internal hemorrhages, and when the man he had chased all over Europe came through on his way to Palestine, he was too ill even to attempt to see him. When Herzl reached Jerusalem on what would be the only visit of his life to Eliezer's city, he missed him again, for he was still ill in Constantinople. Hemda missed him, too, for she was now confined to her bed awaiting the birth of her fourth child, but she sent her stepson, Ben Zion, who now also called himself Ittamar Ben Avi, to greet the Zionist leader in the name of the whole family. The boy came home grinning, for Herzl had called him "the Triple Ben."

After lying in bed in Constantinople for eight months, Eliezer finally decided to go home, but feeling it was imperative to see Herzl, he went to Vienna and there, at last, they met—two ardent champions of Zionism, two men of letters, two bearded journalists, two men alike in some ways but so very unalike in others.

Ben Yehuda congratulated Herzl for all he had done and predicted that history would record that the State of Israel was actually re-created by the First Zionist Congress; but then he criticized him for not supporting the pioneering movement already existing in Palestine, and for concentrating all his efforts on trying to buy colonization rights from the Ottoman Empire, and for ignoring the importance of the Hebrew language-revival. Ben Yehuda outlined to him his own five-point program: the revivial of Hebrew, the purchase of land from individual Arab owners, the fostering of amicable relations with the Arabs, a program of adult political education for those Jews already in Palestine, and a campaign to provide Hebrew schoolbooks for Palestine children who now had to get all their instruction orally.

Herzl showed little interest in any of the suggestions. About the language problem, he said, "Let Jews go to Palestine and live there for a few generations. After that they will decide what language they wish to speak." The talk was without a single positive result. Back in Jerusalem, Hemda, now nursing her fourth child, received a black letter from her husband that concluded, "We will not get support from anyone. We are indeed an unfortunate people."

When he returned home, his shoulders were more stooped than ever; his eyes lacked any trace of sparkle. He brightened up only when Hemda told him that she had obtained in her own name a permit to publish a paper to be called *Hashkafah* (The Review). She was the second woman in history to receive a permit from the Ottoman Empire to run a newspaper. She took out only a few weeks from her task during the next year to have her fifth child.

In 1901, Eliezer drew up what he called a Progress Report on what had been accomplished during his twenty years in Palestine. He had fathered ten children, five still living. Two of them spoke fluent Hebrew. Through all the vicissitudes, he had managed to keep alive a real Hebrew newspaper that was helping to popularize the language for a still only half-receptive public. A modern Hebrew literature had begun. An amateur dramatic group was giving plays in Hebrew. It was not unusual for speeches and lectures to be delivered now in the once exclusively holy language. On the debit side, there was no uniformity to pronunciation, and Hebrew books were heavy and ponderous, with the sense often unclear because of conflicting ideas about the meanings of words. But Eliezer kept telling himself that when his dictionary came out, these troubles would vanish.

So he went back to his schedule of working seventeen or eighteen hours a day. He found that if he wrote for two hours standing at a bookkeeper-type desk, then two hours sitting, he could keep going long into the night. In these years he read through thousands of books and hundreds of private manuscripts. He had become a master of not only written German, English, Russian, French, and Hebrew itself, but of the sister languages of Arabic, Coptic, Assyrian, Aramaic, and Ethiopian. It was taking him so long to compile a modern language because the Hebrew that had survived had a vocabulary of only eight thousand words. (The dictionary he was compiling would ultimately contain almost forty thousand.) It would have been easy just to steal any word lacking in Hebrew from some other language, as the French had done with *rostbif* (roast beef) and English-speaking people had done with words like *chic*. But he wanted to keep Hebrew pure and make it a consistent and beautiful language, without words that grated on the ear because they were inconsistent with the ancient music of the language, so he fought against any bastardization. If it appeared from his studies that the word he needed had never existed in Hebrew, he would either create it, using a Hebrew base, or "borrow" it from one of the sister languages that are close to Hebrew in sound and form. Arabic provided many of the words he needed, because it was the only Semitic language that had remained alive, vigorous, and in current usage down through the ages.

To help launch newly created words, Eliezer would call Hemda and his children—his "army"—into his study and give them the word for the day. It might be a new word for tomato, which the Jerusalemites had been calling *agbanit* and which Eliezer considered ridiculous because it came from a root meaning "to love sensuously." The substitute he created was *badurah*. So the army went from shop to shop asking for *badurah*. When the shopkeeper would shake his head, they would point to the round red objects and if he said they were *agbanit*, he would be told, "Not any more. Now they are *badurah*."

Such tactics generally succeeded, but *badurah* was one example of a Ben Yehuda defeat by the forces of reaction. After years of proselytizing, the only shoppers in Jerusalem who ever called a tomato a *badurah* were members of the Ben Yehuda family.

Soon after he began work on the dictionary, Eliezer founded the Vaad Halashon, or Academy of Language, to pass on words and settle philological disputes.

When the so-called Uganda Plan was suggested, Ben Yehuda wrote many articles supporting it. "This is a great ray of sudden light," he declared. "At last we shall have a shelter, free from persecution; a home where England at least will protect us in our yearning for self-government and peace. Even though it is far away, we will be able to gather there from the four corners of our exile, and there we will be able to learn statehood and prepare for the time when we shall receive our ancient heritage, the land of Israel, for which we have prayed these two thousand years."

The older Orthodox Jews took the attitude that this was fine—now Ben Yehuda and the other rebels and heretics would go off to Uganda, and Palestine would again belong to the religious who spent their days at the Wailing Wall praying for the arrival of the Messiah. But the younger generation, especially in the settlements—men and women who had planted trees and made sacrifices to dig their own roots into the Holy Land—considered Ben Yehuda a traitor. Even Hemda was against moving to a torrid, primitive place, such as the unfathomable wilderness of Africa. Ben Yehuda's oldest son, who by now had become a journalist in his own right, also opposed his family. It was typical of the way the Uganda issue was splitting families everywhere.

For months Eliezer threw himself into the fight. When it was over and it was apparent that he, Nordau, Herzl, and the other Uganda advocates had lost, he returned to work on his dictionary with much of his spirit gone.

"I don't understand, *bitti*," he said one night to his wife. "I pick up my pen, dip it in ink, put the point to paper, but nothing happens."

Herzl's death depressed him even more. He organized a memorial service in Jerusalem, writing out the posters and setting them into type himself. The Ben Yehuda home was converted into a factory for the making of black ribbons for the mourners to wear. The day after the service, Hemda entered her husband's study just in time to see him with a box of matches in his hand, about to set fire to the almost completed manuscript of the first volume of his dictionary.

For an hour, quietly, patiently, she talked her husband out of his black desire to destroy both his work and himself. She promised that as soon as she was able to borrow money for the trip, she would go to Europe and try to find someone to publish his dictionary. A few months later, after giving birth to her sixth child (Eliezer's eleventh), she set forth. Although she was only thirty-six, she looked much older. She was fired by a stern determination not to return without good news for her husband. In Berlin, she found a firm specializing in dictionaries that was willing to publish Eliezer's, providing it was set in type in Jerusalem and that payment for each volume was received in advance. The contract she signed also stipulated that upon Eliezer's death she must complete from his notes all unfinished volumes.

There was a celebration in the Ben Yehuda house in Jerusalem when the first copy of the first edition of the first volume of the first real dictionary of Hebrew ever published arrived by post from Berlin. It is doubtful whether the arrival of any of his eleven children had stirred within him the emotions he had on this occasion.

The first word was *av* (father) to which many pages were devoted, for this was no ordinary dictionary. After each word came the translation into French, German, and English, with references in Arabic, Assyrian, Aramaic, Greek, and Latin. Also, after each word Ben Yehuda had listed all its synonyms and all other words in any way connected with it. The origin of each word was given in detail, as well as an explanation of its construction, a comparison with sister words in other Semitic languages, a history of the changes the word had undergone through the centuries, and a compilation of all its nuances, shades, forms, inflections, and uses. After each word were also what Ben Yehuda called its "witnesses": examples from ancient, medieval, and modern literature of the use of the word. He had dug out, for example, 335 different ways in which the word *lo* (no) could be used. *Ken* (yes) had 210 witnesses, many of them quotations from the Bible or from the works of little-known poets, or from manuscripts that had never been published. These quotations made interesting reading in themselves, giving pictures of the life of the early Jews in their homes, fields, and ghettos. Words that he himself had created were marked with a special symbol.

The first volume was dedicated to Baron Edmond de Rothschild in gratitude for all he had done to make the work possible.

By the start of 1914, five volumes had been published. Each had involved the same problems: months of careful editing of his notes by Eliezer; long trips abroad by Hemda to try to raise money for printers' and binders' bills.

The Ben Yehuda family—husband, wife, and the three smallest children—spent the war years in the United States. They returned to Jerusalem on the first available ship after the armistice, and Eliezer plunged at once into the seething political situation created by the dismemberment of the Ottoman Empire.

During the Arab disorders of 1920–21, Chaim Weizmann, then the "uncrowned king" of the Zionists, came to dinner one night, and while the others were having their coffee he took the frail, bearded philologist into a corner and after a long discussion of the critical situation in Palestine said to him:

"What we need, Ben Yehuda, is a strong, vigorous appeal to our own people. You are the one to write it. We have never forgotten your first and second appeals. Now you must write a third. Write it with all your warmth and with all the magic of your pen. The situation is serious, but your words will enter the minds and hearts of our people and stir them to a realization of the crisis of the hour."

After Weizmann left, Ben Yehuda, still in his evening clothes, went to his study and took up his pen. Hours later he came slowly from the room, saying, *"Bitti,* I don't seem to be able to do it. I fear I am too tired. I shall try again tomorrow."

The next day five doctors tried everything—including an oxygen tent—to save his life. He died that night. He was buried on the Mount of Olives, clothed in a prayer shawl.

His widow and children and a committee called the Eliezer Ben Yehuda Memorial Trust were responsible for putting out eight more volumes of the dictionary. After the revival of Israel, the final three volumes were published under the auspices of the state.

The last word on which Eliezer himself did any work was *nefesh* (soul), but he left behind most of the material for the eleven posthumous volumes.

By the centenary of his birth, in 1958, "his" language was being spoken by most of the million and a half Jews who had come home to Israel.

During his lifetime he was often called a fanatic. The gate over his grave might well have been inscribed:

HERE LIES ELIEZER BEN YEHUDA
faithful fanatic

Chapter 3

Living space for millions,
On both sides of the Jordan.

—Vladimir Jabotinsky

One hot summer evening in 1919, a short, stocky man with pince-nez glasses, black hair, and an overly-large face came to call at the Ben Yehuda house in Jerusalem. The oldest son of the family, Ittamar Ben Avi, greeted the visitor warmly, addressing him by his first name. "It's good to see you, Vladimir! Come in."

When Eliezer Ben Yehuda, working in his study, heard the resonant voice of the guest, he turned out the light over his desk and hurried into the sitting room, eager not to miss a word of the conversation.

The sixty-one-year-old philologist and the thirty-nine-year-old Vladimir Jabotinsky had much in common, principally their great love of Hebrew. Jabotinsky had already done much to popularize the language Ben Yehuda was modernizing. He had translated into Hebrew such diverse works as Edgar Allen Poe's "The Raven" and "Annabelle Lee," part of *Faust* and selections from Dante's *Inferno*. But tonight he had other than philological matters on his mind. He wanted to talk about his ugly premonition that Jerusalem and the rest of Palestine were in for a wave of terrorism. He wanted to express to someone his anger that the British administration not only was doing nothing about it, but was behaving as if it would welcome a little pogrom in order to show London that the Balfour Declaration had been a mistake and that if Jewish immigration continued it would be impossible to hold down the Arabs.

Louis Brandeis, the Supreme Court Justice from America, had been in Palestine in July, and Jabotinsky had made the same prediction to him, "but he wouldn't believe me," the visitor told the Ben Yehudas. "He said it was impossible that pogroms could happen in a land over which the Union Jack was flying." Jabotinsky said he had replied, "We who are of Russian origin are like hunting dogs; we can smell blood from a long way off."

"So what do you propose doing about it?" Eliezer Ben Yehuda asked, knowing that his visitor was a man who always combined his theorizing and academic discussion with plans for action.

"The time has come for us to stop relying on the myth of British protection and take our defense in our own hands."

"You mean armed resistance?"

"Yes. I'm convinced that from now on we must fight for our rights here in Palestine with bullets and bombs."

"You're absolutely right!" Ben Avi declared in his booming voice. "I'm glad you said it. We've had enough of—"

His father interrupted. "The strength of the spirit is greater," he said quietly.

Before their guest could answer, Ben Avi swung around to face his father and loudly declared, "When you were a young man you were a rebel. You fought back. You ignored tradition. Now *we* are young, Vladimir and I and our generation. If we wish to take strong measures, we are entitled to do it without interference from you and your generation."

The discussion went on for hours. Before it was over, Ben Yehuda had admitted that on pragmatic grounds, the two younger men were right. He had great admiration for Jabotinsky, as did millions of others in Europe, America, and Palestine itself. He was a rare combination of poet, political leader, orator, scholar, linguist, diplomat, journalist, novelist, and publicist. For seventeen years he had been devoting his manifold talents to the furtherance of Zionism. He was a master of Russian, Hebrew, Yiddish, English, Italian, German, and French, which he spoke with almost no foreign accent. He could read, write, lecture and quote poetry in nineteen additional languages. He had translated the Hebrew poet Bialik into Russian and had written poems of his own in Esperanto. He had been arrested by the police of Czarist Russia, and although he had no suspicion of it the night he called on the Ben Yehudas, before long he would be sentenced by the British to fifteen years at hard labor. In World War I he had created the Jewish Legion, and with a gun in his hand had helped liberate Palestine from the grip of the Turks. He was pamphleteer and prophet, irresponsible adventurer and searcher after truth. The first forty years of his life had been full of storm and controversy, and there was every reason to believe that as long as he lived he would continue to battle injustice, oppose smugness, and fight for principles he considered superior to those held by his opponents, many of whom were not only fellow Jews but fellow Zionists.

Vladimir Jabotinsky was born on October 5, 1880, in Odessa, the most cosmopolitan city in Russia, with almost half a million inhabitants, one out of every three of them Jews who lived without segregation, isolation, or persecution. Orthodox Jewish customs were ignored by a great many Odessa families, and freethinking was the habit of the community, yet Vladimir learned the Hebrew alphabet when he was six and before long was reading Hebrew poetry. He had a facility with words even as a child. Once when he was asked, "Whose boy are you?" he replied curtly, "I am myself." Until his death half a century later he was always "himself," proud, independent, self-reliant, headstrong.

One day during his seventh year he asked his widowed mother, "Will we Jews someday have a state of our own?" She replied testily, "Of course we will, you little fool!" He did not question her further.

As a schoolboy he wrote such scathing satire and biting verse about those he disliked that a story—probably apocryphal—was told of a teacher who committed suicide because he was unable to face more of young Vladimir's ridicule. While still in school he became one of the editors of a clandestine paper, *Truth*.

Like Herzl and Ben Yehuda, he began his journalistic career at a young age, leaving Russia when he was seventeen. An Odessa paper agreed to print any articles he mailed back, on two conditions: if he wrote from some European capital in which they had no correspondent, and if he wrote "no stupidities."

The *Odessky Listok* had no representative in Bern, Switzerland, so Vladimir went there. On his way he passed through Galicia and Hungary, and for the first time saw his fellow Jews in ghettos, victims of ugly poverty and degrading misery.

One night soon after his arrival in the Swiss capital he attended a lecture, followed by a lively exchange of views between Socialists and Zionists. Vladimir, still only seventeen, was inspired to make the first public speech of his life. If the anti-Semites were correct that Jews were an abscess on the body-politic of other nations, he said, then they should emigrate by the millions to Palestine. When his remarks were translated from Russian into German the audience, containing a large percentage of Jews, decided he must be an anti-Semite himself and were indignant with him, refusing to believe his protestations that he was a Jew.

From Bern he went to Italy, where the *Odessky Listok* also had no correspondent, and for years he called Italy his spiritual fatherland. He remained there three years, learning Italian, studying law, and coming under the influence of Italian scholars. He chose Garibaldi as his hero because he appeared to be a fanatical nationalist and a world citizen, a militarist and a pacifist, all at the same time.

In Rome, where there were only nine thousand Jews scattered among the one million or more inhabitants, young Vladimir almost forgot that he was a Jew. He wrote the same sort of articles for the paper back in Odessa that Herzl had written from Paris for his paper—brilliant but inconsequential essays on local life, art, and letters. Many of them he signed *Altalena,* which he thought was the Italian word for "elevator." (Actually it means "swing.")

When he was twenty-one, he returned to Odessa and took a well-paying position on a local newspaper, writing nonpolitical articles on matters of community interest, including a series on what ten books one would save if all the rest of the books in the world were to be burned. Like Herzl, in his spare time he wrote plays and poems, one of which, *Poor Charlotte,* came to the attention of Maxim Gorki, then Russia's greatest man of letters, who ordered a publishing house that he headed to publish it.

In those days Odessa's intellectuals were talking a great deal about socialism. Jabotinsky went on record as opposing the efficiency of an anthill or beehive organization of human life. For a brief time after his return from Italy his antipathy for socialism was so strong that he seemed about to become an anarchist.

One day in 1902, Odessa police, on suspicion that he might be a Socialist because of some of his personal associations, searched his room and confiscated some articles he had written for an Italian paper. While a seven-week investigation was being conducted he was held in prison, theoretically in solitary confinement, but actually he and his prison mates, most of them Jews, were able to organize lectures and concerts. Three of the lectures were on Zionism and added to his conviction that he was a Zionist ideologically and would like to become one actively.

It was an Odessa Zionist, S. D. Salzman, who spurred Jabotinsky into his first Zionist action. They met at a reception for an Italian opera star. Salzman gave Jabotinsky Pinsker's *Auto-Emancipation* and Herzl's *The Jewish State* as well as reports of the five Zionist Congresses that had already been held. Then he asked Jabotinsky to use his journalistic influence to have several plays by Herzl and Nordau included in the repertoire of the Odessa Theater. When a famous Italian actor came to town, Jabotinsky, at Salzman's urging, persuaded him not to begin his performances with *The Merchant of Venice* in which he played the role of Shylock.

The next spring, an outbreak of violence against the Jews in a small town near Odessa was followed by rumors that a pogrom was being planned in Odessa itself. On his own initiative the young newspaperman sent letters to leading Jewish citizens of Odessa, urging the formation of a Jewish defense force. To his astonishment he received not a single reply, but one of his letters found its way into the hands of a group of students who already had just such a program as Jabotinsky was suggesting, so they invited him to join them. He assisted in the mimeographing and illegal distribution of ten thousand leaflets and then persuaded M. J. Disengoff (who years later became the founder and first mayor of Tel Aviv) to help collect funds for the cause. In one evening together they collected the equivalent of almost three thousand dollars. With the same fanaticism and aggressive energy that both Herzl and Ben Yehuda had displayed in their early days, Jabotinsky, who was just beginning to discover his own Jewishness, threw himself into the fight.

The Odessa pogrom did not materialize, probably due to the self-defense activity of Jabotinsky and the student group, but not many days later, in far-off Kishinev, capital of Bessarabia, the Jewish community was subjected to three days and three nights of massacre, pillage, rape, and terror which outraged decent-minded people all over the world and inspired the younger generation of Jews throughout Russia to make extensive plans for self-defense.

Just as the Dreyfus Case in later years was credited with being the event that goaded Herzl into action (a myth that he himself at one time encouraged), so the Kishinev pogrom was often mistakenly attributed as the spur to Jabotinsky's Zionist activity. What the Kishinev killings actually did for him was to convince him that self-defense in itself was not the answer; there were too many anti-Semites and too few Jews willing to fight back.

In 1903, Jabotinsky was named a delegate from Odessa to the Sixth Zionist Congress. When the twenty-three-year-old poet-journalist entered the crowded Congress hall in Basel, he found himself in a bewildering world that he little understood. At the Fifth Congress an opposition group had been formed. Among its leaders were Chaim Weizmann the chemist, and Martin Buber the theologian. Jabotinsky was so impressed when he was introduced to the tall, distinguished-looking Weizmann, with his black goatee and imperial manner, that he impulsively decided he also wanted to be in the opposition, although he was not quite certain what was being opposed.

The next day he was slightly discouraged when in a café he approached Weizmann as he was talking to friends and said, "Would I disturb you if—" To which Weizmann growled, "You *are* disturbing me!" and turned his back.

There was a tacit agreement among delegates from all factions that they would not embarrass their president, Theodor Herzl, by opening up a discussion of his recent negotiations with the Czar's Minister of the Interior, Plehve, who was considered by many to have been the instigator of the Kishinev Massacre. Unaware of this, young Jabotinsky in his first speech to any important gathering tried to defend Herzl, already his idol. His argument was that ethics and tactics should never be confused. While the first few minutes of his remarks were being translated from Russian into German (the language of the Congress) with frequent interruptions from angry delegates, Herzl rushed onto the platform from an adjoining room where he had been in conference and demanded to know the cause of the turmoil. "What," he asked, "has this young speaker been saying?"

"Nothing but nonsense!" Weizmann replied.

Thereupon Jabotinsky's idol wheeled on him and spoke the only words he had ever said to him—or would ever say to him:

"Your time is up!"

In humiliation Jabotinsky left the platform. He took no part in the subsequent debate over the British offer of land in East Africa for a Jewish settlement, but he voted with the minority against the plan and walked out with the other Russian delegates when the vote was announced.

Despite his disagreement with Herzl on the Uganda issue, despite the personal rebuff, despite the fact that he never saw or heard Herzl again, the fanatical genius of the man from Vienna led Jabotinsky to use many superlatives about him. He often referred to him as a "prophet." He wrote that he never forgot Herzl's resounding voice as he made his pledge to the minority who had voted against him: "If I forget thee, oh Jerusalem. . . ." For the rest of his life he remained a faithful disciple of the father of modern Zionism.

Soon after his return from Basel, Jabotinsky was the victim of an insult that changed the course of his life. One night he was sitting in the Municipal Theater in the fifth-row seat that was permanently assigned to him as the dramatic critic of the *Odesskiya Novosti*—the paper for which he was now working—when a police officer in the audience, assuming that he had sneaked down from a seat in the balcony, publicly upbraided him. Jabotinsky created a scene more dramatic than anything on the stage that night by giving the officer a sample of his ability at picturesque denunciation. When he was informed several days later by the Governor of Odessa that he would in a short time be subjected to severe punishment, he took a train for St. Petersburg. There he went to work for a new monthly Zionist magazine, writing brilliant tirades against both Socialists and assimilationists. He denounced his own people for engaging in a wholesale desertion of Jewish culture and pleaded for a national Jewish renaissance.

When Herzl died in 1904, Jabotinsky felt a keen personal loss. There were many other speakers on the program of the memorial service held in the Great Synagogue of St. Petersburg, but Jabotinsky's speech that day established his reputation as a brilliant orator and started him on a career of public speaking that occupied much of his time during the rest of his life. Almost at once he became a traveling salesman for Zionism. He developed many tricks of oratory. At times he thundered with such passion that he could almost pull his listeners out of their seats. At other times, in more subtle tones, he would seek a way to their hearts, ouls, and minds. Once he kept a packed hall in suspense for ha f an hour as he expounded on the pronunciation of a single Hebrew word. Before long there were many cities in Europe that had no halls large enough to hold the crowds that came out to hear him, and he would be invited back again and again. One night in Vilna, Lithuania, an innkeeper remarked, "Do you realize, Mr. Jabotinsky, this is the fifty-fifth time you have spoken in Vilna and the fifty-fifth time you have stayed in this hotel?" On one occasion he delivered a speech one-quarter in French, one-quarter in Italian, one-quarter in Russian, and one-quarter in Hebrew.

But before long his oratorical success began to bore him, for he told a friend that he no longer got pleasure from seeing four hundred perfectly coiffed college girls in the first few rows of his audience; that he was going to revise his delivery so that future lectures would attract no more than forty Jews who might have as few as forty hairs between them but who would have a serious interest in what he was saying. As he put the threat into practice, his brilliance of delivery became overshadowed by his passionate earnestness.

He still devoted a major portion of his time to writing, and in 1906 made this prophecy: "My faith tells me the day will come when my people will be great and free, and through the sweat of her sons Palestine will scintillate. . . . My craft is the craft of one of the masons building a new Temple for my supreme God, whose name is the Jewish people."

When he was twenty-five, Jabotinsky ran for the second Russian Duma or parliament. He looked so young that the doorkeeper at one political rally told him to "go home and do your schoolwork." During the campaign he put out an open letter containing this passage: ". . . nobody can demand from the Jews to take an oath that they shall remain where they are at any price, even in spite of the elemental force of social circumstances; and nobody is entitled to make their civil equality dependent on taking such an oath."

He lost the election to an older man, but the second Duma was dissolved within a few months and Jabotinsky ran again. Once more he was defeated, this time running fourth in a field of four candidates and receiving only one-third the Jewish vote. That same year he married a girl to whom he had ingratiated himself when he was fifteen and she was only ten by addressing her as *mademoiselle*—the first time anyone had ever called her that. She was Jewish, was from Odessa, and was not a Zionist. Almost immediately after the wedding their paths temporarily separated, Jabotinsky going to Vienna for what he called a "recuperative spiritual bath" and his wife going to Nancy, France, to take up the study of agronomy. During the next twenty-five years they spent exactly one-fifth of the time together. They celebrated their silver wedding anniversary by exchanging affectionate telegrams.

In Vienna, Jabotinsky learned two new languages, Croat and Czech. Then he decided to try for a law degree back in Odessa, but he had never finished the *gymnasium*, or high school, so at the age of twenty-eight, after months of reviewing such subjects as Latin and algebra, he took the gymnasium examinations. He passed, although he received bad marks in Russian composition despite his reputation as one of Russia's most brilliant young writers.

In 1908 a revolutionary group, the Young Turks, overthrew the Sultan, whom Herzl had spent so much time wooing, and Jabotinsky went to Constantinople in a journalistic capacity. Many of the new Ministers in interviews with him asserted their willingness to see Jews settle in any part of the new constitutional monarchy. Then he made a quick trip to Palestine. He was impressed by the self-defense measures he saw in some of the Jewish settlements. While there he decided the two greatest requisites for a settler were to learn to speak Hebrew and "punch hard."

Back in Constantinople, he found that Zionist leaders from Europe were about to establish a small chain of French, Spanish, and Hebrew newspapers, dailies and weeklies, to take advantage of the new, relatively liberal atmosphere of Turkey. He agreed to take charge of the entire operation, at a great reduction in income. He quickly built the French weekly into one of the most influential papers in Constantinople and expanded the size and circulation of all the others. In his spare time he converted to Zionism two Jewish members of the Turkish Parliament. But it was a discouraging period for he realized, long before many others, that the Turkish revolution was going to open no doors. Jews might not be persecuted in Turkish lands, but they were expected to assimilate. Gradually he acquired an intense loathing for what he called "the East." Even the "picturesqueness" of the Bosphorus and the "charm" of Stamboul seemed exaggerated. To him, the Turks became "a yelling rabble." Then he had trouble with David Wolffsohn, president of the Zionist Organization, who accused him of exceeding his authority, of trying to make policy in Constantinople for the entire Zionist Organization, and of insubordination. In accepting the inevitable resignation, Wolffsohn called Jabotinsky "this gentleman who may be a passable Zionist but who lacks even a trace of responsibility and discipline. . . ."

The feud between Jabotinsky and Weizmann began in 1913 when the Eleventh Zionist Congress, meeting in Vienna, authorized a commission to prepare the groundwork for establishment of a Hebrew university in Jerusalem. Jabotinsky was named a member because for the past three years he had spent much of his time campaigning in Russia for the more widespread use of Hebrew, the establishment of schools in which the language would be taught, and a gradual approach to the day when in all Jewish schools of Russia, Hebrew would be the language of the curriculum. He was fought by lovers of Yiddish to whom that language was as important a part of their Jewishness as the Torah, and whose sentimentality about it was impervious to all attacks of logic. They called Jabotinsky "Hebrew-mad" and attacked him with fury.

Weizmann, who had submitted at Vienna the proposal for the establishment of a Hebrew university, had a positive idea what it should be: small schools of medicine, law, and political science, or, as Jabotinsky explained it, "merely research institutes in which scientists would work and strive to win the Nobel Prize, and not a school in which students would study." Aware that Jews were being discriminated against in most of the universities of Europe, especially in Russia, Jabotinsky wanted an educational institution in which these victims of anti-Semitism could develop their minds and prepare themselves to lead useful lives. The conflict grew acrimonious, with Weizmann writing words of bitter contempt about the young man from Odessa. World War I put an end to the quarrel—and to plans for the university. After the war, in 1918, the cornerstone was finally laid, but Jabotinsky had lost a battle, for it began as a collection of research institutes, just as Weizmann wished.

When war broke out in 1914, Jabotinsky, like many other Jews who had lived under the oppression of the Czarist regime, had one burning desire: for defeat of Russia. But when Turkey entered the war on Germany's side and thus became an opponent of Russia, he suddenly reversed himself and decided he wanted to contribute to an Allied victory. He boldly predicted that whatever happened to Germany, Turkey would be destroyed like a wooden hut in a fire. With permission of his employer, now a paper in Moscow, he went on a tour of Arab countries. In Alexandria, quite by chance, he discovered 1,200 Palestinian Jews whom Turkish police one day had rounded up on the streets of Jaffa—apparently on the whim of the ruling Pasha—and had shipped to Egypt. They were scattered through dozens of second-rate Alexandria hotels. Many were distinguished Palestinians: doctors, lawyers, businessmen, students. They spoke twelve languages beside Hebrew, which all the children (thanks probably to Ben Yehuda) and some of the adults understood. Jabotinsky took an immediate interest and persuaded British authorities to house them in some vacant barracks, the largest called "Gabbari," a word that before long was being used to designate the entire Jewish camp.

Jabotinsky gave up his room in Constantinople's best hotel and moved into Gabbari. Partly because of his organizational ability, partly because of his immediate popularity with the refugees, the disorganization, confusion, and depression quickly disappeared and Gabbari became a well run and orderly camp.

Joseph Trumpeldor, who had the distinction of having been the only Jewish officer in the Russian Army, was living at that time in Alexandria and one night Jabotinsky, burning with a new idea on which he needed help, called on him. The two men had many points of divergence. Trumpeldor was a Socialist, a Pacifist, and a vegetarian. Jabotinsky had tried vegetarianism for two weeks in Bern as a young man and then had given it up. He had never been tempted by pacifism, and he had already begun to fight socialism. But they were both Russians, both Jews, and by coincidence each had just celebrated his thirty-fourth birthday. Trumpeldor, who had started out as a dentist in the Caucasus, during the Russo-Japanese War was in a regiment at Port Arthur that was under siege for eleven months, during which he lost his left arm to the shoulder. It was a legend among Russian soldiers how he had insisted on returning to the fighting line as soon as he left the hospital. When Port Arthur fell, he was taken prisoner and in captivity became an active Zionist leader, organizing societies and collecting funds for colonization in Palestine from Jews and non-Jews alike.

Jabotinsky explained in a mixture of Russian and Hebrew that he wanted to organize a legion made up exclusively of Jewish soldiers, to fight on the side of the Allies in Palestine for the liberation of the Holy Land from the Turks. It took him less than fifteen minutes to convince his host and receive his promise of support.

Mass meetings were held and before long at Gabbari several

hundred of the refugees were undergoing voluntary, self-directed military training. Then Jabotinsky and Trumpeldor—the latter with his four St. George crosses pinned on his chest to try to make an impression—called on the general in charge of British forces in Egypt, who listened attentively to their idea but replied that foreigners could not be used in fighting units. When he saw their disappointment he offered a compromise: he would let them form a mule corps exclusively of Jews. Jabotinsky indignantly turned down the suggestion. Trumpeldor, after some hesitation, accepted it, and a few months later went off to Gallipoli with 600 Jewish muleteers who during the next year performed so well that the story of the Zion Mule Corps became the first modern saga of Jewish bravery under fire and led Jabotinsky to admit that he had been wrong and Trumpeldor right.

During that year, Jabotinsky pounded on doors all over Europe, trying vainly to excite some statesman or militarist into approving the idea of an all-Jewish army. Even most Jews—leaders as well as the rank and file—were against it. Yiddish papers in New York ridiculed not only the idea but Jabotinsky himself, calling him the Jewish *enfant terrible* and a foolish Don Quixote. Even the Zionist Organization condemned a Jewish Legion and urged all good Zionists to oppose it. The feeling in Russia against the originator of the idea grew so strong that one of the most celebrated Russian Zionist leaders, meeting Jabotinsky's mother on the street one day, told her, "Your son ought to be hanged!" One of the few exceptions was Baron Edmond de Rothschild. Another was Dr. Weizmann, who in the past had often used scathing words in print and in speeches to describe the young upstart from Odessa. Now the two men suddenly became warm friends and Jabotinsky not only was a frequent guest in the Weizmann home in Manchester, England, but roomed with the chemist and his wife for three months in their town house in London. Often for hours they would mix intellectual discussion with Zionist daydreaming.

Through personal friendships Jabotinsky was able to get the *London Times* and the *Manchester Guardian* to carry editorials favoring the Legion idea, although most of the Jewish press throughout the world was against it. Month after month, year after year, this resolute fanatic kept up his one-man campaign.

He had no organization, no funds, and little assistance. Often he grew discouraged. In the East End of London, where there were tens of thousands of Jewish refugees from Eastern Europe, he tried to collect the signatures of men willing to serve in a Jewish Legion if one were ever formed. Often at mass meetings he was pelted with rotten vegetables. Once his glasses were broken. After weeks he had just 300 signatures.

But on August 23, 1917, his three years of hard work were rewarded when an official announcement appeared in the London *Gazette* that a Jewish regiment had been authorized. General organization was put in the hands of Colonel John Henry Patterson, who had been commanding officer of the Zion Mule Corps and whom Jabotinsky described as "one of the most remarkable Christian figures our people ever encountered on its way through all the centuries of the Dispersion." Jabotinsky enlisted, was made a lieutenant, and was given charge of recruitment. Non-Jewish soldiers in other British units, uncertain how to pronounce his name, nicknamed him "Lieutenant Jug-o'-Whisky."

February 4, 1919, was a day Jabotinsky never forgot. It was cold and wintry, but the Jewish Battalion, its bayonets shining, paraded through the financial district of London to the cheers of many who so short a time ago had so violently opposed the idea. It was a bright moment in a long dream.

The 38th Royal Fusiliers, as the battalion was technically called, landed in Alexandria in March 1919. On the eve of Passover this first all-Jewish military unit in so many centuries reached Palestine. Soon it was in bloody action at the front, midway between Jerusalem and Nablus, in an area of high hills and deep valleys. Later the battalion was given the task of capturing both sides of a ford across the Jordan called Umm Esh Shert. By now it was summer, an unusually torrid one, and this area—one of the deepest spots in the world—was also one of the hottest. The main operation was entrusted to Jabotinsky. Umm Esh Shert was taken, as ordered.

The instant the war ended, anti-Zionist British military authorities wanted to start immediate demobilization of the 38th Royal Fusiliers, the 39th, that had been recruited in the United States and Canada, and the 40th, made up of Palestinian Jewish volunteers. Jabotinsky felt that in the confusion following the breakup of the Ottoman Empire, "the mission of the Jewish battalions is much more important than it ever was before."

But this time he was fighting against overwhelming odds. He had against him not only most British military authorities, but the Legionnaires themselves; with the war over, most of them wanted to go home. At the end of one year, only 300 remained in uniform.

Soon after the cessation of hostilities, the Zionist Organization was permitted to send a commission to Palestine to advise the British in all matters affecting the Jewish population. It was headed by Dr. Weizmann, with Jabotinsky as its political officer, although he still remained in the army. In this capacity he wrote numerous reports for the commission on what he called "the growing Arab impudence." Inciting speeches were being made by Arab leaders, while British authorities, he reported, were discriminating against Jews and behaving as if the Balfour Declaration had never been issued. In one of many letters to Dr. Weizmann he said, "I did not participate in my youth in the organization of self-defense in order that I should now sit quietly and complacently watch while Arabs have it drummed into their ears that it is possible to get rid of us if they only give us a hard enough kick." Dr. Weizmann, annoyed at what he termed Jabotinsky's lack of "poise, balance, and mature judgment," summarily dismissed him from the commission. Six months later he was also discharged from the British Army and went back to journalism, remaining in Palestine and writing for a new paper, *Hadashot Haaretz.*

The winter of 1919–20 in Jerusalem was the coldest and most severe within memory. The streets were so deep in snow that many families were unable to leave their homes. (Arab propagandists blamed it on Jabotinsky and other Russian Jews, saying they had brought typical Siberian winter weather to Palestine to torment the heat-loving Moslem population.) That winter Jabotinsky lived in an unheated apartment and wrote his newspaper articles with a wool scarf around his neck, heavy gloves on his hands, and galoshes on his feet.

When his wife, son, and mother arrived from Russia, the Jabotinsky home became a gathering place for great numbers of immigrants, especially from Russia, who came to discuss all the problems and prospects of this newly liberated land. Moshe Shertok (who later changed his name to Sharret and became Foreign Minister, then Prime Minister) often came to discuss Hebrew poetry. Colonel Storrs, the British Governor-General, was also a frequent visitor. The one house rule was that all conversation must be in Hebrew, with nine-year-old Eri in charge of the box into which violators had to drop money to pay their fines.

That same winter, Jabotinsky was deeply affected by the death of Trumpeldor and six companions who were killed by Arabs while trying to defend four isolated settlements in Upper Galilee. Jabotinsky had argued that the settlements were indefensible and that Trumpeldor and the others should be told to leave Upper Galilee at once. He was opposed by a majority of the Jewish leaders, who insisted that the defense of Upper Galilee was a matter of national honor. But the assistance they dispatched arrived too late.

Organized self-defense in Palestine was consolidated at a conference called late in 1919 by Jabotinsky, at which all Zionist bodies were represented. Leaders of the labor groups insisted on a clandestine force, while Jabotinsky argued that there would be great political advantage if they operated in the open. His viewpoint was approved by the majority and he was asked to take charge of the organization of Jewish manpower for self-defense. Within a short time he had signed up his first 400 volunteers. Jews who had weapons of any sort were asked to turn them over to *Haganah,* the Hebrew word for self-defense. To augment the few guns that were turned in, purchases were made surreptitiously from an old Armenian arms dealer in Jerusalem who charged Haganah exorbitant prices but supplied them with weapons they could not obtain elsewhere. The Jabotinsky apartment was converted into an arsenal. Every night drills were held; every morning a roll call and inspection; every weekend forced marches to condition the recruits. One of Jabotinsky's instructions read: "If an Arab walks up to you and insults you, never strike him, but if he hits you, return the blow twice as hard." Jabotinsky informed Colonel Storrs that Palestine's Jews were henceforth going to defend themselves. Storrs expressed no objection. The Zionist Commission, headed by Dr. Weizmann, was also informed and advanced some financial support. Extremely religious Jews provided the only opposition. Some of them threatened that if Haganah men tried to patrol the streets of their quarter, they would demand that the British arrest them.

The Moslem feast of Nebi Moussa early in April 1920 brought thousands of Arab pilgrims to Jerusalem. Under the spell of inflammatory oratory, they began attacking Jews on the streets. Then they marched to the Jewish quarter in the Old City and started a pogrom that lasted two days and two terrible nights. Only a few Jews were killed, but several hundred were wounded, many seriously. A number of girls were raped and there was widespread looting. Jabotinsky set up Haganah headquarters in the Zionist Commission offices and gave up sleeping and eating to direct the attempt at self-defense. He tried to send two companies of his men from the New City to the Old City, but they were turned back by the British.

As the pogrom wore itself out, the British authorities finally went into action—against Haganah. In a house on Jaffa Road a modest arsenal of three rifles and two revolvers was confiscated. Then Jabotinsky and nineteen Haganah members were arrested and put into solitary confinement in a former Turkish prison at Jaffa. Finally they were given a preliminary hearing. Surrounded by Arab guards armed with Turkish lashes, they faced an Australian captain and his Arab secretary who tried to do the cross-examining.

"What is your name?" he asked Jabotinsky in Arabic. When there was no answer, he repeated the question in French, then English. Jabotinsky continued to stare into space, his lips tight shut. When the captain angrily demanded that the prisoner answer, Jabotinsky said, "I shall not answer a court secretary who belongs to the group of murderers who have been attacking innocent people. . . . Furthermore, I shall answer no questions unless they are in Hebrew, my language and the language of the Land of Israel." Eventually the questioning was done in Hebrew.

Jabotinsky's friends called the case a legal monstrosity and Jabotinsky himself said, "I am happy to be imprisoned for such a cause as the defense of unprotected Jews against blood-thirsty hooligans." Thousands of Palestinians put their names to a document expressing support of the twenty prisoners, while most Haganah members signed a petition to the British court asking that the defendants be released or that the entire membership be committed to trial.

After five days of solitary confinement, the prisoners were tried by a court-martial of a British major and two captains. The nineteen were sentenced to three years at hard labor. In order to be able to demand the death penalty for Jabotinsky, the British prosecutor dug up an old article of the Ottoman Penal Code, which he was accused of violating. The charge said ". . . that he did arm the inhabitants of the Ottoman Dominions against each other with the evil intent of bringing about rapine, pillage, devastation of the country, mutual homicide . . . and that as a result of this action disorders came about."

Jabotinsky, conducting his own defense, pointed out the basic irony: that no action had been taken against those who had conducted the pogrom; that only those who had tried to defend themselves were now being prosecuted—or persecuted. But the court found him guilty and he was sentenced to fifteen years of penal servitude, after which he was to be deported from Palestine.

The Jews of Jerusalem reacted almost unanimously—and with indignation. Shops and schools were closed. Newspapers suspended publication. The Rabbinate proclaimed a day of general fast and mourning. Most of the Jewish political parties decided to put Jabotinsky's name at the top of their lists of candidates in an election about to be held for a Jewish assembly.

For the first seven days Jabotinsky was kept in a dungeon in Jerusalem with a dirt floor, moldy walls, and no bed. When he demanded Kosher food they gave him a piece of Arab bread spread with chopped onions. On the eighth day, Colonel Storrs called on him and had him moved to a well-furnished cell and arranged for his wife to bring him several suitcases of clothes, books, and personal items. The next day, having decided to consider them political prisoners, the British announced that all twenty would be shipped at once to a prison in Cairo. When their train stopped at Lydda, several hundred men—the remnant of the old Jewish Legion—appeared at the railroad station to pay their respects to "the father of the first Jewish Army in more than 1,800 years."

When they reached the Egyptian frontier, Lord Allenby ordered them turned back, declaring that he wanted no "Palestine criminals" in Egypt, so the first deportation of Jews from the Holy Land in a long time was reversed and they were sent to Acre, just north of Haifa, where the British had converted an ancient fortress into a prison. That same day, when Jabotinsky heard a report that Sir Herbert Samuel, a prominent British Jew, was about to be named the first British High Commissioner for Palestine, he remarked, "A good *goy* [non-Jew] would be better for us. . . . A Jew's hands will be tied by his super-caution."

The Acre prison had the reputation of being one of the worst in the world, but Jabotinsky and his nineteen companions were given special treatment. Mrs. Jabotinsky visited the prison almost every day, bringing Eri, whose father gave him long instruction in history, geography, and both ancient and modern languages. While a prisoner he also translated into Hebrew the *Rubáiyát of Omar Khayyám,* several of A. Conan Doyle's detective stories, and a few stanzas of Dante's *Divine Comedy.* Also, he wrote a poem, "The Song of the Prisoners of Acre," in memory of Trumpeldor. He and the other nineteen formed an orchestra, using pots, pans, dishes, and cutlery for instruments.

Meanwhile, the outside world was reacting with indignation to news of the case. Several London papers nicknamed Jabotinsky the Jewish Garibaldi. New York papers said the British had insulted the whole Jewish people. Petitions demanding the release of the prisoners were circulated in many countries. In the House of Commons, repeated questions were directed at Cabinet members. In the face of such pressure the British Government finally reduced Jabotinsky's sentence from fifteen years to one year; the sentence of the others from three years to six months.

Early in June one of the nineteen suggested a hunger strike. Jabotinsky was against it, but when they took a vote and the majority was for it, he agreed to put his name to the ultimatum they sent to the commander of the garrison: if they were not

freed in eight days they would stop eating. As soon as the ultimatum was announced they were bombarded with letters from
the Chief Rabbi of Palestine, from Ben Yehuda, from friends
and from strangers, all begging them to reconsider. On the day
the hunger strike was to have begun they decided to give in to
public opinion.

One month later Sir Herbert Samuel arrived and began his
administration by announcing an amnesty for all those who had
been imprisoned in connection with the Jerusalem riots. Jabotinsky was against accepting, because two Arabs imprisoned for
raping some Jewish girls were included in the amnesty, but
again he was outvoted and again he abided by the will of the
majority.

They spent the first day of their freedom in Haifa, where
Jabotinsky delivered to a mass meeting one of the most brilliant
speeches of his life. Then he went to Jerusalem, where he was
hailed as a national hero by thousands of cheering men, women,
and children.

In 1921 he joined the Executive of the Zionist Organization
and left Palestine to live and work in London. Now he was a
member of The Establishment. It was the only period in his life
when he was not a rebel fighting against those in authority. Yet
he still had strong ideas of his own, and was not hesitant in expressing them. One of his first struggles while "working within,"
as he put it, was to persuade his colleagues to oppose Sir Herbert Samuel's idea of a mixed militia, which would naturally be
composed mostly of Arabs and therefore would turn into a pre-
dominantly anti-Jewish, anti-Zionist "pogrom army." Instead,
he wanted the 38th, the 39th, and the 40th Royal Fusiliers built
up into a powerful all-Jewish military unit. He was opposed
in London by Shertok and David Hacohen, both members of
the labor group, who were collecting funds to buy arms for
Haganah, and in Palestine by Eliahu Golomb, Haganah commander. They all contended it would take time to reestablish
the Legion; that the loss of a number of lives in a recent pogrom
in Jaffa proved the need for immediate strengthening of de-
fenses.

During a three-day debate of the Zionist Action Committee
in Prague in the summer of 1921, Jabotinsky made this state-

ment: "I warn you not to . . . place arms in the hands of Jewish adolescents who know no military discipline. Arms are only for adults who are under military command. A Jewish self-defense force of ten thousand will stir up the Arabs more than two thousand Jewish soldiers would. The only way is to renew the Legion. Without the Legion a colonization of Palestine is not possible. . . ." At the end of a two-hour speech he threatened that if his Legion idea was rejected he would resign. The Committee finally voted to take steps to revive the Legion.

Late in 1921, Jabotinsky went to the United States for the first time and in a letter to Mrs. Weizmann observed, "America is a dull country. Thus far I haven't seen anything for the sake of which it would be worthwhile to cross the ocean." (On subsequent trips he changed his opinion drastically.) In seven months he spoke in sixty American cities, raising funds for Palestine.

On his way home, when he stepped from a boat at Southampton a messenger handed him a large envelope which he hastily opened. It contained a copy of a White Paper the Churchill Government had just issued. It apparently had been drafted at the suggestion of Lord Herbert Samuel and was aimed at appeasing the Arabs by giving them all of Palestine east of the Jordan, and limiting the creation of any Jewish homeland to that small percentage of Palestine lying west of the Jordan. The Zionist Executive had been informed by the British Government that unless acceptance of the White Paper was received by morning, the entire idea of a Jewish homeland would be reconsidered, and perhaps dropped.

When Jabotinsky reached London, Dr. Weizmann explained to him that energetic steps had been taken to dissuade the Government, but without success. Jabotinsky urged that acquiescence ought to be qualified in some way, but out of loyalty to his colleagues he did not oppose sending the letter of approval.

In the ensuing months it became more and more obvious that a break between Jabotinsky and Weizmann was inevitable. The two men were totally unalike in temperament, background, mentality, personal characteristics, and political philosophy—too unalike to work together for very long. The wonder was that they were close personal friends for as many years as they were. Late in 1922, Jabotinsky drafted a memorandum calling on the Zionist Executive to take a firm stand against British policy; to do everything possible to force London to live up to the terms of its mandate; to insist on the removal of all anti-Zionist officials from the Palestine administration. Early in 1923 the Actions Committee met and rejected his ideas, whereupon he resigned, declaring, "I can no longer remain a mere critic of our present policy. . . . I must become a fighter, a rebel. . . ." The political break with his friend Weizmann was never repaired.

From London he went to Berlin, where he put politics momentarily aside and became a book publisher, joining with several friends in an ambitious plan of publishing, in Hebrew, textbooks for schoolchildren, and such works as *Robinson Crusoe* (which had had such an effect on Ben Yehuda's life), *Uncle Tom's Cabin, Gulliver's Travels,* the Sherlock Holmes stories, and even a book on table manners.

In 1924 he moved to Paris and announced that he was establishing an organization of all groups opposed to the policies of the Zionist Organization. They would call themselves the Revisionists, because their aim was to revise the program, the tactics, and even some of the principles of the organization. Their basic aim was to return to what Jabotinsky called the principles of Herzl. Support came from groups scattered across Palestine, Great Britain, Germany, Austria, France, Poland, Greece, Latvia, Russia, and Bulgaria. The first conference was held early in 1925 in a café in the Latin Quarter in Paris at which they stated their policy as ". . . the gradual transformation of all Palestine, including Trans-Jordan, into a self-governing Commonwealth under the auspices of an established Jewish majority." Jabotinsky himself wrote the party song that soon was being sung at all Revisionist gatherings, the refrain of which said:

> *Two banks to the Jordan;*
> *One is ours, so is the other.*

Along with the Revisionist Party he also organized a youth movement, *Brit Trumpeldor,* named in memory of the one-armed hero of Gallipoli and Tel Hai. For short it was called *Betar*, an abbreviation of its full title and also the name of the town where Jewish fighters held out against the Romans during the Bar Kochba Revolt. Members were called *Betarim* and Jabotinsky himself was the *Rosh Betar*, or leader. The Betar doctrine that Jabotinsky formulated and preached to them was a vague mysticism, combined with his insistence on military-like obedience to strict rules of personal behavior he laid down for them. More important than anything else, he told the Betarim, was *hadar*, which in general meant an inner glow of goodness and an outward brightness; a way of life based on truth and beauty. On one occasion he said *hadar* "consists of a thousand trifles that collectively form our everyday life. . . . You must be generous if no question of principle is involved. Every word of yours must be a word of honor, which is mightier than steel. A time should eventually come when a Jew, desiring to express his highest appreciation of human honesty, courtesy and esteem, will say, not as now, 'He is a real gentleman,' but, 'He is a real *Betari!*' "

At the same time the Rosh Betar insisted that his young followers learn to speak quietly in public, that they shave every day, that they keep their faces, hands, ears, and bodies scrupulously clean, and that they check every morning to be sure their fingernails were not dirty.

The secret of Jabotinsky's success with the Betarim seemed to be that he offered to the Jewish youth of his day a positive, romantic, and creative alternative to the confusion they saw all around them. Betar became almost a religion to them and they gave their leader a devotion that approached fanaticism. After his death they voted that no one else could ever be called by the exalted title of Rosh Betar.

Branches of Betar were organized not only in Palestine but also in Europe and the United States. By the start of World War II there were 80,000 members in 25 countries. Jabotinsky's friends said his real objective was to try to create a new type of young Jew in the Diaspora, as well as in Palestine.

At the Fourteenth Zionist Congress in Vienna, Jabotinsky "poured acid on open wounds," as one observer put it, by reminding the delegates how badly Zionism's accomplishments compared with its goals.

In 1926, he made a professional lecture tour of the United States, attracting large crowds and sparking many lively discussions of Palestine's future. Then he went back to the Middle East where during one month it was estimated that at least a quarter of the entire Jewish population of Palestine heard his public addresses. Wherever he went, crowds lined the streets, children showered him with flowers, and he was wildly applauded. Even those who opposed almost everything he said were spellbound by his oratory. Then to Germany, where he lectured in rapid succession in fourteen cities.

In the Fifteenth Zionist Congress in Basel, Jabotinsky headed a Revisionist delegation that now numbered nine men. He shocked the Congress with statistics designed to prove the mathematical impossibility of the situation in Palestine, where, he said, the 750,000 Arabs were multiplying so rapidly that soon they would number a million, while Jewish immigration was adding no more than 10,000 souls a year to the total, so the minority was becoming year by year smaller and smaller. He also spoke out for the industrial development of Jewish Palestine.

In 1928, Jabotinsky went back to live in Palestine, this time in the capacity of managing director of an insurance company. But soon he was also the editor for the first time in his life of a newspaper of his own, *Doar Hayom*. The third World Congress of his Revisionist movement took place in Vienna late that same year, with seventy delegates from eighteen countries, and with Jabotinsky delivering a two-hour, thunder-and-lightning address. His movement was growing, but already so many internecine feuds had broken out that in dismay he asked a colleague, "Why is it that even here at a conference of the movement I have created, there is so much opposition, even among my closest friends?"

The rebel was having rebel-trouble of his own.

The Sixteenth Zionist Congress in Zurich was preceded by a meeting in Jerusalem of the Elected Assembly, where emotions became so inflamed by organizational arguments that Revisionists and labor delegates often came to blows, and once someone seized from Jabotinsky's hand a cane with which he was making angry gestures. The Jerusalem experience cut a deep gash in his mind. He never forgot the antagonism he saw displayed there against his followers. He commented sadly on the expression of "inhuman hatred I have not seen even in Russia, even among the Arabs during the pogrom days in Jerusalem . . . and a great part of this hatred is directed against my own humble person." In a book published four years later he wrote of being haunted by "a hundred pairs of eyes." He added, ". . . eyes that belonged to the best youth that our people have possessed since the days of Bar Kochba look at you with a deep and almost inhuman hatred and boo, 'Down with him!' . . . 'Break his bones!' "

In his address to the Congress he defined the Jewish home-land in unequivocal terms: "It is an area whose essential geo-graphical characteristic is that the Jordan River flows not along its frontier but through the middle of it." The purpose of Zionism, he said, was not only to "create a Jewish majority in Palestine, but to create living space for millions on both sides of the Jordan."

The worst massacre in modern Palestinian history occurred in August of that year (1929) when an Arab mob began swarm-ing from the Old City into the New City of Jerusalem. Almost at once the contagion of disorder spread to other parts of Pales-tine, until 250 persons had been killed, a majority of them Jews. In order to testify before a British commission of investigation that had been sent out from London, Jabotinsky, who was in Europe, rushed back. His friends insisted his life was in danger so they established a 26-man bodyguard for him. At hearings of the Shaw Commission his newspaper was blamed for incit-ing Jewish public opinion and provoking violence. The trouble in Jerusalem had begun, witnesses told the Commission, when a group of young Jews held a protest demonstration at the Wailing Wall against Arab interference with Jews trying to use the Wall as a place of prayer. Witnesses said these demonstra-tors were members of Betar.

In the six years of its existence the youth organization had become as emotionally important to Jabotinsky as he was to its members, and when it was charged with fomenting the Arab-Jewish trouble he denied it as indignantly as if his own

son were the accused, at the same time declaring that if Betar
had been involved he would be proud of it, because he felt the
time had finally come for Jews in Palestine to say, "This far
and no farther!" in order to let the Arab world know that
they did not consider themselves just "tolerated guests" in
Palestine.

In his testimony before the Commission, Jabotinsky described
Eastern Europe as "a zone of incurable anti-Semitism." As for
the goal of Zionism, he said he and his Revisionists would be
satisfied if they could get "the measure of self-government
which, for instance, the State of Nebraska possesses."

Despite the cancellation of his reentry visa by the British at
this time, making it impossible for him to return to Palestine,
and despite the opinion of a majority of Zionists that the
British Empire was close to the point of disintegration, Jabotinsky was loud in contending that "England will always be
our friend; she will keep her word." (After 1930, the British
never permitted him to return to Palestine.)

By 1931 the Revisionist movement had grown so rapidly
that he led a delegation of fifty-two to the Seventeenth Zionist
Congress in Zurich. But the more the movement grew, the
more internal troubles it had. In a despondent mood he wrote
this self-revealing sentence to a friend: "There is no need to
tell you how bitter it is for me to see Revisionism break up,
but I prefer to go the right way with half the movement, or a
third, or even a dozen people than finish my Zionist days as
the opposition to a crowd of spiritual 'opposition' calling themselves the Z.O., a crowd I coldly and infinitely despise."

In the Seventeenth Congress, Jabotinsky fought against a
watering down of the goals of Zionism by Weizmann and his
followers. He argued for using the word "state" instead of the
ambiguous "national home," declaring: "The Albanians have
their state, the Bulgarians have their state; a state is, after all,
the normal condition of a people. If a Jewish state were in
existence today, nobody would think that it is abnormal." Pro-
phetically he added, "We want a home for all the suffering
Jews, and nobody can predict how many Jews there will be
who will suffer during the next few generations." At the Congress the internecine conflict became so violent that at two

o'clock one morning Jabotinsky jumped onto a chair, shouting, "This is not a Zionist Congress any more," tore his delegate's card into small pieces, and was carried from the hall on the shoulders of some of his supporters. Although he had more to do with Weizmann's defeat for the Congress presidency that year than anyone else, the Revisionists were unable to muster enough votes to elect him as Weizmann's successor.

There was also dissension at this time within the self-defense organization called Haganah. Jabotinsky's followers, contending that it was virtually under the control of Histadrut (the Jewish federation of labor) finally split away and formed what they called Haganah Bet (a second Haganah.) For five years Jabotinsky was not formally associated with this group, which was composed not only of Revisionists but of members of all the nonsocialist parties.

At the Fifth Revisionist World Congress in 1932, during debate on a proposal to give the president dictatorial powers, Jabotinsky made a strong statement on what he thought of dictators. "I believe" he said, "in the ideological patrimony of the nineteenth century, the century of Garibaldi and Lincoln, Gladstone and Hugo. . . . Today's ideological fashion is: a human being is in essence dishonest and stupid, and he should not, therefore, be given the right to govern himself; freedom leads to perdition, equality is a lie, society needs leaders, and a stick . . . better not to live at all than to live under such a system."

Yet it was only a few months later that he suspended the secretariat of his own organization and announced that he was assuming personal direction of the World Union of Zionist Revisionists. His opponents called it a *putsch,* so he put the action to a vote of the membership and received the approval of 93.8 per cent. Yet the charge of dictatorship kept cropping up. Jabotinsky himself then went on record as saying, "As I near old age, I am beginning to agree with the belief in the inevitability of personal leadership." There was no question about the dynamism of his leadership. Not even his most bitter opponents ever denied the hold he had on his followers. They were not only swayed by his oratory and dazzled by the sparks that flew from his brilliant mind, but they felt an idealistic and emotional attachment to him so strong that many would have been willing to give their lives for him.

A murder in Tel Aviv formed the background for the fight he led in the Eighteenth Congress against The Establishment. The dead man was Chaim Arlosoroff, head of the political department of the Jewish Agency, who had been sent to Germany to try to find out how serious Hitler and his Nazi regime were in their intimation that German Jews would be permitted to leave the country if they went quickly. On his return, while walking along the Tel Aviv waterfront with his wife on a warm June evening, Arlosoroff was approached by a stranger who asked him the time. As he reached into his pocket for his watch, a shot rang out. He fell, mortally wounded, and his assailant fled. Three days later, police arrested Abraham Stavsky, a young Revisionist who had recently arrived from Poland and who, Mrs. Arlosoroff said, resembled the assassin. The Revisionists charged their political enemies with a frame-up. David Ben-Gurion, expressing belief in the guilt of Stavsky, said that Jabotinsky, as the Rosh Betar, was the one really responsible. At the time, Jabotinsky was on a speaking tour of Poland, where feelings over the case was running so high that he was given a bodyguard and a permit to carry a gun. When he spoke in Stavsky's home town of Brest-Litovsk an angry crowd stoned him. Elsewhere in Poland demonstrators shouted "Murderer!" at him, and one night in the capital of Lithuania they threw stones on the metal roof of the meeting place throughout his lecture to harass him.

This was the atmosphere when the Eighteenth Congress opened in Prague, where Jabotinsky aired his contempt of the Jewish leadership in Palestine, especially for contemplating the plan Arlosoroff had been investigating in Berlin.

From a distance he helped with Stavsky's defense, which was financed by a wealthy South African Zionist who had long been a Jabotinsky admirer. When the court sentenced Stavsky to be hanged, Jabotinsky went to London to try to arouse British opinion. Two months later the Court of Appeals acquitted Stavsky. (Fifteen years later he, in turn, was killed not many feet from where Arlosoroff had fallen.)

Three months after Adolf Hitler became Chancellor, Jabotinsky issued a call for a worldwide boycott of Germany and addressed 69 mass meetings in Eastern Europe as part of this campaign.

After his first visit to Palestine, Jabotinsky had written, "I consider the socialization of the means of production an inevitable and desirable result of the social process." Later, however, he repudiated this point of view and became a sometimes violent critic of any form of socialism, to the extent that many of his political enemies called him the leader of Jewish fascism and the spokesman for an "outdated and reactionary bourgeoisie." He often criticized Histadrut as being monopolistic and "a malignant tumor," and called at least for its truncation. Yet in October 1934, he agreed to meet his arch enemy, David Ben-Gurion, the dominant figure in the current Palestinian labor movement, who, since the temporary enforced retirement of Weizmann, had been Jabotinsky's greatest opponent in Zionism. Ben-Gurion had called Jabotinsky a "Zionist Trotsky" and "Vladimir Hitler." On his side, Jabotinsky had used almost as uncomplimentary names about Ben-Gurion. They met in the London apartment of Pinhas Rutenberg, to whom Jabotinsky had handed over command of Haganah when he went to prison. At their first session they talked for four hours, and two weeks later for an entire day and night. The agreement they finally signed promised an end to acts of terror, and to all libel, slander and insult, Jew against Jew, with expulsion from the Zionist Organization as the penalty for serious violations. This agreement was later approved by the Revisionists but not by Ben-Gurion's party. They also initialed a working agreement between Histadrut and a small opposition labor organization Jabotinsky had formed, but this agreement was rejected some months later by the Histadrut members in a referendum. Although nothing permanently constructive came from the Jabotinsky–Ben-Gurion meetings, the personal relationship between the two men improved, with Jabotinsky writing Ben-Gurion a letter of "friendship and respect," and Ben-Gurion replying with reciprocal warmth.

In 1935, Jabotinsky made another trip to the United States to try to persuade Americans to put pressure on England to implement its old Jewish homeland promise. This time he found it "a land of great yearnings" and wrote eulogistically of its tempo and the pioneering urge of its people. There were 400 outstanding American-Jewish personalities on the Jabotinsky reception committee. A Chicago newspaper said his popularity was due partly to the fact that he resembled in some ways both Theodore and Franklin D. Roosevelt, and one of his introducers called him "the second Herzl." But Albert Einstein had a different idea. He warned against the "sirens of Revisionism who are as much a danger to our youth as Hitler is to German youth." In the magazine *Opinion,* edited by James Waterman Wise, son of the Zionist leader, Rabbi Stephen Wise, an editorial described him as "a reactionary, a militarist, a vain and conceited demagogue who had sent brown-shirted soldiers to Zionist Congresses to cause trouble." The article urged those who had joined the Jabotinsky reception committee to withdraw. The editor's mother, Louise Waterman Wise, was one of the members. Jabotinsky wrote to her complaining about her son's attack. He received a reply not from her but from her husband, who wrote that he was "deeply concerned about . . . the fascist tendencies of Revisionism" and added, "A fascist and undemocratic Jewish state in Palestine would be to me an abomination to be destroyed, not an ideal to be cherished." Even though the New York rabbi reiterated his "personal affection and admiration" for Jabotinsky, and even though he joined his wife on the reception committee, he was the target a short time later of a cruel blast from the Revisionist leader, who in a printed statement said, "Dr. Wise has one great quality, he says what he thinks. But he has one great defect, he doesn't think."

As the Zionists of the world were preparing for their 1935 Congress, Jabotinsky suggested to his followers that they withdraw from the World Zionist Organization and form a new, independent World Zionist body of their own. While he awaited the results of a plebescite, he consoled himself with the thought that if his idea was rejected he could return to being a writer. ("I have a hundred books in my head.") The vote was 167,000, yes; 3,000, no. At the founding convention in Vienna of the New Zionist Organization the only requirement for voting was that each delegate sign a statement that his aim was a Jewish state on both sides of the Jordan and "social justice without class war." Jabotinsky was elected president and the Congress approved the idea of transferring a million and a half new immigrants to Palestine within ten years.

Early in April 1935, he sent a long cable from London to the British High Commissioner in Jerusalem about disturbing rumors of plans for anti-Jewish demonstrations in Palestine and asked what steps were being taken to avoid them. He received no reply, but exactly two weeks later the killing, looting, and burning began. It was the worst outbreak of violence to date.

Early in 1937, he went to South Africa to try to win support among the large Jewish population there. In pleading for immediate evacuation of the Jews of Eastern Europe he likened the situation to a fire in a crowded theater. ("People begin a frantic stampede to get out, but all the doors and windows are hermetically sealed.")

About this time, anticipating that the British would soon make some attempt to satisfy the ever-growing desire for a Jewish state, the official Zionist leadership attempted to bring about a merger of the two underground armies. Even Colonel Henry John Patterson, one of Jabotinsky's most intimate friends and commander of the 38th Royal Fusiliers in World War I, implored him by cable to confirm the agreement. But Jabotinsky was adamant in his opposition. Meanwhile the Haganah Bet commander had proceeded with the merger. The result was confusion, with Eliahu Golomb, commander of the official Haganah, claiming that half the 3,000 members of Haganah Bet were now under his command, but with Jabotinsky declaring that such a figure was grossly exaggerated. Those who did not merge regrouped and called themselves the *Irgun Zvai Leumi* (the National Military Organization). At first Jabotinsky had no rank or title in the Irgun. Later he became its supreme commander. Even when he was away from Palestine there was no appeal from his orders on major policy.

While he was in Alexandria on his way back from South Africa he met with Irgun leaders who wanted to discuss ending the policy of self-restraint called *havlaga*, which Haganah had always followed. It meant that the underground fighters acted only in self-defense and organized no acts of retaliation. Jabotinsky in many of his writings had supported this idea. Once he wrote that even if history at times demands that people struggling for freedom and independence engage in extra-legal political activities, "such actions must not, of course, be contrary to moral law, in particular to the principle of the sanctity of human life, unless in self-defense." He was now faced with a difficult decision. These young Irgun leaders wanted permission to begin retaliatory acts of terrorism against Arabs. His answer to them was a classic: "I can't see much heroism or public good in shooting from the rear an Arab peasant on a donkey carrying vegetables for sale in Tel Aviv." The Conference finally decided to prepare for retaliation but to engage in no large-scale action until a cable was received from Jabotinsky. Regardless of what it might say, if it was signed "Mendelson" *havlaga* should be abandoned.

Irgun began its campaign of retaliatory terror, with Jabotinsky's permission, that same autumn. Arabs had murdered five Jewish workmen. On Black Sunday, Irgun members made an attack on an Arab market place in Jerusalem. There were not many casualties, but it was the first piece of open, daylight, Jewish terror. Jerusalem was stunned. The gunmen escaped but British police later arrested twenty Revisionists, including Jabotinsky's own son, Eri. They were imprisoned at Acre. Jewish Agency officials said the terrorists had marred the moral record of Palestinian Jews. In reply, Jabotinsky defended the right of Jews to "hit back" and said he was proud that his son was among those arrested. Yet three years later, at the time of his death, Jabotinsky was still not reconciled to indiscriminate acts of terror.

One Irgun leader who caused him especial annoyance was Abraham Stern, who tried to undermine the authority of the Rosh Betar by instructing men who belonged to both Betar and Irgun that they owed no loyalty henceforth to Betar leaders. Stern also engaged in a long and bitter feud with David Raziel, the Irgun commander. Jabotinsky supported Raziel and called on Stern to submit to organizational discipline. But one month after Jabotinsky's death, Stern split with Irgun and formed his own terrorist band, the Fighters for the Freedom of Israel, more commonly called the Stern Group, which was later officially blamed for the assassinations in Jerusalem of Count Bernadotte and in Cairo of Lord Moyne, who had reacted to a plan of saving a million Jews by saying, "What would I do with a million Jews?"

Although Irgun after Jabotinsky's death made him their idol and spiritual father, his close friend and biographer, Joseph B. Schechtman, quotes him as saying about the men of Irgun, "What kind of people are they? I know them very little. Their plans, their innermost thoughts, just don't reach me."

When the British closed the doors of Palestine to Jewish immigration, at a time when millions of Jews in Europe were faced with the now-or-never need of going somewhere, Jabotinsky's followers played impressive roles in smuggling them into Palestine. He has even been called "the father of illegal immigration." As far back as 1932 he published an article on Adventurism in which he urged young people to laugh at laws about visas and defy the authorities by emigrating and immigrating as they pleased. Later he ordered his followers to organize the smuggling of Jews into Palestine. Yet even this activity had its internecine problems. Irgun and Betar squabbled so bitterly over which group was to manage *Aliyah Bet* (illegal immigration) that Jabotinsky called an emergency conference in Paris to try to work out a division of authority.

Toward the end of 1938, when more than a thousand Jews were being smuggled into Palestine each month, he suggested that this be made the new Jewish national sport. He also began preaching belligerency, urging parents to teach their children not only to read and write, but to break windows and learn to shoot.

One of Jabotinsky's devoted followers in those days was Dr. Reuben Hecht, who aroused the wrath of his wealthy Swiss family by using business funds to help finance the smuggling of Jews across European frontiers to Palestine. It was typical of Jabotinsky that he offered to bail the young Swiss Revisionist out of his family trouble with his own funds and with party assets, if necessary.

While Jabotinsky was in Alexandria on his way home from South Africa, the Peel Commission, sent to Palestine to investigate the 1936 riots, issued a 400-page report recommending the partition of Palestine into a Jewish state and an Arab state, with 75 per cent of the land, including the Negev Desert, going to the Arabs. To a mass meeting of 6,000 people Jabotinsky denounced the plan and sneered that it was nothing but *chiu-chiuchiachia,* an Italian word meaning "a lot of nonsensical talk."

That same year, in what was to be the last book he would ever write, Jabotinsky said, "Palestine, astride the Jordan, has room for a million Arabs, for another million of their eventual progeny, for several million Jews, and for peace." Despite his own anger with England, he still argued publicly that "the British Government is and will continue to be the government of a well-disposed mother."

The last major battle of Jabotinsky's life was over his insistence in lectures, conferences, and newspaper interviews in Poland in 1936–37 that several million Jews must be evacuated immediately from Eastern Europe. Sholom Asch, who was visiting Warsaw at the time, declared, "One has to have a heart of stone and be devoid of any feeling for human suffering to be so brazen as to come to Poland with such proposals at such a terrible time." In New York, London, Paris, and even Jerusalem, there was also opposition, but Jabotinsky spent most of the next two years trying to arrange with leaders of the Polish Government for a large-scale exodus. He was received by the Polish Prime Minister, who said his government could not possibly cooperate because the world would consider it a colossal piece of anti-Semitism. Because there were three-quarters of a million Jews in Rumania, Jabotinsky interceded with King Carol and received assurances of cooperation, but no action. Then he saw Edouard Beneš, President of Czechoslovakia, who was sympathetic, but nothing more. Then the Foreign Minister of Latvia, the President of Lithuania, and President Eamon de Valera of the Irish Free State. He toured most of Eastern Europe and the Balkans. Everyone was kind and understanding. But that was all.

Jabotinsky's ire was aroused in the spring of 1938 by the Ben Yosef case. It began with an Arab attack on a bus loaded with Jewish men, women, and children, fourteen of whom were killed. Four of the women were raped. In retaliation, three teen-aged Betar members in a nearby settlement attacked an Arab bus. Their plans misfired and no one was even wounded, but the British military court before which they were tried condemned two of them to be hanged. Jabotinsky wrote scathing attacks on the British for their double-standard of morality, demanding to know why action was never taken against Arab terrorists. Then he began pounding on doors in London, begging, pleading, insisting that the miscarriage of justice be reversed. One sentence finally was commuted to life imprisonment, but the General Officer Commanding British Forces in Palestine confirmed that Shlomo Ben Yosef must "hang by the neck until dead," at 6 A.M. London time, on June 29. All the afternoon of June 28, Jabotinsky argued with British officials. It was almost 5 P.M. when he left the office of Colonial Secretary MacDonald, who snarled at him that unruly elements in the Jewish population must be taught a lesson. At 9 P.M., Ben Yosef's attorney telephoned from Tel Aviv that he had found a case during the Boer War that provided a precedent for appealing to the Privy Council. Jabotinsky rushed to the House of Commons and persuaded the librarian there to let him and two young English lawyers make a desperate search for records of the case. They worked for many hours without success. At midnight a Member of Parliament whose services had been engaged came from a conference with the Attorney General shaking his head. At 2 A.M., they began searching in the cellar of the High Court by candlelight for some trace of the South African case. At 3:30 A.M., after finally finding it, they awoke MacDonald's private secretary. Greatly annoyed, he said the Colonial Secretary was spending the night out; no one knew where. It was now 5 A.M. London time, June 29. It was too late to do anything more. Jabotinsky went home. His wife said he cried that morning for the first time in his life. At 6 A.M. London time, young Ben Yosef was "hanged by the neck until dead." In Acre prison, as he walked to the gallows, he said, "Tell Jabotinsky I will die with his name on my lips." True to the principles he had learned as a Betari, he had brushed his teeth just before leaving his cell.

In May 1939, the British issued a White Paper providing for a drastic restriction of the little Jewish immigration that was being permitted and of Jewish land-buying. It also provided that all of Palestine would ultimately be made into an Arab state. Jabotinsky, who had defended the British on so many occasions, now finally turned against them. In a letter to a friend he said, "Palestine seems destined to become in the very near future the country of active, systematic, and poisonous official anti-Semitism, *par excellence.*" In *A Call to Jewish Youth* he flatly said, ". . . the only way to liberate our country is by the sword." He even conceived a wild plan for a countrywide armed uprising. He sent all the details in an elaborate code in three separate envelopes to Jerusalem from Geneva, Switzerland. In a simultaneous attack in the three cities of Palestine, the Irgun would seize all British government buildings. A ship of illegal immigrants would arrive at the height of the *putsch* with himself aboard. He and enough other Jewish leaders to constitute a full cabinet would barricade themselves as long as possible inside Government House in Jerusalem and would proclaim a Jewish state. At the same time a provisional government would be set up in some city outside Palestine to serve as a government-in-exile after he and his cabinet had been captured and imprisoned—for inevitably the British would put down the revolt and take power back in their own hands again. But the net result would be that a Jewish state had been proclaimed, even though its leaders might be killed or imprisoned. While Irgun leaders debated the idea in the autumn of 1939, world events suddenly forced its abandonment.

Jabotinsky's preoccupation that summer with the British did not sidetrack him from his fight with the Jewish authorities of Palestine. When *they* made speeches against British policy, he ridiculed them, directing most of his fire against David Ben-Gurion.

Less than six months before the start of World War II, Jabotinsky made the most serious miscalculation of his life. In letters to friends and members of his family he insisted, with all his customary vigor of expression, that there was not the remotest chance of war; that in two or three months "German insolence" would subside; that England and Italy would become friendly; and that, in an atmosphere of worldwide peace, a Jewish state would be proclaimed by the spring of 1944.

But as soon as events proved him wrong, he began once more the campaign on which he had spent so much energy a quarter of a century earlier—for a Jewish army. Only this time, as he pounded on doors and interceded with politicians and statesmen, he added two conditions: the Jews of the world must be represented at the peace conference, and the creation of a Jewish state must be one of the declared war aims. His campaign took him in the spring of 1940 to the United States, where he found "the war news on the second page of the newspapers" and American Jews astonishingly shy about speaking out, "lest they be charged with warmongering." At his behest the British Ambassador to Washington cabled London suggesting the immediate authorization of a Jewish army of 100,000 men, plus an Air Force squadron. While Jabotinsky was hopefully waiting for London to approve the idea, he went for a weekend visit to a Betar camp 130 miles north of New York City. There, on August 3, 1940, he had a heart attack. Death was almost instantaneous. His last words were, "I am so tired!"

With 150 cantors taking part in the service, he was buried in a Jewish cemetery on Long Island, in accordance with his will, which asked that he be interred "just where I happen to die; and that my remains, should I be buried outside of Palestine . . . not be transfered to Palestine unless by order of that country's eventual Jewish government."

Seven years and nine months later the State of Israel was proclaimed. Revisionists, who changed their name to the Herut (Freedom) Party, made immediate attempts to have such an order issued. After 14 years they still had not succeeded. Prime Minister David Ben-Gurion remarked that what Israel needed was "live Jews, not dead Jews." Jabotinsky's partisans said their leader, even in death, was a victim of politics. But whether his bones were on Long Island or Mount Herzl, his place in Israel's history was fixed. By golden oratory, an almost hypnotic personality, indefatigable work, and burning conviction he had created a following of men and women who would have obeyed almost any command he gave them. Their ardor, inspired by him, helped to re-create Israel.

Chapter 4

I am not yet too old
To dream dreams.

—HENRIETTA SZOLD

VLADIMIR JABOTINSKY had just finished washing the dishes that he and his nineteen fellow prisoners had used for the midday meal—he insisted on sharing in the chores, even though they had elected him "commander"—when a guard announced that he had another visitor. In his two months of incarceration in Acre prison he had grown accustomed to a parade of well-wishers—friends and opponents alike. It had become a fashionable pastime for Palestinian Jewish society to call on him; he was somewhat cynical about it, but he was impressed by today's guest. She was a robust, buxom woman with soft brown eyes, white hair, and a sweet gentleness that made her seem incongruously out of place in prison. It was the last day of spring 1921. Already it was hot, even inside the great stone fortress, yet Henrietta Szold stayed a long time chatting. As a humanitarian and a pacifist she had never fully agreed with Jabotinsky's ideas or his methods. She considered him militant and aggressive, qualities that had no appeal for her. Yet, writing later of her first personal encounter with him, she said that she had found him "a whole man and a fascinating one," and that when one listened to him, his ideas "assume charm as well as cogency." She added,

"My visit with him will be a memory I shall always want to recur to."

Although she was sixty, Henrietta Szold was actually that day in 1921 only at the start of her real career. The remaining 25 years of her life were to prove that even when one reaches sixty, what has already happened may only be preparation for the flowering of a life. She herself had been tragically unaware of this. As a thirty-one-year-old schoolteacher, weary of correcting examination papers, she had written, "I am getting old!" At forty-two, when death took her father, to whom she had been daughter, son, secretary and literary collaborator, she was certain her usefulness in life had come to an end. At fifty, writing in her journal about the sad denouement of her first love affair, she said, "My only real happiness in life has been killed by a single word." Yet despite these periodic feelings of frustration and uselessness, by the time of her death she would have become a worldwide symbol of Jewish humanitarianism, her name a household word in most Jewish homes in America and Palestine.

Henrietta Szold was born in Baltimore on the day in 1860 when her family and other good Jews were lighting the second Chanukah candle, December 21. Her father was a Conservative rabbi who looked like Lord Tennyson and could quote Horace, Homer and the Talmud with equal facility. A born humanitarian, he had fought on the barricades of Vienna in 1848. Eleven years later he answered a call to become the rabbi of a congregation in Baltimore that had been meeting on the third floor of a coach factory, but now had acquired a Presbyterian church for conversion into a synagogue. Following the Civil War, he was among the first of the city's liberal-minded citizens to join a society to help the newly freed Negroes obtain an education.

The real story of Henrietta Szold begins in the three-story brick house on Lombard Street, Baltimore, into which her family moved when she was thirteen. As an old lady looking from the window of her Jerusalem home over the majestic beauty of the Hills of Judea, she would recall walks she took in her youth through the Maryland woods near her home. Or, serving tea to a friend in her Jerusalem garden (the inevitable tea, in a land of Russian Jews and English! Miss Szold couldn't stand it; she preferred hot water), she would smilingly tell of the spring day in 1874 when the Szolds moved to Lombard Street. Bag and baggage were loaded, but Papa could not be found. Finally they left without him. When they arrived at the new house, there was Rabbi Szold in the garden, planting his vine and fig tree. This was typical of the Judaism that permeated the Szold household; it was not only law and tradition, but a way of life that left imperishable memories for all who came in contact with it. Yet Rabbi Szold's liberalism extended to permitting his children to read the New Testament so they would have tolerance based on understanding; the rabbi himself attended services in some of the Christian churches of Baltimore.

Henrietta, as the eldest of eight daughters—three died in infancy—learned to accept responsibility early in life. *"Mein Kamelchen* [My Little Camel]," her mother laughingly called her, because she insisted on assuming so many burdens. In this family of girls she occupied the place usually reserved for the firstborn son. She sat at her father's right at table and was his intellectual companion in his library-study. At the age of twelve—a brown-haired girl with a pert, intelligent face—she helped him read the German proofs of the new prayerbook he was compiling. In her early teens she was already acting as his secretary, taking down his letters and speeches.

When she was thirteen she entered Female Western High School, two years younger than most of her classmates and the only Jewess in the school. Her brilliance was such that immediately upon graduation she was appointed acting principal of the high school during the principal's illness. About the same time, she became a regular contributor to the *Jewish Messenger,* writing under the pen name *Sulamit.* Her articles were pungent and unconventional, on subjects as varied as the troubles in Turkey and what she thought of her fellow Jews of Baltimore, whom she flayed without mercy, accusing them of replacing Judaism with charity and pandering to materialistic values. "Apparently there are but two central ideas to which all is subservient: business and pleasure; the fluctuation of prices or a round of dissipation." (She was only eighteen when she wrote that, but her opinion of materialism did not change during the next 67 years.)

The more Henrietta grew in wisdom and knowledge, the closer became the tie between her and the rabbi. Soon she was even referring to herself in letters and conversation in the third person as "her father's daughter." Now she was able to read books in Hebrew, German and French, hold profound discussions of philosophy, and talk intelligently about the history and literature of many lands. Her father grew more and more dependent on her, discussing with her every project he contemplated, as well as the subject of next week's sermon, the notes for an essay, and how a certain letter ought to be answered. He wrote his manuscripts in a longhand which often only Henrietta could decipher. All this work she did in her spare time, for when the high school principal returned to duty she joined the teaching staff of the Misses Adams School, an institution for respectable young ladies, run by three spinster sisters whose aristocratic Southern family had never recovered from the financial shock of the Civil War. For $15 a month she taught almost every subject on the curriculum of a young lady of quality.

Meanwhile the house on Lombard Street became the gathering place of a wide variety of young intellectuals, among them Abraham Flexner, an undergraduate who one day would become head of the Institute for Advanced Studies at Princeton and have the honor of inducing Albert Einstein to come to America; Harry Friedenwald, son of the family doctor, who would become an internationally famous ophthalmologist and whose first important operation was the removing of a cataract from the eye of the Szold cat; and Morris Jastrow, a handsome young man with curly hair, short-cut chin whiskers, and an immense Windsor tie, who was helping to put himself through the University of Pennsylvania by writing a column for a San Francisco paper. When he asked Henrietta to jot down each week a few notes for his column, she responded by virtually writing his column for him, from then on. It might have developed into something more than a one-sided literary collaboration, except for Henrietta's concentration on work and her father-idolatry. From those who came through the doors of the house on Lombard Street, Henrietta received much intellectual stimulus. It was a full and rich life for the serious-minded young girl, although not a completely happy one.

When she was twenty-one, she took leave of the Misses Adams to go to Europe with her father. Young Jastrow, having just obtained his bachelor's degree, was to meet them in London. On the Continent, they visited Berlin and Dresden, Prague and Paris—places Henrietta had dreamed of and now found more exciting than she had imagined—except that everywhere there were relatives. She counted up forty first cousins! Several uncles thought she would make a good match for their sons, but such suggestions neither she nor her father even considered. The long-lasting importance of the trip was that for the first time Henrietta came in contact with her Jewish past. In her father's native city of Bratislava (Pressburg, as the Germans called it), she saw the sufferings of European Jewry at close range. In London they missed Henrietta's young suitor by 24 hours because of a delay in the sailing of his ship. It would have been a tragedy if either had seriously been in love with the other.

Back home, father and daughter discovered that Russian Jews, fleeing the pogroms that had followed the assassination of Czar Alexander II, were pouring by the hundreds into Baltimore. They were not being well received by most members of the well-to-do Jewish community, largely of Western European origin. Instead of using her pen in attacking those guilty of this snobbery, Henrietta and her father—from whom she had acquired her tenderheartedness—went every day to the wharfs to meet ships loaded with bewildered refugees, to whom they gave packages of food, wallets of money, and a friendly welcome. They were drab people, unattractive in many ways, but they struck a cord of sympathy in Henrietta's heart. She wrote to a sister, "I feel very much drawn to these Russian Jews. There is something ideal about them. Or has the suffering through which they have passed idealized them in my eyes? At all events, I have no greater wish than to be able to give them my whole strength, time and ability." A little later she wrote, "I eat, drink, and sleep Russians. . . . In fact, the Russian business so absorbs my thoughts that I have gone back to my early girlish longing to be a man. If I were, I am sure I could mature plans of great benefit to them."

THEODOR HERZL

ELIEZER BEN YEHUDA

VLADIMIR JABOTINSKY

HENRIETTA SZOLD

CHAIM WEIZMANN

RABBI ABRAHAM
ISAAC KOOK

BARON EDMOND
DE ROTHSCHILD

A. D. GORDON

Zionist Archives and Library

ORDE WINGATE

DAVID BEN-GURION

RACHEL ZELTZER

ZIVIA HABSHUSH

Fritz Cohn

But she was being modest. She and her father did much for the horde of refugees from the East. If a younger sister who managed the family finances had not watched them, they would have completely emptied the family exchequer. Rabbi Szold on several occasions gave the coat from his back to a shivering man just off a refugee ship. Henrietta got up at 5:30 every morning, and her workday now counted 17 hours. Soon she was referring to them as "my Russians" and was lavishing on them the affection she would give to the children she wanted to bear yet somehow knew she would never have. ("I would exchange everything for a child of my own," she once lamented.) Her "baby" became a school she and her father helped found to teach the immigrants English. It opened one November night in 1889 in a small loft room with 30 immigrant students. The next evening a second class was formed. Then a third and a fourth. Soon there were 600 students. Then an entire building was rented. By the time the city took over the project, 5,000 immigrants had been helped over the first hurdles in becoming Americans. Meanwhile, her father from his pulpit thundered denunciations of the Czarist regime that sometimes made his congregation squirm. ("I say that so long as a single Jew in any corner of the world can with impunity be insulted on account of his faith, this long, not a single Jew anywhere is free!")

It was what she had seen in Europe and her work with "my Russians" that combined to strengthen her Zionism and make her more convinced than ever that self-respect and dignity could be restored to the Jewish people only through the establishment of a national homeland. As she herself put it, "I became converted to Zionism at the very moment I realized that it alone supplied my bruised, torn and bloody nation, my distracted nation, with an ideal. . . ." In the autumn of 1894, the Zionist Association of Baltimore was founded, an outgrowth of the Hebrew Literary Society of which the rabbi and his daughter had been active members.

Meanwhile the volatile, energetic Henrietta had not lost her interest in education. She was still a young woman when she told the Maryland State Teachers' Association in a memorable address, "Not knowledge but the capacity to acquire knowledge is power."

Henrietta and a few other Jewish intellectuals joined, in 1888, in forming the Jewish Publication Society to revive interest in the Jewish cultural heritage. She was the only woman charter member and became one of the editors, correcting manuscripts, translating, even writing parts of some of the books herself. Her ambition was boundless. After the Baltimore synagogue pensioned off her aged father and he thus had less need of her at his side, she accepted a position in Philadelphia as executive secretary of the publication society. The step was taken with much hesitation, but Philadelphia and Baltimore were close and she promised her father to spend all her holidays with him.

In the summer of 1903, Rabbi Szold, his wife and Henrietta went to their favorite resort, Berkeley Springs, West Virginia. There the ailing rabbi almost invited death by refusing to eat, to be fed, or to take medicine. Henrietta, whose greatest wish now was that when her father died he would die in her arms, stayed up night after night watching over him. Finally early one morning exhaustion overcame her and while she slept, her father died. She felt she had failed him, and so in addition to the awful void, she was lashed by a sense of guilt. It did not help that on the table beside his bed lay the Talmud open to a passage they had been discussing only a few hours before she had dozed off.

A younger sister, worried by Henrietta's despondency, suggested she do something with the voluminous manuscripts the rabbi had left behind; after all, only Henrietta could read his handwriting. She agreed, but she needed more knowledge—she had never been trained in rabbinics—so she applied for admission to the Jewish Theological Seminary in New York. No woman had ever been admitted, but an exception was made on her assurance she did not want a rabbinical diploma.

The forty-two-year-old coed, her mother and a younger sister found an apartment across the street from the seminary and a new life began for all of them. Henrietta became deeply interested in the new Zionist movement in New York and joined a group called the Hadassah Study Circle that met in the temple of Dr. Judah Magnes. In many ways this was the happiest period of her life. Her literary brilliance, her warmth of character, and her keen intelligence made her popular in New York academic circles. She acquired many new friends, among them a young professor 13 years her junior, who physically resembled her father when he was young, intellectually seemed as brilliant, and like her father welcomed the literary help and companionship she gave him. He came to depend more and more upon her, until soon he had not only taken the place of her father, but had made her aware of what it was that had been missing in her life.

Then one night he told her he was engaged to marry a girl his own age. The announcement caused her to write secretly in her journal, "My only real happiness in life has been killed by a single word. Since then I have hardly been conscious of living. There has been only suffering, nights and days, days and nights of suffering."

Henrietta and her mother sailed for Europe on the S.S. *California* on July 31, 1909. Perhaps a trip abroad would bring some relief from the nervous collapse she had suffered. They went to Edinburg, London, Paris, Munich, Vienna, Pressburg, Budapest, and finally down to Palestine. For four weeks they toured the Land of the Book. Henrietta's reactions were mixed. She was astonished at the poverty, misery, ignorance and disease. Yet she fell under the spell of the land. ("I learned to love its grayness, its stones, its terraces, its varied richnesses. It is the only possible refuge of our people.") She also saw the need, and the opportunity. If only she were 20 years younger, she lamented. (She was now just forty-nine.)

Back in New York, she made a report to Hadassah Study Circle members, who were impressed, but it was two years before they finally issued an invitation to all interested women to attend a meeting. Thirty-eight women appeared on Purim, the Feast of Esther, and joined in founding what they called the Hadassah chapter (Hadassah being Queen Esther's Hebrew name) of a national organization, the Daughters of Zion, with Henrietta Szold as president. They set as their first goal the establishment of a system of visiting nurses in Palestine and Zionist study groups in America. Before the year was out they had 200 members and $542 in the bank. They had sent to Palestine two nurses who were giving trachoma treatment to a never-ending stream of sufferers. They had opened in their living quarters Hadassah's first clinic, a mother-child welfare station from which they distributed fresh milk, a luxury in those days. (Since then Hadassah mother-child clinics have always been called *Tipat Halav,* Drop of Milk.)

When the outbreak of war forced the nurses to return to America, they brought back graphic stories of the need for Hadassah to expand its work as soon as it was able. ("You should see the people in the streets! They are perfect studies in pain, misery and starvation.")

In 1914, Miss Szold presided at a national convention in Rochester at which Hadassah was adopted as the name of a national body which she herself described as "an organization of Jewish women who believe in the healing of the daughter of my people, in the healing of the soul of the Jewish people as well as its body; who believe that only there in Zion can a normal Jewish life be established."

After the liberation of Jerusalem, the World Zionist Organization asked Miss Szold if Hadassah could send a medical unit to Palestine. She agreed, but $25,000 was needed. To raise it, she urged her 2,000 followers to walk instead of taking a trolley car and to give the money to the medical fund. Soon 44 doctors, nurses, sanitary engineers, and dentists were on their way. They were greeted by news of a cholera epidemic in Tiberias and were rushed to that corner of the country. Thereafter they were like a fire department, receiving frequent calls about emergencies only they could handle.

Henrietta Szold went over in 1920, thinking she would stay for just a few months; unaware that she would never live permanently in America again. She had been in Palestine less than three years when the doctor in charge of the medical unit returned to the United States, leaving her in complete command. She was frightened, at first, by the responsibility. She had to supervise more than 400 employees, hospitals in Jerusalem, Jaffa, Safad and Tiberias, a nurses training school, laboratories, mother-child welfare stations springing up everywhere, and a school hygiene program. She had never had any medical training and she was sixty-two years old. But in some ways she felt much younger than 20 years ago, when her father died and she was certain her usefulness in life had come to an end. No matter how hard she would work during the week, she would always relax on Friday evenings when friends would gather at her home to sing American folk songs. Then there was the peace of the Sabbath, which she strictly observed throughout her life.

But there was sorrow, also. In America she had been an active pacifist. Killing, in any form, for any reason, was repugnant to her, emotionally and intellectually. But her sense of justice was outraged as day after day she heard how British soldiers would disarm Jews, often at the very moment when they were about to be set upon and butchered by Arabs.

Being ultramodest, she tried to limit the field of her work, but she was drawn deeper and deeper into public life. After the Zionist Congress of 1927, she was made one of the three members of a committee responsible for health and education.

In 1930, she went to America to be feted by Hadassah on her seventieth birthday and in a burst of sincere confusion wrote, "My mind is a blank on my future. I cannot decide where to spend the balance of my days, in America or Palestine." She added that she was finding it difficult to "adjust to contemporary life in America"—which was another way of saying that her work in Palestine was calling. Others made up her mind for her. She was asked to organize a Department of Social Welfare for the Jewish community of Palestine. Her comment was one of her charming pieces of naïveté. "What do you think of my temerity in undertaking such a task?" she asked a friend. "When I came to Palestine I acted as though I were an expert on medical affairs. Fate made me pretend to be an expert on educational affairs in 1927. And now, in 1931, having passed the Psalmist's term of years, I dare go into another field in which to expertize is imperative."

Little did she know that her greatest work still lay ahead.

In 1932, in Berlin, a group of young Zionist high school and university students called on Recha Freier, a rabbi's wife, to discuss what could be done to help save the Jewish youth of Germany. Out of that meeting grew a lifesaving movement, at first called Jewish Youth Aid, later Youth Aliyah. The first group sent off by Jewish Youth Aid numbered 18 girls and 24 boys. They arrived at Haifa port in February 1934. Henrietta Szold, now in her seventy-fourth year, was at the water's edge to meet them. Soon the young of Europe began arriving in an endless stream and the problem at the receiving end was to find homes for them. Most were sent to kibbutzim (collective settlements). Then two children's villages were established. There were large problems of finance, housing, and education, as well as small human problems of homesickness in a strange land, the heartache of orphans who craved affection, the need to make these small wandering Jews feel that this really was home. Miss Szold worried about every detail of the lifesaving movement. Rescuing the young became an obsession with her. "I have a great new work ahead of me," she said on her seventy-fifth birthday. "I must get the young Jewish people out of Germany, and after that out of France, Lithuania, and Russia. What does age mean? Nothing!"

From her own mother she had learned, "It is only in rearing children that service piled on minute service counts. . . . In a mother's life, ability to lose one's identity in details is the greatest thing for the future of mankind." Her own family was growing now. Soon she was being hailed as "the mother of Israel," which was some compensation for the personal childlessness she had never ceased to regret.

With the outbreak of war in 1939, Henrietta Szold, in her seventy-ninth year, discovered more work than ever to be done. "I find that, old as I am, in a certain sense I have never stopped growing. . . . While my intellect is an organ of narrow limitations, my inner world—perhaps it is my world of feeling, of instinct—expands."

In 1942 came the Teheran children—an almost legendary group, part of a struggling mass of 14,000 Poles, who had been wandering on foot for hundreds of miles through forests, across deserts, from country to country, since Poland was torn apart by Germany and Russia. Finally 933 Jewish children in the group, from one to eighteen years old, half naked, half starved, ridden by disease, reached a Joint Distribution Committee camp at Teheran. After a brief rehabilitation they were shipped by rail to Karachi, by troopship across the Arabian Sea, up the Red Sea to Suez, then by train to Palestine. Miss Szold met them and tried to talk to each of the 933 personally. For her 933 children were 933 souls, 933 individuals, 933 sparks of life. Writing of her work during this period, she said, "And for the first time I saw one of my hopes connected wih Zionism realized. . . . I faced a human problem in which Jews are concerned, and alone concerned, and I forgot wholly that they were Jews, and so did they."

Now in her eighties, she still looked ahead, rarely back. Operation Jewish Future was her blueprint for meeting the needs of the flood of immigrants she was certain would be pouring in as soon as the war was over. "As you see," she said, "I am not yet too old to dream dreams."

But about the time of her eighty-fourth birthday, her life finally began to slip away. She was taken to the great hospital on the crest of Mount Scopus that had been built by her Hadassah. There on February 13, 1945, she quietly died.

On her eightieth birthday she had said, "The greatest of all arts is the art of living. . . . Men and women need the preparation given by a cultivated heart."

Henrietta Szold had a cultivated heart.

Chapter 5

We had Jerusalem,
When London was a marsh

—CHAIM WEIZMANN

Two MONTHS BEFORE HER DEATH there was a marked improvement in Henrietta Szold's condition, so a few carefully selected callers were admitted to her hospital room. One afternoon, just six days after her eighty-fourth birthday, she had as a visitor the tall, distinguished-looking president of Hebrew University, Judah Leib Magnes. Although he was seventeen years her junior, they had much in common. He, too, had been born in the United States—at San Francisco. More important, like Miss Szold he was a gentle person who all his life had been a pacifist. This was one reason he had been advocating for a quarter of a century the transformation of Palestine into a binational state in which Jews and Arabs, as he envisioned it, would live at peace, running the country jointly. This "phobia," as some called it, had caused an ever-widening rift between him and the Zionist leaders, especially Dr. Chaim Weizmann, then president of the World Zionist Organization. After a short visit, Dr. Magnes said he had to call on someone in the next room and so bade Miss Szold *au revoir.*

A few moments later the nurse admitted the next guest, another tall man, somewhat older, bald, with a small mustache and spade-shaped goatee. He greeted her warmly, for his admiration was deep. (In the memoirs he had already started to write, he would refer to her as "one of the most remarkable figures of modern Jewish history.") After they had chatted about the recent assassination of Lord Moyne and other acts of Jewish terrorism against the British, a twinkle came into her soft brown eyes and she said, "Dr. Weizmann, there's a friends of yours in the next room who just paid me a call. I'm going to send for him." When the startled Dr. Magnes reappeared, she took one of his hands and said, "I have told Dr. Weizmann that of all the service he has rendered to Zionism, I think his coming here at this time is the greatest of all, because of his attitude to England. There is another thing on my heart, and this gives me great joy—to see you two together." Dr. Weizmann took her free hand. Both men smiled down at her, then left the room together. In the corridor Dr. Weizmann said to Dr. Magnes, "We must never quarrel." Dr. Magnes replied, "No, we seem to have received an injunction from on high."

Henrietta Szold had less than eight weeks to live; Dr. Weizmann, eight years. In this twilight period of his life he would perform even greater service in furthering what he called "the holy mission" of his people; upon establishment of the State of Israel he would be hailed by his most bitter political enemy as the person who had done more than any other to bring about the miracle of the rebirth; he would be unanimously elected the first President of the new state; he would go down in history as a man who devoted most of his manhood years to fighting, in many world capitals, the diplomatic battles of a state that existed then only in the dreams and spiritual yearnings of a relatively small band of iron-willed people. His most important contributions were persuading the British to issue the Balfour Declaration and President Truman to announce immediate recognition of the State of Israel. Had he never been born these two diplomatic victories might have been won by someone else. If not, the State of Israel eventually, somehow, would have come into existence and survived. Yet Chaim Weizmann without doubt was, for Israel, the right man, in the right place, at the right time.

The highest compliment ever paid to him—by the distinguished British philosopher, Sir Isaiah Berlin—was that he was

the first totally free Jew of the modern world, and that the State
of Israel was constructed in his image. What many of his fellow
Jews liked was that he pleaded their cause in high places effectively yet with dignity. In him there was no groveling, ever.
He walked with shoulders square and head high—a mien that
announced, before he had said a word, that here was a man of
distinction, representing a people of distinction. He could trade
quips with Winston Churchill, put Benito Mussolini in his
place with a well-directed barb, exchange pleasantries with His
Majesty King George V, argue effectively with the suave Franklin D. Roosevelt, vent his fury on members of the Chamberlain
cabinet, establish a close *rapport* with Ian Christian Smuts, and
entertain in his home such diverse characters as T. E. Lawrence,
Orde Wingate, Leon Blum, Lord Cecil, and Rabbis Stephen S.
Wise and Abba Hillel Silver. He met all these people always on
an equal footing, yet he never denied by a single act, word, or
gesture his Jewishness. Always and forever it was an organic part
of his being. He abandoned in no way his Jewish background
and tradition, or his Jewish piety and learning. He even re-
tained his Jewish mannerisms and inflexion. It was impossible
for him to conceive of a Jew being anything else. When an Arab
witness before the Ad Hoc Committee of the United Nations in
1947 declared that Jews were not Jews at all but Khazars or Tar-
tars, Weizmann answered with magnificent simplicity, "I feel
like a Jew and have suffered like a Jew."

Many of his own people back in Europe respected him because he acquire a private fortune not in the world of com-
merce and money changing, but as a distinguished scientist, and
became a gentleman in the accepted British sense, a man of
taste and good manners, equally at home in a French salon or
the drawing rooms of British nobility, yet still one of them—an
Eastern European Jew. Most people were impressed by the
warmth of his personality.

As a public speaker he was effective not because of the thunderous quality of his oratory, nor because, like Jabotinsky, he
could obtain striking effects with his voice, but because he
seemed to capture the wisdom of Jewish life in what he said. As
his American Zionist friend Louis Lipsky put it, in the stateli-
ness of his presentation "he seemed to speak ex cathedra for the

silent Jewish people." Lord Balfour once described a speech of Weizmann's as being like "the swish of a sword."

Aphorisms were sprinkled through all his writings and conversations. The one most widely quoted was, "To be a Zionist it is not absolutely necessary to be mad, but it helps"—a remark which since he made it has often been paraphrased and distorted. To an American audience he once said, "We are told we are dealers in old clothes and junk. We are perhaps the sons of dealers in old clothes, but we are the grandsons of prophets." On another occasion he said, "I believe in miracles, but you have to work very hard to make them happen!" Writing of his own student days, he said, "Poverty loses most of its pangs when it loses its disgrace." Some of his most brilliant remarks were so sharp that they were like rapier thrusts. ("It's hard to be a Jew; it's still harder to be a Zionist! it is triple-hard to be a Zionist and live in Israel.") He could illustrate almost any point he wanted to make with a story from the Bible, from the Talmud, or from his rich store of Yiddish humor.

By defining and redefining what Zionism meant to him, he made a major contribution to the development of Jewish thinking in the first half of the twentieth century. Once to a member of the British branch of the Rothschild family, at whose home he had recently dined, he wrote: "We who come from Russia are born and bred in an inspiration toward a new and better Jewish life. It must not only be a comfortable life but a Jewish one, a normal Jewish life, just as an Englishman looks for a normal English life."

Years later he declared that he was one of those who believed that "in the slow and difficult struggle with the marshes and rocks in Palestine lies the great challenge to the creative forces of the Jewish people, its redemption from the abnormalities of exile." He never tired of reiterating that if Jews were ever to become free men, it could happen only in Palestine; that there alone they could secure for themselves the basic human rights without resorting to intrigue, servility, and self-abasement to obtain them.

Like all great men, he acquired opponents, critics, and detractors as he went through life—men eager to point out that his virtues were balanced by negative qualities. They especially criticized him for his conceit and for the arrogance he often showed to those he decided were no longer of any use to him. *Chalutzim* (Palestinian pioneers) who had fought malaria, marauders, and misery to dig their roots into the Promised Land criticized him for waiting until he was thirty-three years old to pay his first visit to Palestine, then spending so little of the subsequent 45 years there. They said in some ways he became more British than the British; that his children were brought up in England; that one son died fighting for England while the other remained all his life a British citizen and resident. They called him a cosmopolite, at home anywhere in the world, and were critical that throughout the war he maintained luxury quarters in one of the best hotels of London's West End. Some went so far as to label him a snob, a reactionary nineteenth-century nationalist, and an enemy of social welfare. They argued that when he came to Palestine on visits it was always as the *grand seigneur.*

He was involved in many political feuds, always with a personalized antagonist. Some of the feuds almost tore the Zionist movement to pieces, especially those with Herzl, Jabotinsky, David Ben-Gurion, and Louis D. Brandeis, the American Zionist leader who became a U. S. Supreme Court Justice. About some of these men he wrote bitterly. After meeting Herzl at the Basel Congress in 1898 he decided that the father of modern Zionism was naïve in many ways, lacked any real Jewishness, and was not "one of the people." He was distressed because of what he called Herzl's leanings toward "clericalism" and by the "touch of Byzantinism in his manner." He called the diplomatic work Herzl was trying to do "nebulous negotiations." He had a warmer feeling for Jabotinsky, who was a frequent visitor in his home, but criticized him for being "utterly un-Jewish in manner, approach, and deportment" and for "a certain touch of the rather theatrically chivalresque, a certain queer and irrelevant knightliness, which was not at all Jewish." His feeling about Ben-Gurion was so strong that he rarely mentioned his name. In the 300,000 words or more of the Weizmann memoirs the words "Ben-Gurion" appear just four times—almost all of them unavoidable references. Martin Buber, the theologian, he described as "the son of a rich father, a rather odd and exotic figure. . . . I was often irritated by his stilted talk, which was . . . without, it seemed to me, much clarity or great beauty."

During World War I, the British gave him a secret diplomatic mission: the task of keeping former U. S. Ambassador Henry J. Morgenthau, Sr. and Professor Felix Frankfurter (later U. S. Supreme Court Justice) from carrying out a diplomatic assignment they had been given by President Wilson. Writing of the incident, he said he took "an instantaneous, cordial, and enduring dislike" to one of Mr. Morgenthau's aides. This was typical. His reactions to people were rarely indefinite.

He was not religiously orthodox, although a man of profound natural piety. Politically he never attached himself to any party; he seemed to have little sympathy for anything but the theoretics of statehood. The political tug-of-war between the left, the right, the religious parties, and the middle-of-the-roaders annoyed him, or at least bored him. He was out of touch—and perhaps out of sympathy—with the politicians and practical men of affairs who would ultimately have the task of making a functioning Jewish state out of the British Mandate. A few months after independence, the Zionist Organization of America published a booklet of short biographies of the Prime Minister, his cabinet and the other key figures in the government. Of the 34 listed, only 7 are even mentioned in the voluminous Weizmann memoirs and most of them merely in lists of names. Whereas Herzl in his excitement dreamed of Utopia—even of such minute practical problems as the construction of tunnels under city streets to carry the pipes and wires of the public utilities— Weizmann's great concern was with the diplomatic problems involved in obtaining a state, and in the spiritual qualities of Zionism. Sir Charles Webster, British historian, called him the greatest diplomatic statesman the First World War produced, explaining that if the main objective of diplomacy is to obtain what one wants without recourse to violence, then Weizmann was a supreme diplomatist.

Motol, the village of Chaim Weizmann's birth in 1874, was close to the Pripyat Marshes of White Russia, in one of the most dismal corners of the Pale of the Settlement—that vast and mournful ghetto in which most of the Jews of Czarist Russia were compelled to live. One-third of the 600 families of Motol were Jewish. Although Chaim's father, who was engaged in cutting and transporting timber, had an annual income never in excess of $300, the Weizmanns were considered one of the well-to-do families of the village, for they had a seven-room house, several cows, a servant or two, enough to eat, and one by one the twelve children (three others had died in infancy) were being given an education. The house was crammed with books in Russian, Yiddish and Hebrew: religious works side by side with Gorki, Tolstoi, and Chekov; textbooks on medicine, engineering, and dentistry; tracts on Zionism.

Chaim's sharpest memory of the *cheder* or religious school he attended was of the day the teacher smuggled into class a book in Hebrew on chemistry. It was his first contact with the branch of science in which he would make a career. When he was eleven he was sent to a high school in the nearby city of Pinsk, a stronghold of Zionists, among them the family of Moshe Shertok (Sharret), future Foreign Minister of Israel. In Pinsk, while still twelve, he sent a letter to his old schoolmaster back in Motol which 75 years later would be studied with interest by those seeking the origins of his almost mystic faith in England. In it he wrote: "Why should we expect mercy from the kings of Europe? In all the countries of Africa, and especially in the State of Morocco, they beat us and have no mercy upon us. Let us carry our banner to Zion and return to our original mother on whose knees we were reared. . . . England only will have pity on us." At twelve he was already both a Zionist and an Anglophile. He was so impressed when he heard that a Pinsk Zionist, Aharon Eisenberg, was about to set off for Palestine that he went to the farewell reception for him, although he had received no invitation. When he reached the house he was too frightened to do more than peek through the keyhole at this wondrous man whose feet would soon be walking on the soil of the Promised Land. While still a boy he tramped the streets of Pinsk collecting money for Zionist causes. He read daily and weekly papers in Hebrew and was especially influenced by the articles of Achad Ha'am, whose literary style Jewish students not only in Pinsk but all over Russia were trying to imitate. By parental order he conducted all his correspondence with his father in

Hebrew. The one time he forgot and wrote in Yiddish the letter was returned, unanswered.

At eighteen he went to a Jewish boarding school in a small German city, then to the *Polytechnicum* in Berlin. He was there when *The Jewish State* gave a sudden concreteness to the rather vague Zionist dreams in which he and so many of his fellow students were indulging. When the First Zionist Congress was called he was elected a delegate from Pinsk, but the vigilance of Czarist police in Moscow caused him to miss the historic gathering. He had gone there to try to sell his first important chemical discovery to a dye plant. Unable to obtain the permit any Jew needed to travel beyond the Pale, he spent so much time dodging the police that the Congress in Basel was over by the time he had concluded his business.

His desire for the best possible scientific education led him next to Switzerland. At Bern and Geneva he clashed in volatile debates with Russian revolutionaries who were contemptuous of those who put their Jewishness ahead of Russian nationalism. Defying them, young Weizmann joined with other Russian students in issuing a call for a founding meeting of a new Zionist society to be called The Dawn. Although their revolutionary opponents removed and hid all the chairs in the meeting place, they met, remained in session for 60 hours, and enrolled nearly 200 students willing to revolt against assimilation.

From now until the end of his days Weizmann would be dominated by first one then the other of his two passions, chemistry and Zionism—often by both, almost simultaneously. He began attending all the Zionist Congresses, critical from the start of Herzl's ways. He ridiculed the Congress President for wearing white gloves when he shook hands and for requiring delegates to don frock coats. ("It smacked of artificiality, extravagance, and the *haut monde.*") It was while serving as a lecturer in chemistry at the University of Geneva that Weizmann met a medical student seven years his junior, Vera Chatzman from Rostov-on-Don, a pensive, almost sad girl whom he nicknamed "The Distant Princess" and to whom he became engaged.

While at Geneva, he sold a patent to the I. G. Farben Company of Germany. ("Hardly anyone thought of it then as the focus of German military might and German dreams.") He also began to have visions of a Jewish university at Jerusalem. After the Kishinev massacre he visited the larger centers of Jewish life in the Pale, organizing defense groups.

At the Sixth Zionist Congress the Weizmann family provided good proof of the schisms caused by the Uganda proposal. While Chaim campaigned against it, his father and a brother, also delegates, were working just as actively for it. ("For the only time in our lives there was a coolness between us.") In meetings of the Russian delegation Chaim made what he later admitted was a "violent" speech, accusing Herzl of hysteria. ("Nothing good is ever produced by panic.") He was certain that he turned against Uganda many who had been uncertain.

Despite his feeling about Herzl personally, and his political opposition to him, when he died the next year Weizmann wrote to his own fiancée: "His death at this time is a tragedy. Wear a black armband on your sleeve. We are all doing this."

By now he was a part-time research worker in a dye plant at Manchester, England. It had been an "inner voice" that had commanded him—in his thirtieth year—to leave Geneva for England. That was as well as he could explain it, even to his fiancée. In London he found himself socially and intellectually isolated, cold-shouldered by the Herzl supporters, avoided by many because he knew no English. Yet it apparently never occurred to him to argue with the quiet voice. He had a fatalistic belief that England ruled his destiny and that there was no escaping it. He picked Manchester as the place of his self-imposed exile because it was the center of the chemical industry, and because he thought that there he could get away from Zionism, at least temporarily. But Charles Dreyfus, managing director of the dye works, was also head of the Manchester Zionist Society and chairman of the Conservative Party of the city. If he had not been all three, young Weizmann and a Conservative politician named Arthur James Balfour might not have been brought together, and if that meeting had not taken place, twentieth-century Jewish history might read quite differently. Balfour was running for Parliament from Manchester and Dreyfus suggested he give the young chemist 15 minutes of his valuable time to straighten him out on Uganda. The meeting, in Balfour's room in the Queen's Hotel on Piccadilly, lasted over an hour. In trying to explain the romantic and spiritual appeal Palestine had for Jews, Weizmann suddenly said, "Mr. Balfour, suppose I were to offer you Paris instead of London, would you take it?"

Balfour looked startled and replied, "But Dr. Weizmann, we have London."

"True," Weizmann quickly retorted, "but we had Jerusalem when London was a marsh!"

Instead of Balfour convincing the young chemist that he had been wrong in opposing the Uganda plan, the opposite happened. As the hour drew to a close, Balfour remarked that Weizmann was not at all like other Jews he had met, to which Weizmann replied, "Mr. Balfour, you have met the wrong kind of Jews."

He was thirty-two years old when he and the girl from Rostov-on-Don, who had passed, brilliantly, the examinations for her medical degree, were married in a village near Danzig. There was no time for a honeymoon. Weizmann had to rush off to Cologne to attend a meeting of the Zionist Action Committee. He took his bride with him, but she saw little of him. One morning he arrived back at their hotel bearing a large bouquet of flowers and a basket of fruit to camouflage the fact that it was 5 A.M.

He was thirty-three years old and his wife had just had their first child when he paid his initial visit to Palestine, which impressed him as a "dolorous country." He found there were seven Arabs to every Jew, that the 25 agricultural settlements were in a sad condition, that most of the Jews lived in Jerusalem, Safad, Haifa, or Jaffa and were objects of charity, supported by alms from abroad. Many had come merely to die in the Promised Land. One of the trip's bright spots was meeting Arthur Ruppin, a brilliant young German economist, who was one of the first to dream of establishing an all-Jewish city beside Jaffa. Visiting Rehovoth, Dr. Weizmann met Aharon Eisenberg, the man at whom he had squinted through a keyhole. He was now a well-established Palestinian. Jerusalem he found to be a "miserable ghetto, derelict, and without dignity," in which Christians and Arabs had their holy places, but the Jews had nothing. Nothing but a small piece of wall. Young Weizmann left the

Holy City as quickly as he could—after just a few hours. For years he had depressing memories of it. But the visit had one fruitful consequence: he decided the ideal place for the university of which he had been dreaming would be the top of Mount Scopus.

At the start of World War I all scientists were asked to inform the British Government of any discoveries they had made that might be of military value. Weizmann promptly offered a fermentation process he had worked out. He received no reply from the government, so a year and a half later he sold the process to a private British munitions maker; but just as the "dazzling" contract was about to go into effect, an explosion destroyed the plant and he was asked to release the company, which he did. Then the British Admiralty heard of his process, summoned him to London and asked him to set up a laboratory to see whether with his fermentation process he could make a chemical of which there was a drastic shortage—acetone. After some weeks of experimentation he was summoned into the presence of Winston Churchill, the First Lord of the Admiralty, who gruffly said, "Well, Mr. Weizmann, we need thirty thousand tons of acetone. Can you make it or not?" The startled chemist replied that so far he had made only a few grams in his laboratory, but if he had a pilot plant he might be able to turn it out in quantity. Churchill gave him carte blanche and his first large-scale experiment in making acetone from corn was conducted in a famous gin factory in Bromley-by-Bow. When the German submarine campaign created a scarcity of corn from abroad, he turned to making acetone from horse chestnuts.

In the lives of most great men there is a myth against which their biographers tilt with their spears of truth as ineffectually as Don Quixote against his windmills. In Herzl's life it was the myth of the Dreyfus case, in Jabotinsky's the myth of the Kishinev massacre. The great myth of Weizmann's life was that the Balfour Declaration was his reward for fermenting acetone from corn and chestnuts so that British guns could continue to fire. In denying the myth himself he said, "I almost wish it had been as simple as that . . . but history does not deal in Aladdin's lamps." More important in influencing Jewish history than making acetone was Weizmann's chance conversation at a party one night with C. P. Scott, celebrated editor of the *Manchester Guardian*, who was greatly impressed with Weizmann's argument that if Palestine should fall into the hands of the British during the war, they should make it into a British-protected Jewish homeland. Scott arranged a meeting between Weizmann and Lloyd George, then Chancellor of the Exchequer, later Prime Minister. He, too, was impressed and suggested a meeting between Weizmann and Balfour, now Foreign Minister. Weizmann did not disclose that they were already acquainted. The conference Lloyd George arranged turned into what Weizmann later described as a "tremendous talk" lasting two hours.

Chemistry and Zionism were closely knotted together in these days, as Weizmann worked to create what he called "a network of relationships" to further the idea of a Jewish homeland. He was a whirlwind of activity—lunching, dining, buttonholing, arguing, expostulating with people of all sorts—members of both the British and French branches of the Rothschild family, Christian churchmen, Jewish assimilationists, skeptical Britishers, noncommittal Cabinet members, phlegmatic editors, the Colonial Secretary, anyone who was important and would listen.

In January 1917, he decided the time had come to press the British for a declaration of policy, so he called a series of Zionist conferences at which they worded and reworded and then reworded a dozen times more what at first they called *An Outline of Program for the Jewish Resettlement of Palestine in Accordance with the Aspirations of the Zionist Movement.* They started out speaking only of "Jewish resettlement of Palestine," and the formation of a Jewish company for that purpose. As conferences with British leaders went on, Weizmann talked more and more of a British protectorate. The draft finally handed to Balfour by Lord Lionel Walter Rothschild started out by saying, "His Majesty's Government . . . accept the principle of recognizing Palestine as the National Home of the Jewish people . . . and the right of the Jewish people to build up a national life in Palestine under a protection to be established at the conclusion of peace." Weizmann always believed that this draft would have been accepted had it not been for the opposition of upper-class, British, assimilationist Jews, the most powerful of them Edwin Montagu, Secretary of State for India. Actually it was three and a half months before the declaration was finally issued. Partly because of a passionate speech Montagu made to the War Cabinet, the proposed declaration was so greatly watered down that the Zionists were heartsick. To get some reaction in advance, the Cabinet submitted the proposed text to four Zionists and four non-Zionists for their comment. After reading his copy, Weizmann asked that the declaration be amended to read "re-establishment" rather than "establishment" of a Jewish National Home, and that "Jewish race" be changed to "Jewish people." When he was told the declaration would be issued in the form of a letter and was asked to whom it should be addressed, he suggested the name of Lord Rothschild, even though he himself was president of the English Zionist Federation.

While the Cabinet was having its final discussion of the text, on November 2, 1917, Weizmann sat outside the Cabinet chambers, nervously waiting. Finally the door opened and Sir Mark Sykes, Chief Secretary of the War Cabinet, a devout Catholic who had become sympathetic to Zionism under Weizmann's guidance, appeared with the famous document in his hand, saying, "Dr. Weizmann, it's a boy!"

Running his eye quickly over the text, he saw that "Jewish race" had been changed to "Jewish people," but his other suggestion had not been taken.

Balfour called it the greatest achievement of his life. Zionists all over the world celebrated. One after another the Allied countries endorsed the commitment. To many people it looked as if little stood in the way of a quick re-creation of Israel. Some overenthusiastic American Zionists even began picking a Jewish cabinet to run the new state.

Early in 1918, Weizmann was chosen chairman of a Zionist commission sent to Palestine to prepare for the carrying out of the Balfour Declaration. Before he left London he bought his first top hat to wear to an audience with His Majesty King George V. On arriving in Palestine he inspected the start of a new seaside town of a hundred houses near Jaffa, called Tel Aviv. A British general told him that a great many British officers stationed there had copies of the forged Protocols of Zion in their haversacks and that relations between the Jewish population and the British Army were growing more strained by the day.

Three months after the commission's arrival, the British decided Dr. Weizmann should try to obtain some sort of agreement over the future of Palestine with the Emir Feisal, King of Syria and next to his father the most important of all Arab leaders. He was encamped not far away on the heights of Moab, but because the Turks still held the Jordan Valley, Weizmann and the British officers who accompanied him had to go by military car, train, ship, and camelback on a ten-day, very roundabout circumnavigation. With the Emir they found T. E. Lawrence (Lawrence of Arabia) who fascinated Weizmann with his whimsy, shyness, and "remarkable personality." The talk with the Emir, who was also sympathetic, lasted two hours and led to the eventual signing of an agreement that Jewish leaders thought might herald an era of happy cooperation between their people and the Arabs.

The next month on Mount Scopus the foundation stones were laid for Hebrew University. At first British General Allenby, who had liberated much of Palestine already, was skeptical, saying his army might be thrown back at any moment and Jerusalem retaken, but Weizmann convinced him the ceremony would be a great act of faith.

On November 11, 1918, the day of the Armistice, he had to fight his way through a hysterical crowd surrounding 10 Downing Street to keep an appointment with Prime Minister Lloyd George and give him a report on Palestine.

With World War I over and a Jewish Home Land assured, colonization and development began. Arab property owners suddenly were asking 10 to 20 times the pre-Balfour Declaration price for each dunam of land, which led Weizmann to warn, "We will have to cover the soil of Palestine with Jewish gold."

In 1921, he went on a fund-raising tour of the United States at the head of a delegation that included Albert Einstein. Most of the American reporters, for some reason unfathomable to Weizmann, wrote of him as "the inventor of TNT," and they were more interested in getting some simple definition of relativity from Einstein than they were in Palestine. In pleading for funds Weizmann said the Jewish pioneers of Palestine were willing to go hungry, "but cows must be fed and you cannot feed a cow with speeches." To another audience he said, "They call us the salt of the earth, and there are Jews who feel themselves extraordinarily flattered. . . . Salt is used for someone else's food. It dissolves in that food. It is good only in small quantities. . . ." It was on this tour that he used a simile that became famous: "You will always be treated as a guest if you, too, can play the host. The only man who is invited to dinner is the man who can have dinner at home if he likes. Switzerland is a small country and there are more Swiss outside Switzerland than in it. But there is no such thing as an anti-Swiss sentiment in the sense there is an anti-Jewish sentiment. The Swiss has a home of his own to which he can invite others. It does not matter how small your home is, as long as it is your home."

One month before ratification of the British Mandate over Palestine, while an intensive parliamentary campaign was going on in London for repeal of the Balfour Declaration, a new statement of government policy was issued—the Churchill White Paper. It arbitrarily subtracted from Palestine 77 per cent of the mandated territory, on the other side of the Jordan, which was set up as a separate kingdom under the rule of the Emir Abdullah as a counterweight to King Ibn Saud. It was the first of what would be a long series of blows to Weizmann's faith in England. But he won a diplomatic victory the next month when the League of Nations Council unanimously ratified the Mandate.

The next high point in his career came with the official opening of Hebrew University, in 1925, in the presence of seventy-seven-year-old Lord Balfour, Lord Allenby, the liberator of Palestine, and hundreds of other men of note.

Four years later Zionists and non-Zionists were brought together, largely through his work, in a new body, the Jewish Agency, which under the Mandate would be the intermediary between the Jews of the world and the British. But as its constituent assembly was being held in Zurich, an Arab pogrom caused 150 deaths, filled the hospitals of Palestine with the wounded, and resulted in tragic property losses. The British sent a commission to investigate, then one year later issued another new statement of policy—the Passfield White Paper— which Weizmann labeled as a concerted effort to retract the promise of the Balfour Declaration. It restricted both immigration and purchase of land by Jews. Sadly he admitted it had the effect of "rendering and intending to render our work in Palestine impossible." In protest he resigned as president of the Jewish Agency.

In an interview with Prime Minister MacDonald, commenting on the restriction of Jewish immigration "because of lack of absorptive capacity," Weizmann remarked, "If you want to graze goats where you can have flourishing orange plantations, there is no room in Palestine. . . . You must choose, sir, between a goat and a Jew."

Although the British Government could not lose face by retracting the White Paper, Prime Minister MacDonald sent a letter to Weizmann attempting to pacify the Zionists by permitting the immigration of 40,000 new Jewish settlers in 1934 and 62,000 in 1935. This somewhat revived his faith, but as the delegates began to assemble in the summer of 1931 at Basel for the forthcoming World Zionist Congress, he was well aware of their mood. In his opening address he announced that because of the state of his health, he intended to resign his leadership of the world organization. But his opponents, led by Jabotinsky, insisted on introducing a resolution of non-confidence. In his address to the Congress, Weizmann said that despite everything he still had faith in the English who, he believed, had less anti-Semitism than any other people in the world, and were honest in their desire to help re-create the Home Land. But the voices against him were loud and angry. Emotions were boiling, tempers were not always under control. As a protest against what he considered the hysteria of many delegates, he said, "The walls of Jericho fell to the sound of shouts and trumpets. I have never heard of walls being raised by that means." But the roll-call vote on the non-confidence resolution showed the majority against him.

For 13 years he had been concentrating most of his energy on Zionism. Now that he was no longer president of the world

organization, he went back to his other love, chemistry, opening a modest laboratory in the house of a friend in London. In
1933 he received a series of urgent telegrams from his close
friend Meyer W. Weisgal, who was arranging a Jewish Day at
the Century of Progress exposition in Chicago and who offered
a $100,000 contribution to work he was now doing in resettling
German Jews, for a single speech. It meant a round trip of
8,000 miles and he was not well, but he did it. The next year
he spent five months sight-seeing and fund-raising in South
Africa, where the solicitude shown by the government for wild
animals led him to comment, "It must be a wonderful thing
to be an animal on the South African game reserves; much better than being a Jew in Warsaw, or even in London."

During his four years out of office he spent some of the time
in Palestine supervising construction of the Daniel Sieff Research Institute, the forerunner of the Weizmann Institute of
Science, at Rehovoth, where he and his wife decided to build a
home. It was only after they had chosen "the perfect site" that
they discovered they would be buying it from that same Zionist
from Pinsk, Aharon Eisenberg, at whom he had once peeked
through a keyhole.

As concern began to be felt around the world over developments in Germany, Weizmann in 1935 was again elected president of the world organization and devoted much time in the
ensuing several years to maintaining contact with the governments of those powers that had endorsed the Mandate. He had
three interviews with Mussolini. In the first the Italian dictator
declared, "You know, Dr. Weizmann, not all Jews are Zionists,"
to which he replied, "and not all Italians are Fascisti!" Mussolini suggested that England was using the Zionists as pawns in
her great power game and said Italy, if she chose, could build
a Jewish state *"en toute pièce."* Weizmann smiled and replied,
"I remember that the Romans destroyed it *en toute pièce."*

When the British sent still another royal commission—the
Peel Commission—to investigate why Jews and Arabs were not
getting along better, Weizmann spent two hours and ten
minutes testifying, climaxed by a statement that there were six
million Jews "pent up where they are not wanted, and for
whom the world is divided into places where they cannot live

and places where they may not enter." Why he chose the figure six million he himself may not have known, but it was prophetic. Early in 1937, when the Commission sounded him out on what he thought of a partition of Palestine he replied he could not speak without consulting his colleagues, yet in his own mind he thought it would be much better for the Jews to be a majority in a small area of their own than a minority in all of Palestine. ("It was my own deep conviction that God had always chosen small countries through which to convey His messages to humanity.")

Then, in 1937, another White Paper, based on the Peel report, which recommended severe curtailment of Jewish immigration and land purchasing. Still Weizmann did not completely lose faith, although he wrote a letter to the Colonial Minister in which he told how, to his own detriment, he had defended Great Britain to his own people, from public platforms in all parts of the world. Now, he concluded, it was beginning to look like a one-sided love affair.

As the likelihood of war became greater, the British followed what he called in anger and growing disillusionment, "the technique of keeping a promise to the ear and breaking it to the heart." In 1939 the worst White Paper of all was issued, officially called *Command 6019*. An outline was delivered in advance, for their approval, to members of an Arab delegation then in London. By a clerical error a copy was also sent to Dr. Weizmann. For five years only, limited Jewish immigration would be permitted; after that, none at all, except with Arab permission. At the end of five years, Palestine would become an independent Arab state. It was the ultimate in appeasement by a government that had already appeased Hitler at Munich. Weizmann saw Chamberlain and pleaded with him, declaring that what had happened to Austria and Czechoslovakia would now happen to the Jews of Palestine. Chamberlain sat before him like a marble bust, wordless.

Early in World War II he received a message from President Roosevelt asking him to come to the United States to work on the problem of synthetic rubber. As he and his wife were packing they received news that their younger son, a fighter pilot, had crashed on the coast of France and was presumably dead.

At 10 Downing Street he said good-bye to Churchill, who made a statement to him so amazing that he wrote it down and put it in an envelope that he gave to a colleague, to be opened "should anything happen to me on this journey." Churchill had said: "I would like to see Ibn Saud made lord of the Middle East—the boss of the bosses—providing he settles with you."

In America he worked on fermenting corn to get butyl alcohol, to be made into butylene, to be turned into butadiene, the basis of synthetic rubber.

When, immediately after war's end, the new Labour Government of England repudiated all its old pledges to the Zionists and instead, offered only Foreign Minister Ernest Bevin's thinly veiled anti-Semitism and another investigating committee, Weizmann was blamed by both a large body of American Zionists and the Ben-Gurion faction of Palestinian Jews. Between them at the 1946 Zionist Congress they prevented his re-election. He was tired and unwell, so he retired to Rehovoth. The next year, in testifying before the United Nations Special Committee in Jerusalem, he denounced the current Jewish terrorism as something contrary to Jewish tradition. In a striking aphorism he said, "I have never believed that the Messiah would come to the sound of high explosives." Despite all that had happened, he once more defended the country of his adoption, whose passport he still carried.

Then he went to the United States and at Lake Success testified before the Ad Hoc Committee. His eyesight was growing dim, he was seventy-three and ill, but he lobbied with the energy of youth, trying to persuade various UN delegations to vote favorably when the time came. In November he heard that the American delegation, as a gesture of appeasement, favored giving the lower half of the Negev to the Arabs, so he went to Washington and interceded with President Truman, pointing out that in the thousands of years the Arabs had had the Negev not a blade of grass had grown, but if it were made part of a Jewish state it would soon blossom. He also explained how imperative it would be for the Jewish state to have an outlet on the Red Sea. At the end of the talk Truman promised to communicate at once with the American delegation. And he did. On November 29, by a vote of 33 to 13—England abstaining—the General Assembly approved the partition plan, unchanged.

The battle seemed over now; the victory secure. But in January 1948, as he was about to go from London to Palestine, he received an SOS from Abba Eban, representative of the Jewish Agency in Washington: CRISIS! COME AT ONCE! Part of the crisis was Britain's fault. He knew it. Finally he was really disillusioned. Instead of accepting the decision of the highest international body in the world, Britain was doing everything possible to frustrate it. She was permitting disorder to spread, arming Arabs while disarming Jews, denying a UN committee admission to Palestine, refusing to hand over government services to the incoming Jewish administration, denying Jews the right to a self-defense force, expelling Palestine from the sterling bloc, and creating what he himself called "planned chaos." The United States, also, was behaving badly, having passed an arms embargo that hurt only the Jews, for the Arabs could get all the planes, tanks, guns, and bombs they wanted from the British. Worse, the American delegation in the UN was leading a move to reverse the November 29 decision.

During his first two weeks in America every possible influence was used to get him into the White House, but President Truman, having been greatly annoyed by several incidents involving American Zionist leaders, said a firm "no." As a last hope, someone in the middle of the night of February 20–21 telephoned the President's former haberdashery shop partner in Missouri, Eddie Jacobson, who was told that the fate of a Jewish state might be in his hands. He had never been a member of any Zionist organization but he agreed to help. When he reached the White House the President's private secretary, suspecting why he was there, ordered him not to discuss Palestine. Jacobson replied that that was why he had come and walked into Truman's office. They chatted amiably for a long time, but when he finally asked for an appointment for Weizmann, Truman not only refused but said there was no use discussing the matter. Just then Jacobson noticed a bust of Andrew Jackson on Truman's desk. "Harry," he suddenly said, "all your life you had a hero . . . Andrew Jackson. I remember when we had our store together and you were always reading books and pamphlets on this great American." Jackson was Truman's idol, he said, but his own was "the greatest Jew who ever lived, a gentleman and a great statesman . . . a very sick man . . . almost broken in health . . . but he traveled thousands and thousands of miles just to see you and plead the cause of my people. Now you refuse to see him. . . ."

It worked. Five days later, Dr. Weizmann entered the White House incognito by the little-used East Gate, so that he would not be seen by reporters, and had a 45-minute session with the President. Truman indicated his firm intention of holding out against those who wished a reversal of America's original position. Weizmann left the White House reassured, but the next day Chief U. S. Delegate Warren R. Austin stood up in the Security Council and proposed that partition be suspended and a special session of the General Assembly be called to work out a UN trusteeship over all of Palestine. When Weizmann heard the news he expressed the belief that Truman was a victim of his own State Department, so he wrote a private letter to the President which concluded with a challenge that sounded almost Biblical: "The choice of our people, Mr. President, is between statehood and extermination. Providence has placed this issue in your hands, and I am confident that you will yet decide it in the spirit of the moral law."

Now, from Tel Aviv, he began to receive intimations that the Jewish state was going to come into existence despite whatever happened in New York, Washington, or London, so he began to concern himself, on his own initiative, with obtaining American recognition of the new state whenever it might be declared. On May 13, just 36 hours before the moment when the British said they would terminate their mandate, he wrote another letter to President Truman urging prompt recognition as soon as the state was declared.

On the morning of May 14 (there is a seven-hour time difference between Tel Aviv and New York) word reached Washington, where Truman and his advisers were in consultation on the Palestinian situation, that the State of Israel had just been proclaimed in Tel Aviv. At 6 P.M. the White House issued a statement: *The United States recognizes the Provisional Government as the de facto authority of the new State of Israel.*

While Weizmann was being deluged with felicitations and congratulations, a cable arrived from Tel Aviv signed by Ben-Gurion, his most bitter political enemy, and four other Mapai (labor party) members of the Provisional Government: ON THE OCCASION OF THE ESTABLISHMENT OF THE JEWISH STATE WE SEND OUR GREETINGS TO YOU WHO HAVE DONE MORE THAN ANY OTHER LIVING MAN TOWARD ITS CREATION.

Two days later he received a message that the Provisional Council of the State of Israel had elected him President. His first official act was to accept Truman's invitation to be his guest in Washington. He had intended to stop off in England on his way to Israel, but when he received news that the British-trained, British-equipped, British-led Arab Legion had invaded the state that had just been reborn, he changed his plans and went to France instead. For 44 years he had been loyal to Britain, had suffered because of her, had persisted in his faith in her. Now it was finished. *His* state was being bombed by British-made planes. His fellow Israelis were being killed by British-made bullets. His Promised Land had been invaded by British-led troops. It was a terrible mélange of the bitter and the sweet. A 2,000-year dream had finally come to pass, but five Arab armies were on the march. And his love affair with England was over.

When he stepped from the plane, he took a handful of Israeli soil and pressed it to his lips.

When he walked into the Tel Aviv museum that was still being used as a temporary Parliament building, to assume his duties as President of the Council, a half-whisper escaped his lips: "How long the journey has been!"

After his death, an Israeli biographer told the story of his last four years in a brilliantly written book with a tragically appropriate title: *Hollow Glory.*

He had returned tired, ill, almost blind, and full of bitter grief because no place had been left for his signature on what some were already calling the most important Jewish document since Moses came down from the mountain with the tablets of stone: Israel's Declaration of Independence. Also, he was confused over what his duties and rights as President were to be.

His arch opponent in Jewish ranks in all these years was only twelve years his junior, but as Prime Minister he was assuming one by one all the power, making all the decisions, leaving to the President only the functions of an Elder Statesman, who was consulted just occasionally. If he had been younger and in better health he might have waged war for the power, but as it was he delivered the speeches, shook the hands, and signed the public documents without public complaint.

After a first attack, when his physician asked him how he felt, he answered, "Horribly, Doctor. You can't help me, and I can do my own dying." Months later, after a second attack, he sighed and said, "Man cannot fight the inevitable." He never recovered from the third. He died on November 9, 1952, and was buried at his own request in a shady corner of his own garden. Each year on November 9, Israelis gather there to pay tribute to the man who has been called the first totally free Jew in modern times.

Chapter 6

How gorgeous the vision!
Come all, partake, enjoy!

—ABRAHAM ISAAC KOOK

ONE COLD NIGHT in November 1917, thousands of people poured into Albert Hall in London to celebrate what some considered the most important landmark in Jewish history since the Bar Kochba Revolt: the issuance of the Balfour Declaration. The principal speaker was Dr. Chaim Weizmann, for no one questioned that he had had more to do with wheedling this commitment out of the British than anyone else; but there were many others on the program. One was a man with a wild, uncut beard, shaggy mustache, large dark eyes, and saintly expression. A stranger could sense that here was a genuine man of God. There was something unmistakably ethereal about his expression. He often seemed to be enjoying spiritual experiences beyond the understanding of the average person; to be thinking sublime thoughts; to be staring into eternity.

As he began speaking there was a sudden hush in the great hall, for his voice commanded, not with its force or volume, but with its embodiment of wisdom and gentility.

"I did not come to thank the English people for the declaration it gave us. I came, rather, to congratulate it, with the blessing of *mazel tov,* on its great merit in being the one nation to grant us this declaration."

Rabbi Abraham Isaac Kook, who had been of great help to
Dr. Weizmann when Lord Montagu and other wealthy British
Jews tried to prevent the British Government from making
such a declaration, was born in 1865 in Grieve, province of
Kurland, Latvia. An almost solidly Jewish village, Grieve was
so steeped in religion that the synagogue was crowded each day
from morning until night. Businessmen spent their spare time
studying the Torah, and the ambition of every mother was for
her son to start studying Holy Writ at the earliest possible age.
Abraham Isaac came from a long line of saintly men. His
father, a rabbi, permitted no word to be spoken in the home
on the Sabbath except Hebrew. At the age of nine the boy, by
virtue of spending almost every waking hour with his head in
books, won the title of *illuy,* or child prodigy. He seldom
played; when he did, he drilled the other children in a march
to the cry of "Toward Jerusalem!" Soon he earned the additional title of *masmid,* diligent student.

One day when he was almost fifteen he came home from the
synagogue—in one corner of which he did his studying—his pale
face covered with ugly scratches. His parents, knowing he was
not a child ever to fight, demanded an explanation. With embarrassment he told how every time that day he had seen a female approaching in the streets, he had covered his eyes with
his hands and had dug his nails into the flesh of his face, to
eliminate what he called "strange thoughts" from his mind.

From Grieve his parents sent him to the town of Lutzin, to
continue his studies and become a *yeshivah-bahur.* These pious
religious students in many ways resembled medieval monks.
Some were as young as thirteen, some as old as thirty. They
lived in poverty, sleeping on hard benches in synagogues, which
they used as their study halls as well as their dormitories. Pious
families of the town would invite them for a meal. Thus the
yeshivah-bahur would eat in a different home each day—if he
was lucky enough to find hospitality that frequently. It was a
system unique in the history of learning.

In Lutzin, Abraham Isaac would cry bitter tears as he recited
the story of the destruction of Jerusalem and would tell his
fellow students that his life ambition was to serve as a priest in

the Temple after it had been rebuilt on the sacred mount in the holy city.

When he was nineteen, he went to study in a college in Volozhin, considered one of the foremost centers of Talmudic learning in the world. There his piety created a profound impression; one of his roommates reported, "Every prayer that he uttered was thoroughly soaked in tears."

Marriage was important in the life of a *yeshivah-bahur*, but by custom the "caprice of emotion" (as one of Kook's biographers has put it) was never involved. The prime question was whether there was a good rapport between the young man and the prospective father-in-law, for habitually the *yeshivah-bahur* after the marriage went to board in the home of the bride's parents in order to be able to continue his studies without additional problems. At the age of twenty, Abraham Isaac married the daughter of a rabbi in Ponivesh and went to that place to live. After a brief career as a businessman, which he undertook in the hope of acquiring financial independence so he could study the rest of his life, he became a rabbi.

Once, when a plague was sweeping that corner of Europe, young Rabbi Kook—on Yom Kippur, the most solemn fast day in the Jewish calendar—stood before his congregation with a piece of bread in his hands. After reciting the proper blessing he broke the bread and ate it, advising the astonished worshippers to go home and do likewise, for it was dangerous to fast at such a time as this.

When Herzl published *The Jewish State,* then formed the Zionist Organization at Basel, Rabbi Kook, while greatly disapproving the Congress statement that Zionism had nothing to do with religion, thought only good could come of the movement. He considered the *mitzvah* (commandment) of settling in Eretz Israel as one of the 613 Divine Commandments and looked forward to the day when he could obey it. "We cannot fulfill our all-embracing mission," he wrote, "unless we settle in the Holy Land, for only there can the spirit of our people develop and become a light for the world."

The same year that Herzl died, Abraham Isaac Kook accepted a call to become the Rabbi of Jaffa. Upon landing in that Palestinian seaport city he was in such a religious ecstasy that he ran up to a cow being led through the street, threw his arms around its neck, and shouted, *"Oi, ein Eretz Israeldicke Kuh!* [Oh in the Land of Israel, a cow!]" But he was distressed to find that even in the Holy Land, Jews were fragmented: Ashkenazim from Eastern Europe, Sephardim from the south; Orthodox colonists and freethinking colonists; the Hassidim, who worshiped God with joy, and the Mithnagdim, who were seriously intellectual about their religion.

Almost at once he became adviser and spiritual godfather to the few Jewish colonies that were scattered across Palestine. He underwent considerable physical privation in order to make frequent tours from one to another. Even those colonists who disagreed with his religious attitudes found him a refreshingly new type of rabbi: a saint astride a mule; a man with his spiritual roots deep in ancient teaching, yet with an outlook that seemed to them fresh and modern. He pleased them, for example, when he encouraged them to plant more *ethrogim* (lemonlike fruit used in the Feast of the Tabernacle ritual) and decided that the competing *ethrogim* from the Greek Island of Corfu should be boycotted because they came from grafted trees. He also undertook to popularize Palestinian wine in order to give an impetus to the Palestinian economy.

Although Rabbi Kook had still been in Europe at the time of Eliezer Ben Yehuda's various conflicts with the religious leaders of Jerusalem, he attacked what he called the "nationalistic atheism" of the philologist from Lithuania and his associates. He was especially concerned about a sentence from an article that had appeared in Ben Yehuda's paper in which he defended the Uganda supporters for turning their backs on the entire past of the Jewish people. The article had contained this sentence: "We, all of us, have turned our backs to the past, and that is our pride and glory." Rabbi Kook took this as a challenge to the religious traditions of Israel and in a circular letter pointed out that "a people can have no future if it cuts itself off from the roots of its past." He called on Ben Yehuda and his associates to stop heaping abuse on their own ancestors.

As the year 5670 approached (1909–10 by the Gregorian calendar), the colonists of Palestine were faced with a grave problem. According to Biblical law this was the one year in seven known as the year of *Shemittah*, during which in Palestine no agricultural work was to be done, fields were to lie fallow, fruit and other produce that grew without assistance were not to be harvested, and all outstanding debts were to be canceled. The Biblical punishment for violation was exile. In ancient times this edict had been observed. Then came the Dispersion and there was no problem until Jewish colonists returned to Palestine late in the nineteenth century. When religious leaders figured out that the year 1888–89 would be a Shemittah year, there was consternation among the Jewish farmers, but three great pro-Zionist rabbis conferred and finally issued a unanimous decision: if Jewish orchards in Palestine were sold to non-Jews, the fruit could be harvested as usual, for the Shemittah rule applied only to Jewish-owned land. The sale would be only a formality and would not involve any literal transfer of ownership. It was no different, the rabbis pointed out, than the long-practiced subterfuge before Passover of selling all the food in the house to a non-Jew in order to obey the Biblical law that no leaven food be seen or owned by Jews on Passover.

The 1888–89 decision had caused a cleavage among the colonists of that day, some heeding it, others refusing to harvest their fruit. Now the question had to be decided again. Rabbi Kook did not have the backing of precedent, because the three rabbis in 1888–89 had said their dispensation was only for that one year; that it applied only to orchards and not to other farmland; that the orchards could be worked only by non-Jewish labor. In making a new, 1909–10 decision, Rabbi Kook had to face the organized opposition of some of the greatest rabbinical students of the age, both in Palestine and abroad. His own uncle, religious leader of an Orthodox colony near Rehovat, and his aged teacher in the academy at Volozhin, an expert on Talmudic law, were among the great majority of scholars taking the stand that the fields must lie fallow. They argued that by ignoring Shemittah, one was shutting out the possibility that in the sixth year a miracle would occur whereby the harvest would be great enough for two years, and how could religious Jews close the doors to miracles in the Holy Land?

Rabbi Kook took a realistic viewpoint and instructed the colonists that they need not refrain from work during the year of Shemittah. He argued that the task of recreating Israel as a refuge for persecuted, homeless people was more important than anything else, and therefore it was religious duty to work the fields and not invite economic chaos.

But in his habitual spirit of tolerance and humility—two of his most noble characteristics—Rabbi Kook insisted that those who wished to observe Shemittah must be permitted to do so without harassment. He sounded the key note of his own beliefs by saying, "Let us not offend the religious feelings of any individual." He went so far as to threaten to revoke his decision permitting the working of the land unless those obdurate farmers who wanted to observe Shemittah were permitted to do so. This broad-mindedness made him recognized and respected throughout Palestine and far afield.

In June 1914, Rabbi Kook went to Berlin for a religious conference. He was there the day war broke out and was interned as an enemy alien, since he was a Russian citizen. Finally, however, he got to neutral Switzerland, where for more than a year he lived in St. Gall, writing brilliant religious essays. Then he was invited to become the rabbi of a congregation in London and accepted.

When Lord Montagu led a coterie of wealthy British Jews in a campaign against the Balfour Declaration, Rabbi Kook wrote a scathing reply entitled, "A Manifesto Concerning the Act of National Treachery," which was read during Sabbath services in all the Orthodox synagogues of London. It said in part:

> We are in duty bound to explain to an embattled humanity its obligations toward us. We gave much to humanity. . . . Our wondrous history, suffused with the Divine Spirit, is and will always be the foundation for the purest spirit of humanity, the seed for the development of all human nobility. And the peoples have paid us back very beautifully, by robbing us of our land, exiling us from it, and burning our Holy Temple; with massacres, with pogroms, with the fire of the *auto de fe,* with yellow badges, with the shouts of *hep, hep* in the streets.

While in London, Rabbi Kook, in the intoxication of mystical ecstasy, wrote a small book on the mystical significance of the Hebrew letters, vowel signs and music notes. Also, through mass meetings and a prodigious correspondence, he organized a society, The Banner of Jerusalem, designed to bring about some degree of unity among religious Zionists, to stimulate literary activity, and to establish great schools of learning and a supreme rabbinical court. But although many branches were formed, the organization soon disintegrated. Abraham Isaac Kook, the mystic, lacked the organizational genius of a Herzl or a Jabotinsky. He himself lamented, "I am not a politician and I cannot concern myself with matters which lead to divisiveness of thought."

Soon after the end of the war he was called back to Palestine to become the Chief Rabbi of Jerusalem. His first great achievement was in giving the Jewish religion, homeless all over the world, a street address in Jerusalem. On the invitation of High Commissioner Herbert Samuel he established a supreme religious body for Judaism. It was impossible to have one Chief Rabbi for all Palestine, because of the ritualistic differences between the Sephardim and the Ashkenazim, so each selected its own, with Rabbi Kook becoming the religious leader of all the Ashkenazim in Palestine, and Rabbi Ya-akov Meir the leader of the Sephardim.

Many of Jabotinsky's ideas appealed to Rabbi Kook. When Jabotinsky was imprisoned in 1920, Rabbi Kook not only was the first person to sign a petition demanding his release but even authorized it to be circulated in the synagogues. He also gave permission for signing on the Sabbath by those who normally were forbidden by religious law to use writing materials on that day.

On one occasion, spokesmen for a group of ultrareligious Jews protested the immigration of colonists who believed only in the religion of work, thereby desecrating the Holy Land by their very presence. How, they asked the Chief Rabbi, could he explain his tolerance of such Jews in Palestine? Rabbi Kook smiled and replied that nothing was more sacred than the holy of holies in the ancient Temple of Jerusalem. Only the High Priest was permitted to enter, and then only on Yom Kippur, after he had undergone a service of personal purification. Yet, continued Rabbi Kook, if it was necessary to make repairs in the Temple, ordinary carpenters could enter the holy of holies without any ceremony whatsoever. In Palestine everyone was working to rebuild the Holy Land. Workmen were needed, with all their bravado and vulgar energy, as well as Talmudic scholars. Later, when the task of reconstruction had been completed, there would be time to enforce the rule of piety.

Once a Jew from Denver, Colorado, visited Rabbi Kook and also complained about the irreligiousness of certain colonists. Apparently changing the subject, the Chief Rabbi asked about Denver. The visitor boasted of how famous it was for its hospitals.

"But I hear that your city is filled with tubercular people. Surely this means that you must have a terrible climate."

The visitor quickly explained that it was because of Denver's wonderful climate that tuberculosis victims from all over the country came there.

"Just for this reason," said the Chief Rabbi, "sick Jewish souls from all parts of the world come to sink their roots in the Holy Land, here to be renewed and reinvigorated."

Although the word "saintly" has been used to describe Rabbi Kook by almost everyone who has ever written about him, his son remembers that on one occasion his father behaved with irritation. It was in 1929. A British government official had ordered the Jews of Hebron to surrender their arms. They obeyed, but a few days later they were attacked by Arabs and many of them were killed. Some days after that tragedy the British official, seeing Rabbi Kook at a social function, spoke to him and held out his hand. The rabbi ignored it, explaining, in the words of Isaiah, that he could not touch a hand that was "stretched forth but covered with blood."

When Abraham Stavsky, follower of Jabotinsky, was placed on trial in 1933 and charged with the murder in Tel Aviv of Chaim Arlosoroff, head of the political department of the Jewish Agency, Rabbi Kook came to his defense. It was beyond his comprehension that one Jew might assassinate another for a political motive. It violated his passionate belief in the purity of the Jewish soul. Jabotinsky's biographer called Rabbi Kook's efforts on behalf of Stavsky, who finally was acquitted, the most weighty of all.

More characteristic than anything else about the Chief Rabbi was his capacity for profound religious experiences. Once he turned suddenly to a visitor in his home and said, "It is time to go to the synagogue for worship, but you must excuse me from going with you, for I am all on fire with the love of God. If I should go to the synagogue now, I might be completely consumed. Let us go, instead, for a walk so I can cool off."

On another occasion he rushed from the synagogue and began engaging a gardener in trivial conversation, later explaining that he was so afire with the fervor in his heart that he had to calm down quickly by talking to someone about prosaic matters.

On the first night of Shevouth, commemorating God's gift of the Tablets to Moses on Sinai, the doors of the Kook home always remained open all night, while he preached from 9 P.M. until dawn.

In the winter of 1935, he became ill and his doctors diagnosed the trouble as cancer. Day by day the pain grew more excruciating, but the rabbi, now just seventy, continued to dash through the streets performing small and large services for those who had come to him begging favors. To ease the pain, he tied hot-water bottles around his body under his clothing. Finally the disease progressed so far that he was unable to leave his bed. His dying days were filled with agony, yet between clenched teeth he would speak of the nobility of suffering.

On the third day of Elul the famous physician from Hebrew University who was attending him bent over his bed to catch his last words. In a whisper the dying man said, "I hope the day will come when the Jews who are great will become great Jews."

He died seventeen years to the day after taking office as Chief Rabbi. All over Palestine and Europe, Jews of every shade of belief—and even many without belief—mourned the passing of a great man. Some remembered the majestic flow of his literary style and how he could perform magic with words; some remembered his eloquence and how beauty seemed to return to earth when he spoke. Others thought of the strength of his personality and how he had always seemed to exude love. Still others mourned the loss of a man who had such a firm belief in the inevitability of human progress. Nonobservant Jews respected him for his tolerance. Zionists of all complexions blessed him for what he had done to help prepare the way for the re-creation of the Jewish State.

Perhaps better than anyone else, he had expressed what is deep within the consciousness of every loyal Jew, the abiding conviction of Israel's mission to bring light to the world:

> There is still a long road ahead of us, to finish what we have begun to do. We began to speak a great word, among ourselves and in the ears of the entire world, and we have not yet completed it. We stand in the midst of our speech. We cannot stop it. Nor do we want to stop it. . . . In our inwardness we understand our thoughts, and, in the course of time, our speech, too, will be liberated from the stultifying cobwebs of exile in which it is presently caught, so that we shall be able to speak, portray and explain in clear concepts that which we seek with our whole being. But, until the advent of this Golden Age, we shall not cease our spiritual and practical labors; only a nation that had completed what it began can afford to go off the stage of history.

Chapter 7

---

*Without me the Zionists
Could have done nothing!*

—Edmond de Rothschild

Theodor Herzl tried to convert him to Zionism and failed. Eliezer Ben Yehuda, in gratitude for years of help, dedicated the first volume of the Hebrew dictionary to him. Vladimir Jabotinsky tried—without success—to persuade him to finance the defense of Abraham Stavsky, after the Arlosoroff murder. Henrietta Szold met him on several occasions and found him charming. Chaim Weizmann was on such intimate terms with him that once when the future President of Israel lay ill in a London hospital, he appeared at the bedside with a check for almost a quarter of a million dollars and presented it to Dr. Weizmann saying, "This ought to help bring your temperature down!"

Baron Edmond James de Rothschild differed from most other molders of modern Israel in that he was in no way a fanatic. In the years when he was influencing the course of Middle Eastern affairs more than any other Jew, he was not even a Zionist. By outliving all the other grandchildren of old Mayer Amschel von Rothschild, founder of the greatest banking empire in world history, he acquired the title, "Head of the House of Rothschild." While some others in the family married Roman Catholics, became involved in occasional scandals, or had various eccentricities, the gray French baron was always a model of conventionality and respectability—except for what some of his less Jewish-minded relatives called his "Palestine phobia." Whatever it was—phobia or passion, folly or "a rich man's sport," as Herzl in pique once called it—Baron Rothschild's philanthropy saved the Jewish colonies of Palestine at a critical moment in the history of The Return. Even one of his negative actions had a profound effect on Palestinian history, for had he not been so adamant in his refusal to take Herzl seriously, the young Viennese journalist might not have carried out his threat of organizing a mass movement which in turn, laid the foundation for the revival of Israel.

The Rothschilds trace their ancestry back to Isaac Elchanan, a retail merchant who acquired the name Rothschild because he lived in Frankfurt, Germany, on the Street of the Jews, where each house was marked not by a number but by an emblem, and his was a red shield *(Rothschild)*. Judengasse, actually a 12-foot-wide dark alley, was for 300 years the Frankfurt ghetto. The number of Jews on Judengasse was limited to 500; they were not permitted to acquire land, practice farming, trade in fruit, weapons or silk, leave the ghetto at night or on Sunday, or visit taverns; and only 12 marriages per year were permitted. When anyone shouted, "Jew, do your duty!" Isaac Elchanan had to take off his hat and bow low, while passers-by laughed in contempt. From that background came this family of multimillionaire international financiers.

Edmond, who was born in Paris in 1845, carried on the French branch with the skill of his forebears. He acquired the third largest private art collection in the world (he eventually gave 20,000 engravings to the Louvre), married a member of the German branch of the Rothschild family in an Orthodox wedding ceremony, and developed into a *bon vivant,* with exquisite taste in art, architecture, interior decorating, and men's clothes. He was a split personality, at times shy, gracious, even nervous and ill at ease; at other times arrogant and almost brutal in the use of his power. He might have been passed over with a single paragraph when the family history was written, had it not been for something that happened in 1882. There are two versions. Biographer Frederick Morton gives the credit to Samuel Mohilewer, a rabbi from Bialystok, Poland, who became interested in Palestine as a place of refuge for those fleeing Czarist persecution. Mohilewer paid a call on the great French banker, and by personal magnetism combined with Talmudic dialectics persuaded him to search his soul and decide if he should not put some of his stupendous wealth at the service of the struggling Jewish colonies in Palestine. The other version is told by a recognized authority on Palestine events of that era. Moshe Smilansky, a settler of the First Aliyah and its foremost literary spokesman. He gives the credit to Joseph Feinberg, an engineer from Kiev, one of the handful of intellectuals who came to Palestine in 1882, bought land not far from Jaffa, founded a settlement called Rishon-le-Zion, and attempted to make farmers of themselves. The wells they dug failed to provide sufficient water for human existence; the fields they planted grew thorns and thistles instead of wheat; they were harassed by marauders and plagued with disease; their meager resources ran out; the weakhearted fled back to Russia and its pogroms. But Feinberg, loath to quit the settlement they had established, went to Paris and obtained an audience with the great baron in his mansion on Faubourg St. Honoré, where for hours he talked of the dream and of the return, of the hunger in Rishon-le-Zion, of the bitter depression at Rosh Pinna in the Galilean hills, of the discouragement at Zamarin in Samaria, of the epidemic at Petah Tikvah. He argued that this was a great opportunity for some rich man to save Jewish lives and encourage Jewish colonization. Finally Rothschild agreed to help on two conditions: his name must be kept secret; the number of colonists must be greatly increased.

This was the start. Before long, Palestinian colonies became the baron's obsession. The struggling settlements that already existed were revitalized, a dozen, twenty, thirty new villages were established; a great impetus was given to resettlement in the Holy Land. It was not possible to keep the secret. In Rishon-le-Zion they said prayers each Shabbat for the man they were all calling, now, the Great Well-Known Benefactor, or the Well-Known Great Benefactor. Zamarin was renamed Zichron Ya'-akov (Jacob's Memorial) after the baron's father. From the Faubourg St. Honoré to Palestine flowed a steady stream of golden francs. In France the baron owned some of the finest vineyards of Europe and he decided that this was an ideal occupation for intellectuals trying to reconvert themselves, so he sent them the roots of vines, and built two great winepresses—the press at Rishon-le-Zion was one of the largest in the world. He sent a Russian who had been an orchestra conductor in Kiev to a school of viticulture and then to Palestine to take charge of this new industry. The wine that was produced the baron bought at a price far in excess of its market value. At first, wine bottles were imported all the way from France; then the baron sent Meier Dizengoff (who was later to become mayor of Tel Aviv, a city that did not then exist, even in anyone's imagination) to Belgium to learn the glassblower's art, then back to Palestine to take charge of a glass factory that made not only bottles but chimneys for kerosene lamps.

At Rosh Pinna, mulberry trees were planted and a Palestinian silk industry planned. Jewish farmers were encouraged to grow geraniums and roses on every spare foot of their land; then French chemists arrived to establish a perfume industry. More and more Rothschild gold poured in until it was estimated he had spent between 20 and 25 million dollars on his Palestinian ventures. Schools, hospitals, and agricultural training centers were established, thousands of houses were built, trees were planted along the sides of roads as in France, swamps were drained, new wells were dug. Almond trees, jasmine, mint, and tobacco were planted. A salt works was built and a plant to generate electricity. An envoy was sent to the Sultan to see if he could be bribed to permit many more colonies. In a way, it was a rich man's attempt to create Utopia.

But it had nothing to do with Zionism. Over and over again the baron made this clear. He wanted it understood that this was philanthrophy, pure and simple. Nationalism was beyond his understanding or his liking. He considered Herzl a dangerous and undisciplined man; a visionary and a dreamer—not complimentary words in the baron's vocabulary. He told Herzl face to face he disliked the idea of a Jewish state—even talk about it might anger the Turks and adversely affect the Turkish attitude toward his colonies. His concept of Palestine was a place of refuge, nothing more. He disliked organizations. To

Menachem Ussishkin, Russian Zionist leader, he once exploded, "Why must you people go around making speeches and attracting attention?" There was no sense in speeches; all Palestine needed was money and he had plenty of it. He had no conception of the human problems involved in Zionism: the need to encourage Jewish independence, initiative and spiritual development. When Ben Yehuda paid him a call, he warned the editor-philologist to cease his nationalistic writings. When Ben Yehuda did not obey, he cut his subsidy in half. As much as he liked Dr. Weizmann he accused him, because of his Zionist activities, of being a "Bolshevik," to which Dr. Weizmann quickly replied, "One is always someone's Bolshevik!" A little later, when other members of the Rothschild clan began to show interest in Palestine, the baron thundered to Weizmann, "I spent tens of millions on the project, while they made fun of me; now they want to come in with a beggarly few hundred thousand francs and share the glory! If you need money come to me!"

An anecdote that throws almost a psychoanalytical light on his character concerns his financing of a series of excavations on Mount Zion, where, in the ruins of seven cities, one on top of the other, archaeologists thought they might find the Ark of the Covenant. When Dr. Weizmann asked the baron what he hoped to achieve, he replied, "I don't give a damn about the excavations; it's the possession that counts!"

In 1887 (he was then forty-two years old) the baron paid his first visit to the land for which he had already done so much. Those fortunate enough to be invited aboard the Rothschild yacht at Jaffa were impressed by the silk-lined cabin the Great Benefactor used for prayers, by the mezuzah tacked at the entrance of each cabin door, by the kosher kitchen presided over by a great French chef. The baron, in turn, was impressed by the little empire of factories, settlements, vineyards, and green fields that his money had created. In his exuberance he even tried to purchase the Wailing Wall from the Arabs so that this whole section of Jerusalem could be converted into a Jewish holy place. The Arabs listened with interest to his offer to pay $200,000 and to build substantial homes elsewhere for the Moslems who would be displaced, but Jewish opposition developed and the plan was dropped.

This first visit was marred by trouble with the man who had whetted his interest in Palestine five years earlier. Engineer Feinberg, as spokesman for many of the colonists, complained that everything was not as rosy as it might seem to the Great Benefactor. The administrators he had sent from France to manage the settlements were mostly arrogant little dictators. They had created a paternalistic system under which no freedom of any sort existed for the colonists. It was bureaucracy at its worst. Men who had fled from Russia to live a free Jewish life in the Holy Land were required to play sychophant to these feudalistic overlords, who were trying to kill off the pioneering spirit of the First Aliyah. The settlements were nothing but business establishments. The Jewish landowners were told they must hire Arab labor because it was cheaper. They were ordered what to grow and not to grow. The administrators had no understanding of the colonists and denied them any voice in running their own villages. Financial aid was given out to those who fawned the most on the administrators, who in turn interfered in the most minute details of everyone's life. All initiative was being destroyed. The men the baron had sent out from France were snobs and tried to force everyone to drop Hebrew and speak French. Their wives had established a social heirarchy and flaunted their Parisian clothes and Parisian ways. Many of the settlers had lost hope. Some had left the land; others had gone back to Europe. (Years later Herzl, on his first visit to Palestine, wrote bitterly of the "sniffy baronial administrators" and said that over all the Rothschild colonies hovered fear of "Monsieur le Baron.")

Feinberg had organized a rebellion at Rishon-le-Zion against the local administrator, who in turn demanded the expulsion of the young engineer. When Feinberg finished his story, the baron told him that he was in the wrong and should sell out and leave the settlement.

"Monsieur le Baron," Feinberg was reported to have replied, "all your millions cannot get me out of Rishon-le-Zion."

But when the baron threatened to cut off any further aid for Rishon-le-Zion, Feinberg's friends urged him to give in. Broken in spirit he left the colony he had helped found, and years later died in poverty and obscurity in Jaffa.

After the baron went back to Paris the troubles in the colonies became so widely known that a deputation of distinguished Russion Zionists, including Ussishkin and the writer Achad Ha'am, with Max Nordau as their spokesman, called on the baron and urged him to order certain reforms. His reply was curt. "These are my colonies. I shall do with them what I like."

Evidence that something was wrong finally came in a form that a banker could understand. The silk worm experiment had failed. Perfume from the factory at Yesud ham Ma'ala found no favor among customers abroad and that enterprise had to be dropped. The sand at Tantura was so inferior for glassmaking that the wine bottles broke almost as fast as they were filled and corked. Malaria in some areas was out of control. There were reports of his administrators being stoned by the colonists. And so in 1900, he transferred the management of all his colonies to the Jewish Colonization Association, which had been established by Baron de Hirsch and had had much experience with Jewish colonies in South America. But for the further development of his settlements, the baron wrote out one more check: for almost three million dollars.

Gradually during the next decade his unrelenting attitude toward Zionism changed. Once he had told Nordau that he considered Zionism "dangerous." Like all the members of all the branches of the family, he had taken the position that, while of Jewish faith, he was a loyal citizen of the country in which he lived and made his money, and always would be. But gradually he acquired what Dr. Weizmann called "a deeper understanding of Zionism." He was won over to the support of the idea of a Hebrew university in Jerusalem. He received Jabotinsky and told the future Revisionist leader he was "enthralled" with what the Zion Mule Corps had done and wished him luck in organizing a Jewish Legion. When the Balfour Declaration was announced in the form of a letter to his second cousin, Lord Nathaniel Rothschild, he used his influence to obtain France's assent to the pledge. In 1918 he permitted his son to attend meetings of a Zionist commission of the representatives of Jews in all the allied countries, set up by the British to make plans "in the spirit of the Balfour Declaration." He supported a project to settle 25,000 Jewish war orphans from Galicia in Palestine. He accepted the title of honorary president of the Jewish Agency Council. He finally wound up being what Dr. Weizmann called "a good Zionist." What converted him was apparently what he saw of the fruits of Zionism on his many trips to Palestine. He became convinced that Zionists were not just idealistic agitators and said, "Without me the Zionists could have done nothing; but without the Zionists my work would have been dead." He even declared sadly and publicly, "Never before did I regret so much as now that I cannot speak Hebrew." (This from the man who helped finance the revival of the Hebrew language!)

Nine months before his ninetieth birthday, the Great Benefactor died. After the State of Israel was re-created, a ship of the Israel Navy was sent to France for the remains of the baron and his wife. They were reinterred on the side of Mt. Carmel, on what is now called the Benefactor's Height, a short distance from the settlement named after his father, Zichron Ya'akov. From this spot one gazes out over the Sharon Plain and the mountains of Samaria, dotted with villages that were established by the baron and are named after members of his family. Here the Great Well-Known Benefactor is at home, among his people.

Chapter 8

*Then you shall know
How great is your richness.*

—A. D. GORDON

THERE WAS ONE CERTAIN WAY to start an argument in the Rothschild-supported village of Rishon-le-Zion in the year 1904: to mention the word "Uganda." Those who argued the loudest in favor of accepting the British offer of land for colonization in East Africa were the officials who had been sent out from France to represent the millionaire baron. Not having either religious, ideological, or emotional reasons for being in Palestine, they insisted that nothing could be worse than this place. One of the most vocal of their opponents was a slim youth of eighteen, Shlomo Zemach, who had come from Poland the previous year and already showed evidence of the intellectual brilliance that would someday make him a well-known literary figure. He worked in the winepress, and there one hot summer afternoon during an argument he made a sharp remark to a Rothschild foreman, who by way of reply slapped him across the face.

That night in the barracks, the winepress workers held an impromptu meeting. They were addressed by one of the most recent arrivals at Rishon-le-Zion, a forty-eight-year-old man with a shaggy white beard, a thin nose, and searching, intensely-blue eyes. He had already won the respect of all the other workers, for he was a strange and wonderful character, with a magnetic personality. He looked like a Biblical prophet and his words often sounded as if they came straight out of the holy book. Because he believed that man should respect the rights of even animals to life and freedom, he was a vegetarian. Because he was a gentle person who abhorred violence, he had been shocked by what had happened in the winepress. He told the meeting that no official had the right to strike a worker. These Rothschild men must be taught to respect human dignity. The meeting should demand not only an apology from the administration, but discharge of the foreman who had made the unwarranted attack.

The next day, when the conditions of the demand were not fully met, the white-bearded patriarch led the workers in a protest strike. The incident was characteristic of Aaron David Gordon, who was soon to become celebrated as the Tolstoi of Palestine, a sort of Jewish Rousseau, and a prophet of the religion of labor.

A. D. Gordon (he was always known by the Hebrew initials of his given names, Aleph Daled) was born on the Feast of Pentecost 1857 in a small village of Podolia. As a child in the forests of the Ukraine he developed his understanding of nature. His mother tongue was Yiddish, but he learned Hebrew and Russian in the schools of Vilna, and later taught himself German and French. Wealthy relatives offered to finance a university education; he refused, not wishing to be obligated to anyone. He was told that with as brilliant a mind as his, he should become a rabbi; he rejected this suggestion, too, because a rabbi's position in the community was one of honor and he wished to eschew all honor. When he reached eighteen, his parents offered to buy him off from military service, but he refused, for this would mean someone else would have to be conscripted in his place and that was not his idea of justice. When he returned from the army he married and spent the next two years, by custom, in the home of his wife's parents. Then he joined the staff of Baron Horace Günsberg, head of the vast Günsberg financial interests. Günsberg was one of the most powerful men in Russia, despite his being a Jew in a country in which Jews, if they were not actively persecuted, were at least restricted in

numerous ways. The Günsbergs were to Eastern Europe what
the Rothschilds were to Western Europe. In addition to banks,
gold mining companies, and railroads, they owned extensive
lands. On one of their estates young Gordon became a clerk.
For 23 years he was a faithful employee. His wife bore him
seven children, but five died while still young. During 1903,
both his parents succumbed to fatal illnesses and his only surviving son left home, after an argument with his father, to
spend the rest of his life following a religious career. These
events helped make up Gordon's mind. He gave the money he
had just inherited from his parents to his wife and daughter,
and at the age of forty-eight set out alone for the Promised
Land, to put into practice some theories he had been mulling
over for years.

He arrived in Jaffa without baggage, his only tangible possession a Hebrew dictionary which he had to pawn immediately
to raise the money needed to bribe a Turkish official to over-
look the rule forbidding Jewish immigration. When he applied
for work in the Rothschild village of Petah Tikvah, he was offered a job as a librarian because of his clerical experience with
the celebrated baron.

Gordon, however, announced: "I have come to help redeem
Eretz Israel as a common laborer." When the incredulous Rothschild administrator finally agreed to hire him as a common
farmhand he was delighted.

From the start of his Palestinian experience Gordon was a
man apart, considered by many as a saint or a prophet. Frail
and aesthetic-looking, he reminded some people of the rabbis
Rembrandt had painted. He was modest in the extreme, tolerant of everything but cruelty or stupidity, and sociable on all
occasions, even when staggering in from the fields, dead-tired.
He had no respect for money, believing that the purpose of
work was the work itself and not its financial return. Whatever
money he received over the cost of his simple needs he gave
away. Several times when he was in dire straits he did transla-
tions for a fee, but he consistently refused to accept money for
anything else he wrote. If he was sent a fee anyway, he gave it
away. He loved children, nature, and animals. Some of his
colleagues were also vegetarians, but he was one out of love for

animals he was not ashamed to express. He had a way of talking to them so that they seemed to understand whatever he said. When the midday bell sounded and the other farmhands tied up their mules and rushed off to eat, Gordon would linger, picking grass and feeding it to his mules while he talked softly to them.

It was a pleasure to watch the way this man, with more than three-quarters of his life already spent, would work in the fields. Whether it was a scythe, a mattock, or a pitchfork he was using, he handled it with a rhythmic swing that advertised joy. When he was given a piecework job, such as digging ditches for the planting of almond trees, at so many piastres per hundred ditches, he worked with the same slow perfection as when he was paid by the day—every ditch a small masterpiece. This was the way he always worked, whether it was writing a philosophical article, making a bed, sweeping a floor, or spreading manure.

The workers lived in barracks, many men to a room. Gordon always arose at 3 A.M. and in order not to bother the others would take his kerosene lamp into a corridor and sit on the floor with a pad on his knees, writing for two or three hours until it was time for breakfast. His handwriting was so fine that he could get as many as 52 lines on the back of a small postal card.

The joy of work was his religion. He practiced it as well as he preached it, thus giving vital meaning to his ideals. He said no people could be truly happy unless they had a living relationship with the soil and with nature, and could experience the excitement of a good harvest, and the moods of the changing seasons.

"Only when a man works with his hands on the land are the barriers between him and the deep cosmic forces of the universe removed," he wrote. "Like air to a bird, like water to the fish, is the environment of nature to man. To the degree that he removes himself from it, his life force, his basic feelings . . . dwindle in vitality."

Gordon's joy, however, had a deep intellectual quality that sometimes seemed paradoxical. There was always a trace of sadness and inner pain behind the smile. Some saw in him even occasional signs of great intellectual gloom. Once he said, "Give me ten despairing men and I will transform the world." His colleagues explained that he meant men who despaired of their old life and had set out in search of new physical and spiritual horizons.

The workers of the Second Aliyah (immigration) were mostly idealists and intellectuals, and they understood Gordon. They had been looking for a spokesman, a prophet, a seer. They found all three in this frail aesthete who preached that the commandment to earn bread by the sweat of the brow was not a curse but an invitation to a sort of joy that they had seldom if ever known in the black days of their dispersion.

Gordon always wore a Russian-style shirt that hung down like a coat, the collar hidden by his bushy white beard, and shapeless trousers, the bottom of each leg tucked into rubber boots.

After some months in Petah Tikvah he moved on to Rishon-le-Zion and then to Mikveh Israel, where he fell ill with malaria. These were bitter times for the men of the Second Aliyah. They had many enemies. Their bodies, accustomed to the intense cold of Russian winters, did not adjust easily to the scorching desert heat. Malaria was only one of many diseases that plagued them. Jewish farm owners were reluctant to employ them because, although most were young and strong, they were inexperienced, and Arabs could be hired for much less. The overseers sent out by Rothschild treated them with arrogance, almost as if they were slaves. The Arabs themselves considered them unfair competition. Other Jews treated them as *miskenim,* unfortunate creatures who might deserve sympathy but surely not respect.

Then there was religious conflict. Many of the men of the Second Aliyah were freethinkers, while the older colonists were mostly Orthodox. It was a religious argument that finally led the Town Council of Petah Tikvah to make a drastic decision. One morning handbills were distributed on the streets saying: *It is forbidden to employ Jewish workers, or to rent living quarters to them, or to have any dealings with them. Violators of these rules will be severely punished.* Some of the Jewish farmers immediately evicted their Jewish workers. That evening so many of them gathered at Gordon's quarters (he had recently moved back to Petah Tikvah) to argue over what to do, that they overflowed the room. Their white-bearded host smiled. "Gentle-men," he said, "let us go into my parlor" and he led them out-side. As they sat in a circle on the ground he pointed to the hills and valleys, saying, "Do you know of any man who has a room with such a wonderful view?"

The battlecry of the evening was sounded by Gordon him-self, who said, "We have been expelled from Spain. We have been expelled from Germany. We have been expelled from many other countries. Now we are faced with a new expulsion—by our own people in our own land."

As they discussed what to do he pointed out that they had struggled and suffered for years to gain the right to labor on the land of their ancestors, and that they should not now surrender. The more practical asked how they would subsist if the land-owners refused to back down. Gordon proposed an emergency fund from which everyone in need would draw four piastres a day (a few cents, by American standards). Four hundred francs was quickly collected, mostly from recently arrived immigrants who still had money left. They voted to inform their employers that they would not leave their living quarters under any cir-cumstances. Late in the evening they adjourned and paraded defiantly through the streets, led by a white-bearded man sing-ing at the top of his voice.

At least one of the Jewish landowners refused to abide by the Town Council's injunction and continued to employ Jewish workers. Others, seeing a chance to profiteer, offered to retain them but at greatly reduced wages. When the Petah Tikvah Council tried to get other towns to join in the ban, Gordon sent three workers on a tour of the colonies by foot. Not only did the boycott of Jewish workers fail to spread, but it finally collapsed, even at Petah Tikvah.

Gordon went from Petah Tikvah to Rehovot. His illness had left him weak. He was now a frail, delicate man in his fifties, yet he was given a job as stoker of a furnace in the winepress where alcohol was distilled. He was paid two francs per night. The boiler room became the meeting place of workers who gathered each evening to discuss the day's events and to listen to Gordon's philosophical remarks on the importance of the life they were leading. Later he was given a job uprooting diseased grapevines, a task he relished because he said he felt he was eliminating badness from life.

After he had been in Palestine four years, his daughter arrived to join him. He went to Jaffa to meet her.

"You are terribly thin, Father!" she exclaimed as she embraced him. "And your clothes—how ragged they are!"

He smiled and indicated by gesture that to him such matters were of no importance. She told him that in her luggage she had a great fur coat she had brought for him from Russia. One unusually cold night the following winter, while walking to Jaffa, he was waylaid by three masked men on horseback who robbed him of his only earthly treasure, the fur coat, and left him by the side of the road, severely beaten. He suffered less from his wounds and the loss of the coat than from what he called "the human degradation" of the experience; the firsthand proof that men could commit such a crime against a fellow man. He was in a Jaffa hospital almost a month—the most unhappy period of his life because he was unable to work. To pay the hospital bill, he translated a book. Finally his wife came from Russia and for a few months father, mother, and daughter lived happily in a small rented cottage in a workers' village, Ein Ganim. Soon, however, the two women contracted malaria and were taken to a hospital in Jaffa, where Mrs. Gordon, after months of suffering, died. For many months after that, Gordon continued to nurse his daughter. When she finally was well enough they returned to Ein Ganim. The other workers greeted the white-bearded man eagerly and again he joined them in physical work and in singing and dancing when the day's labor was done. But they noticed that his blue eyes seemed to have lost some of their twinkle.

After eight years in the general neighborhood of Tel Aviv, Gordon went to Galilee. During the next three years he moved from settlement to settlement—Migdal, Sejera, Uriah, Kinneret —until finally in 1915 he settled down at Degania, which he called home during the final seven years of his life.

This kibbutz, or collective settlement, had been established in 1908. Thus it had been in existence only six years. It was not yet the showplace and rural paradise it was eventually to become. The land was still strewn with hundreds of tons of rocks. Malaria had not been conquered. Housing was crude. The diet was sparse and the work hard. But here Gordon was happy. Although he was one of Degania's most celebrated residents, he never became a member of the cooperative. He agreed with the kibbutz principle that the individual possession of money or "things" was not a prerequisite to a full and happy life, but he discounted the socialist theory that economic conditions are responsible for the evils of society. Deep within man himself, Gordon argued, is the source of all his trouble, the wellspring of evil. The problems of society, such as slavery, economic misery, and exploitation, he said, are made by individual man and not by society. He often denounced the hypnotism of power. Men too frequently cast off their own chains in order to enslave others. He preferred the kibbutz way of life to any other, yet he thought no social or economic form was a virtue in itself. He preached a theory that nothing could change man but man himself. He was certain that the secret of happiness was for man to get himself in tune with nature and the universe.

In one of his essays he answered the question: How shall the Jews throw off 2,000 years of the Diaspora? His answer: "We are an alienated people with no roots in the soil. We are thus deprived of the power of creativeness. We are a people who have lived as parasites in towns and cities, and to whom by force of circumstance this has become second nature. We must return to the soil, to independence, to nature, to a regenerated life of work."

Once, in trying to explain the joy and cosmic meaning of labor, he wrote: "Life is only a continuously extending ladder of goals, and we will never do more than climb toward those goals. Hence, we must find life in the climbing, in the preparation, for there is nothing else."

Joseph Baratz, one of the original settlers of Degania, once said, "Many of us planted more trees than Gordon, but nobody planted them so neatly, so beautifully. Everything he did was like this. . . . So a man works when he works not for duty but for love."

Menachem Ussishkin, distinguished Zionist leader from Europe, once came to see Gordon and found him spreading manure in the fields. Without stopping his rhythmic motion, the frail aesthete said, "You see, when you stand like this and use your fork like this, you feel so well, so good. You feel that you actually have a right to live."

At Degania, dancing was part of the community life. Workers would come in from the fields dead-tired. After a shower they would eat the evening meal, then sit and rest. A discussion would begin, often led by Gordon. Then someone would start strumming a guitar or put a harmonica to his lips. Suddenly, tired muscles would be forgotten as the farm workers—in heavy boots, or perhaps in bare feet—would join hands and start a *hora*. Gordon, more than twice the age of most of them, always took his place in the circle. Whenever he danced he closed his eyes, as do the Hassidim in their dances of religious ecstasy. The faster the beat, the more animated his thin gaunt body would become, until finally the music stopped and they would all drop with exhaustion. Often they danced all Friday night. Gordon, even when he was in his sixties, would stay up as late as any of them; then, after all the others had gone to bed, he would get pencil and paper and write for another hour or two.

Sometimes he put his mystic ecstasy onto paper.

> Then in that day, Son of Man, you shall raise your eyes, you shall raise your eyes upwards and you shall see the land and the creation and all which is in it. . . . Then you shall attain the eternity which is in the moment. Then you shall know how great is your richness, how great is the blessing which life bears for you. . . . And on that day you shall love all that exists, you shall love man, and you shall love yourself, for your heart shall be full of love. And you shall have faith in yourself and faith in man . . . and you shall be completely filled with life.

Because he was a champion of ideas, Gordon was an enemy of mere words, empty phrases, oversimplification, pat slogans, whether used with intent by exploiters and politicians, or innocently by the unthinking. He repeatedly warned his readers and listeners not to be hypnotized by the "enslavers of mankind."

One day during lunch at Degania, while the mail was being distributed, a letter was handed to Gordon. He put down his knife and fork, opened the envelope carefully, read the letter, then slowly got up and went to his room. For half an hour he lay on his bed; then, when the bell rang, he took his hoe and went back to the fields, speaking no word to anyone. It was days before the others at Degania found out what the letter had said. It was an announcement of the death of his only surviving son, who had refused to join him in Palestine. Gordon believed in silent mourning.

In the early days of World War I, the Turks conscripted healthy young Jews into their labor battalions. Although he was nearly sixty, Gordon insisted on being taken, too. He explained to friends that he had heard stories that the conscripts were given such arduous work that they often fainted from exhaustion. The food was so bad they suffered constant pangs of hunger. He felt it his duty to share this ordeal with them. But he was not permitted to remain in the labor battalion for long.

Now the valley around Degania began to fill up with refugees, for the Turks were expelling the Jews of Jaffa and seaboard settlements. Food became scarce, disease widespread, and the death rate mounted. The Turks doubted the loyalty of any Palestinians, especially of Jews who had come from Russia, Turkey's enemy. As the British advanced northward, the Turks arrested more and more Jews on suspicion of spying and took them to Kinneret for questioning. When Gordon heard about the torture to which they were being subjected, he walked from Degania to Kinneret, found the building in which the prisoners were being interrogated, smuggled himself into the lineup, and when shrieks of pain came from the room in which the suspects were being given third-degree treatment, he raised his voice in a Yiddish song that began, "As they draw my blood, I sing a merry tune."

At one point Turkish troops occupied Degania. One by one the men were questioned and beaten, among them frail, aging Gordon. The soldiers established themselves in all the houses of the village, forcing the settlers to sleep in makeshift tents. When an epidemic broke out among the children, Gordon worked night and day, without rest, as a nurse. One night while the rest of the village slept, a young settler who had recently arrived from Russia committed suicide, leaving a note that said, "You hope for a better future. I leave you my part in it. You have faith. I have lost mine." But the grimmer life became there on the edge of the Sea of Galilee, the more Gordon became a source of encouragement and inspiration with his humor, his faith, and his imagination. He was constantly telling first one and then another, "Be strong, it will pass!"

Finally came war's end. Now the Third Aliyah began. Immigrants streamed in from all over Europe, hoping the British would keep their promise of the Balfour Declaration. Many came to Degania. Gordon, joyous over this return of Jews to the land, tried to imbue them with his feeling about the importance of labor. His saintly appearance impressed them, and to many his words sounded like poetry and philosophy combined. At night when he came in from the fields they would cluster around him, listening and questioning.

He told them that "instead of trying to fight the darkness, man should try to increase the light." He insisted to them that "the evil men do to one another does not result from men being basically bad, but from men not understanding each other." In a book of aphorisms he wrote: "Man sometimes regrets; nations never. Man can be punished, but not a nation." Once he was asked if he thought religion was passé. "Passé?" he repeated. "It has not arrived yet." In one of his last essays he wrote: "There is no escape from life, neither in poetry nor in song, neither in literature and art nor in the intimate selfish limitation of one's ego; neither in aesthetics, belles-lettres, beauty or refinement of spirit. The sublime soul is only life. Life in all its fullness and completeness. A great supreme life. Life in tune with the universe. Life must sing and man must be a vital force in it. We cannot divert from life, not for a moment."

Gordon's simplicity, especially in his last years, won him many friends among the children. A five-year-old boy once said, "Grandpa Gordon is just like all of us except he has a beard."

In the spring of 1920, he grew paler and thinner than ever. When the Degania doctor hinted that it was probably just old age, he concentrated all his will power on trying to hold back the process of human deterioration. "If I can only work to my dying day, I will meet death with joy," he said. But X-rays taken in Jerusalem showed that he had cancer of the esophagus. He was not told this; it was merely suggested that he should see a celebrated doctor in Vienna. But he sensed the truth, for while in Vienna he wrote "The Memoirs of a Man About to Die." He even penned a death request. "Those who wish to honor me after I am gone should honor me in silence. There is no greater respect than silence. Can there be anything better than the quiet tear in the far corner? For one year after I am gone no one should speak or write about me."

After six weeks in Vienna, he returned to Degania. "The doctor was afraid to tell me the truth, but I know, because he said I had better go back home."

He told his daughter, "I know that the future does not belong to me, but I am so much interested in everything!"

Because he was unable to leave his bed, the men, women and children of Degania flocked to his room to be inspired by his cheerfulness, and to share his last thoughts. One day they brought him news that a bridge was being built over the Jordan.

"By our people?" he asked.

"Yes, entirely by Jewish labor," someone replied.

The old man smiled. "This is as it should be. The first Jewish bridge in two thousand years! Just imagine!"

One afternoon, with an excited look in his soft blue eyes, he described—to his daughter Yael, who never left his side—the exalted future of man: he would begin to find and to exhume that which is hidden in his soul. The hidden light would burst forth and illuminate and perfect the relations of man until he reached the level of a new sky and a new earth.

He talked to her often about death, which he called "just a new chapter in life." His only complaint was that the human mind could not grasp the cosmic transition from life to death. Once he awoke from a short nap with his eyes bright and his face aglow and said, in ecstasy, "Such moments as that are worth something!" What he meant he never explained. His daughter could only guess.

As he felt life slipping away faster and faster he asked for his only tangible possessions, his pencils. Borrowing a knife, he lay in bed putting a sharp point to each of them. Then he asked that the children of the settlement be sent for. As they paraded by his bed he handed each a pencil. They ran off, shouting to their parents, "Look! Grandpa Gordon has given us the pencils he loved so much!"

His daughter was by his side the night in 1922 when he died. His last words were for her, yet for all his people:

"You *must* believe in a bright future for Israel and for all mankind!"

Then the sixty-six-year-old poet of labor went to sleep.

He was buried in a grove of pines, deep in the earth he so greatly loved. For one year, as he requested, the people of Degania neither talked nor wrote about him. But then, as a memorial, they erected Gordon's House, a museum of nature and agriculture, now containing tens of thousands of books on those subjects in Hebrew, English, French, German, Russian and Italian. One room has been reserved for Gordon's personal possessions. It is a small room. It contains little besides books and manuscripts, and a bare kitchen table on which he often wrote, for Aaron David Gordon was a man of the spirit for whom the material objects of life were of almost no importance.

He was of such stuff as saints are made.

Chapter 9

I count it my privilege to
Help you fight your battle.

—ORDE WINGATE

ALTHOUGH A. D. Gordon was a pacifist, both in principle and in practice, he insisted on taking his turn at standing night watch when a self-defense system was inaugurated at Degania to protect the settlement from Arab marauders. Instead of arming himself with a rifle, however, he stood guard with a whistle. This was as far as he would go, even in self-defense.

A. D. Gordon and Orde Wingate never met. The poet of labor died several decades before the man who wanted to be commander in chief of an all-Jewish army arrived on the scene. This was just as well, for although they both called Degania their favorite spot in the world, they would not have understood each other.

Orde Wingate was a strange man, even in appearance. He was of less than average height, with rounded shoulders, an aquiline nose that led many people to think he was Jewish, and blue eyes that had the peering-into-the-distance quality of a sailor's eyes. He was as intent as a thunderstorm and as brilliant as a streak of lightning. His voice, when he was not excited, was low but insistent. Everything about him was insistent, even his gestures. He had more qualities of a university don than a soldier. He was a man to be liked or disliked, but never ignored. He upset all the preconceived ideas a foreigner might have about an Englishman. Some of his eccentricities may have been culti- vated to gain attention, but most were sincere expressions of his personality. Nakedness for him was a natural state, not a fetish. If he was alone in his flat or his home—be it London, Jerusalem, or Addis Ababa—he often answered the ring of the bell by throwing open the door and standing before his caller, male or female, stark naked. Once in Jerusalem, when Eliahu Epstein (later Elath), a celebrated Orientalist who was eventually to be- come Israeli Ambassador to the Court of St. James's, came to in- troduce himself and discuss Oriental literature, Wingate not only answered the door unclad, but remained in that state throughout a serious intellectual conversation that lasted for several hours.

He believed that eating raw onions frequently was conducive to good health and that rancid oil rubbed into the hair pre- vented baldness. Often he would make a meal of a bunch of grapes or a dish of olives. His idea of perfect bliss was to lie completely nude on a bed massaging various parts of his anat- omy with an old toothbrush and eating onions, while reading the Bible and listening to Bach. Even before his conversion to Zionism, he said that Christian music and the Hebrew prophets made a delightful combination. Once at a formal dinner party he kicked off his shoes under the table, then worked his socks off, and finally leaned down and began massaging his toes with a pencil. He had no respect for "important personages" and kept on hand a grease-stained uniform he would wear to show his indifference toward them. However peculiar these aberra- tions seemed to the conventional, Orde Wingate was a man of sharp intelligence, deep moral convictions, and profound loy- alty to a cause once he embraced it. He also was somewhat of a mystic.

Although a Christian, he won a place in Jewish history by proudly identifying himself, at great personal cost, with the struggle for a Jewish state. His conception and organization of what he called Special Night Squads put an end to the *havlaga* (self-restraint policy) of Haganah and its purely defensive mili- tary tactics. Wingate's SNS was a daring experiment in how to protect pipelines, roads, and settlements by going onto the of-

fensive against the bands of Arab brigands that had been harass-
ing Jews almost everywhere in Palestine. He looked upon
himself as the father of the army of the Jewish state he was certain some day soon would be brought into existence.

Orde Wingate was born in Naini Tal, India, on February 26,
1903. He was the son of a British Army colonel and grandson of
a wealthy Glasgow businessman who suddenly in middle life decided he owed something to the Jews of the world, abandoned
his business career and devoted the rest of his life (he lived to
be ninety-one) to the attempt to convert the Chosen People to
Christianity.

On his mother's side, Orde Wingate was a distant cousin of
T. E. Lawrence, whose romantic Arabian adventures may have
had something to do with young Orde's love of a game he
played with his six brothers and sisters. They called it *Lodolf,*
the name of a mythical kingdom they had invented in which
great battles were always being fought and in which the constant struggle for power was generally won by King Harold—
the role invariably played by Colonel Wingate's eldest son,
Orde.

Besides his sometimes reckless imagination, Orde's other dis-
tinguishing youthful trait was his serious interest in the Bible,
with emphasis on the Old Testament. At eighteen, he went to
the Royal Military Academy. Two and a half years later he began his military career as an ensign in the Royal Artillery. During his young manhood he frittered away much of his time on
race horses and fast automobiles, but in the autumn of 1926 he
decided to study Arabic. He no doubt was influenced partly by
reading the exploits of his distant relative, who at this time was
the idol of most English schoolboys. He was also encouraged by
his father's cousin, Sir Reginald Wingate, who had been Lord
Kitchener's successor as British Governor-General of the Sudan,
then High Commissioner in Egypt. (He was known to all the
Wingate family as Cousin Rex.) While Orde studied Arabic at
the School for Oriental Studies in London he lived in a garret
in High Holburn. In the dark streets of London's East End, he
tried out what he learned in the classroom in conversation with
the Arab seamen he sought out.

Then, deciding that he wanted to eat, dress, and live like an

Arab as well as talk like one, he headed for Egypt. Traveling by bicycle across France, Germany, Czechoslovakia, Austria and Yugoslavia, he averaged 70 miles a day. He was robbed in Prague, arrested in Vienna, and sold his bicycle in Yugoslavia. Then he took a train to Genoa and a boat across the Mediterranean. He cared little for either Alexandria or Cairo, so he was happy when he was posted by the British Army to the East Arab Corps in the Sudan. For the next six years his duty was to train primitive Sudanese tribesmen in the art of modern warfare. He was monarch over 300 men and their families in this remote outpost of empire, and for a time was not only content but "delighted," he wrote to a friend. "I would have been perfectly happy to concern myself with their affairs indefinitely."

Later he served on the frontier of Ethiopia, where his job was to try to prevent poachers and slave-raiders from slaughtering elephants for their ivory and kidnaping children and young women for sale in Addis Ababa. It was there that he began to develop his theories about the best way to ambush infiltrators. In 1933, he made a one-man expedition across the Libyan Desert in a futile search for a certain lost oasis. Some months later, on board a ship for Europe, he met and fell in love with a girl of sixteen, although he then was thirty-one. They were married two years later.

By the spring of 1936, Arab troubles in Palestine began to cause serious worry in London. Smugglers were running arms into the mandated territory from neighboring countries. Jewish settlements were being attacked indiscriminately, orange groves destroyed, buses fired upon, women and children killed. There was no respect for law and little semblance of order. That was the situation when the British Fifth Division was ordered by ship to Haifa, with Captain Orde Wingate as an intelligence officer. He had been picked because he was an Arabist with some Middle-Eastern background. He had been in Palestine just once, for a few days on a visit from the Sudan. Not even Jerusalem had impressed him. Although he was vaguely aware of the goals of Zionism he had little interest in it. A Jewish acquaintance in London in his riding-racing days had tried to explain it all to him, but he had been bored with it.

Wingate remained in Haifa three and a half months. By the

end of that time he was a Zionist, openly, admittedly, boast-
ingly. What caused the sudden conversion? Christopher Sykes,
his brilliant British biographer, spent years digging in files,
notebooks, and people's minds trying to get the answer. He decided it was partly because Wingate found that he had hereto-
fore been seriously misinformed about Jews—their general
characteristics, their problems, their behavior. Also, he had a
passionate sympathy for oppressed people, and during those
first months in the country, discovered that it was the Jews of
Palestine, not the Arabs, who were being exploited. In their
eagerness to purchase land from Arab owners, they were swin-
dled, robbed, and even terrorized, until they were forced generally to pay many times what the land was worth. He saw
the Jewish-Arab conflict as a David-Goliath contest, with millions of Arabs ranged against a handful of Jews who were trying
to hold on with their fingertips to their small stake in the land
of their own ancestors.

Once Wingate himself explained it this way: "When I was at
school I was looked down on and made to feel that I was a failure and was not wanted in the world. When I came to Palestine
I found a whole people who had been treated like that through
scores of generations, and yet at the end of it they were unde-
feated, were a great power in the world, building their country
anew. I felt I belonged to such people."

It is not belittling his idealism to point out that he was a man
who enjoyed being in opposition, rather than one of a crowd.
In Palestine, "the crowd"—most of the British stationed there—
was thoroughly pro-Arab. It was natural, then, for Wingate to
be on the other side. What is not true is the gossip of those days
that his real name was Weintgartner; that somewhere in his
background were Jewish genes, or that his wife was Jewish.

In his first few months in Palestine he had the good fortune
to meet some key figures of Haganah and the Jewish Agency, all
men of integrity and intelligence, all strong personalities, many
of them distinguished by a blunt, realistic frankness that appealed to the unconventional Englishman. One was David Hacohen, who had served in the Turkish Army and was now head
of Solel Boneh, Histadrut's mammoth construction company.
During World War II, Hacohen was to play a major role in the

Allied scheme of recruiting Jews from Southeastern Europe to be parachuted back into Nazi-occupied countries for espionage and sabotage work. And after the creation of the State of Israel, Hacohen would become the first Minister to Burma. When Wingate was introduced to him as a "different sort of Englishman" who was already professing a sympathy for Zionism, Hacohen, in his typical brusque manner, fired a volley of fast questions at him.

"What do you know about Zionism?"

"How many Jews have you ever met?"

Wingate liked the bluntness and replied in kind, asking Hacohen if he had ever read the Koran, and without listening to the answer said he himself had read the whole thing in Arabic and found it a "heap of pompous verbiage."

After many meetings he told Hacohen, "I count it my privilege to help you in your battle. To that purpose I want to devote my life."

Hacohen became convinced that Wingate was in earnest and was not, as many others believed, playing a double game. He introduced Wingate to others in key positions. When he met Emanuel Wilenski (later Yolan), an intelligence officer for Haganah, Wingate quoted to him the Bible in Hebrew and the Koran in Arabic, then gave him a voluble lecture on what was wrong with Haganah; to wit, that it must get off the defensive, take up arms, and give battle. Whether Wilenski realized it or not, Wingate said, a state of war now existed between Jews and Arabs. Before the rather one-sided discussion was over, Wingate said what was needed was a real Jewish Army and he wanted to live long enough to be its first commander in chief.

Later he met Eliahu Golomb, then Commander of Haganah, and lectured him on why the self-restraint policy was wrong and how Haganah must go on the offensive.

"With what?" Golomb asked bitterly. "With the antiquated rifles, the few grenades, and the odd machine guns we have stolen from you British?"

At first Hacohen was chided by his friends when he expressed belief in the sincerity of the mad Englishman. Palestinian Jews had reason to be suspicious in those days of anyone who pretended friendship, for it was a period of cross and double-cross;

of agents provacateur; of spies everywhere, Sarcastically they would refer to Wingate as "that friend of yours." But gradually, as his sincerity became certain to more and more people, the sarcasm was dropped and his code name in Haganah became simply *Hayedid*, "The Friend."

Hacohen took Wingate to his first kibbutz, Degania, in Galilee at the point where the Jordan flows into the Lake of Tiberius. The Englishman's reaction was instantaneous. Degania quickly became—and remained—one of his favorite spots in Palestine.

The more Wingate saw of Jews and their life as pioneers in their old-new land, the more his respect grew and the deeper became his Zionist convictions. Soon he was more Zionist than the Zionists; a fanatic with an intensity that was almost frightening.

Captain and Mrs. Wingate met Dr. and Mrs. Chaim Weizmann at a Government House dinner party and struck up such a spontaneous friendship that Dr. Weizmann suggested that they all go to his house to continue their talk after dinner. It was almost dawn when they finally parted. This Wingate-Weizmann friendship became a deep one. Weizmann often called Wingate "my favorite madman." In his autobiography he said he and his wife "both loved and revered him."

After Wingate had been in Palestine just four months, he wrote a long memorandum to Cousin Rex, giving a plan for what the British should do in the mandated territory, including: purging the administration of all pro-Arab, anti-Jewish officials; removing the High Commissioner ("He has lost all grasp of affairs"); recognizing the rights of Jews to unlimited immigration as long as land was still available; raising at once two Jewish Brigades to take over the internal and external defense of the country. He said if this plan were followed, Palestine could be secured for the Empire and the Empire for the world. He heaped lavish praise on Palestinian Jews for what they had already done: "You would be amazed to see the desert blossom like a rose; intensive horticulture everywhere; such energy, faith, and inventiveness as the world has never seen."

Next he buckled down to a study of Hebrew and before long was boasting that with his thousand-word vocabulary "I know more Hebrew than any officer in the British Forces." He pored over maps until he knew the geography of Palestine better than some who had been born there. In a way he had felt at home from the moment of arrival, for he was familiar with the Holy Land from his Bible reading. He liked to visit spots where great Biblical events had taken place and to recite aloud, for anyone to hear who would listen, his own version of what had happened there. If it was a battle scene, he was likely to expound on the military errors that had caused the defeat of such a Hebrew hero as Saul. He talked Zionism from morning until night. His tremendous energy had found, at last, its perfect outlet; his idealism was now channeled. It was certainly the happiest period of his life. He reread familiar passages in the Bible and memorized the Psalms, which he would sing in a booming voice when he was alone. He fell into the habit of using "us" and "we" when he spoke of the problems Palestine's Jews faced. Once to Dr. Weizmann he said, "Do you know what the first thing is *we* should do after the state is established? Bring back the bones of Herzl from Vienna and bury them on Mt. Carmel."

From Haifa he was sent to Jerusalem and given a desk job in General Archibald Wavell's headquarters. He annoyed his fellow officers by answering the phone or saying hello and good-bye to visitors with the Hebrew word *"Shalom!"* which the Palestinian Jews used as a greeting. They accused him behind his back—and sometimes even to his face—of having "sold out" emotionally and intellectually.

The murder in the autumn of 1937 of the British Acting District Commissioner of Nazareth and his police escort by Arab terrorists, was the peak of many months of intensified banditry, raids, and indiscriminate killing. Much of it was done by Arabs under the direction of Fawzi Kawakji, a fierce Syrian guerrilla leader. The British Army seemed unable to cope with the situation. The Arab marauders were clever about getting across the frontier at obscure points, cutting the oil pipeline from Mosul to the British refinery at Haifa, committing a wide variety of terroristic acts, and then getting away safely. Most of the million Arabs of Palestine were ready to give aid and comfort to the raiders, or were intimidated into doing so. It finally reached the point where no one with any regard for his own life used the roads at night. In some areas the police were instructed not to leave their barracks after dark. The Arabs boasted, "The night belongs to us!" And it just about did.

This situation gave Wingate his chance. He wrote a memorandum to General Wavell stating the pressing need of accurate and detailed information on Arab methods of infiltration and suggesting that he make the investigation himself. The permission was granted and the mad Englishman, heavily armed, set off for the Syrian frontier alone in an old automobile. Some days later he arrived back at the Jewish settlement of Afikim. Darkness had fallen and the settlement gate was closed, so he climbed over it. As he dropped to the ground he felt the muzzle of a rifle against the small of his back. The gun was in the hands of a Haganah girl he had already met somewhere.

"*Shalom,* Ruth!" he said.

"*Shalom,* Captain Wingate. How did you get in?"

"I climbed over the gate."

"Well, you'll have to climb back," she said in dead earnestness, "and then I'll open the gate and let you in. Otherwise I will have to shoot you."

He often repeated the story. It illustrated for him the soldierly efficiency of these kibbutznik-soldiers and their intense dedication to duty.

The settlements were under the unofficial protection of Haganah, but Haganah existed illegally and had to obtain what weapons it could illegally, and keep them hidden for fear of confiscation by the British. Wingate stayed up all that night lecturing the Haganah leaders of Afikim on what was wrong with their system of defending their settlements; how they must take the attack to villages across the frontier from which the Arab infiltrators came.

From his tour of the frontier he now knew what he wanted to do: organize patrols of Haganah men, sprinkled through with a few picked British officers, to operate at night against the raiders, on the raiders' own territory. And he wanted to lead them into action himself. But he needed official permission; after all, he was only an intelligence officer. Both of Wingate's biographers agree on how he obtained that permission, although it seems uncertain exactly where, how, and when the dramatic incident occurred. One version is that Wingate heard that on a certain day at a certain hour General Wavell would be going through a certain village on the Jerusalem-Nazareth road. Wingate stationed himself there behind a tree. When the outriders had passed and the general's car appeared, he stepped into the road and held up his hand. As the car stopped, he opened the door, got in, and told the driver to proceed. This effrontery might have led to court-martial, except that Wavell had already met and been impressed by this unconventional young officer. He listened while Wingate with fervor and convincing eloquence explained his idea of organizing Special Night Squads to deal with the gangs of infiltrators. Before he left the general's car he had received the permission he sought.

Now his task was to persuade Haganah to assign some of its best men to him. He went to see Golomb, who was delighted at the prospect of a legal military unit, recognized by the British, in which his men could play active roles, so he immediately agreed to cooperate. Encouraged by this promise of help, Wingate set off for Galilee. He went first to Hanita, a settlement on the Lebanese frontier that had been under frequent Arab attack. Its cluster of prefabricated houses had been brought in by a fleet of 300 trucks and erected in 48 hours. The Haganah commander had been killed in the first skirmish with raiders. Hanita was considered such a danger spot that no children were permitted to live there. Although Wingate bore a letter from Golomb, the men of Hanita were suspicious of him. One of them later explained: "When you have been plowing all day, and repelling snipers and infiltrators at night, and when you have gone out to relieve a sentry post only to find the girl who manned it dead and mutilated, you are not particularly glad to see strangers, especially British military intelligence officers. I admit I was suspicious."

Because of this suspicion, Zvi Brenna, a Haganah leader from Afikim who had been sent to Hanita to help in its defense, slept in the same tent with Wingate to keep an eye on him. During one of the short naps Brenna took that first night, Wingate vanished. No one was permitted to leave Hanita without the commander's permission, because in the darkness beyond the fences there was danger and almost certain death. But night after night Wingate, alone, went off on one-man investigating trips to learn from close personal observation the ways of the Arab infiltrators.

Then he went to the settlement of Ein Harod on the Plain of Esdraelon to set up headquarters. Because of his strong Biblical sense he probably chose this place knowing how much history it had already seen. Nearby was the capital of the ancient Kingdom of Israel, and the River Harod was the one involved in the Biblical story of how Gideon chose his men by watching whether they drank "as a dog lappeth" or by "putting their hand to their mouth." Wingate was already imagining himself a modern Gideon.

Haganah at first supplied 80 picked men. From the Royal Ulster Rifles, Wingate got a few officers and from the 16th Infantry Brigade, 36 British soldiers. This was the nucleus of his first Special Night Squads. He organized a school for them and personally gave them instruction in guerrilla tactics, with a good sprinkling of religion, psychology, and philosophy thrown in. ("Remember that out of ten thousand candidates Gideon chose just three hundred because they were not gluttons.") He invented a special signaling device—a torch on a long pole—so that his men could communicate over the scrub. For uniforms he chose blue police shirts, linen trousers, and tennis shoes, but he insisted that this typical attire for kibbutzniks be topped off with something to distinguish the men as members of an elite corps. What he wanted, he told Wilenski, was a large, distinctive Australian hat for each man. They could be ordered from London. Wilenski consulted Shertok. Shertok at first said the Agency had no funds to spare for "such nonsense." But eventually Wingate's SNS men wore expensive Australian hats.

When the SNS went out on an operation, the men were transported by civilian trucks. Since Arab spies were always watching, Wingate trained them to leap from the trucks while they were in motion, hide for a time in a ditch, then make their way to the predesignated assembly point.

In most of their raids, deep into Arab territory, they were successful in inflicting severe casualties on the enemy while losing few men of their own. They seized large quantities of arms and ammunition. Sometimes they got possession of papers that told of future Arab plans. In one raid Wingate was shot in both legs and one arm and had to spend several weeks in the hospital. It brought him a promotion and a decoration, the D.S.O. On his return to Ein Harod, the settlers gave him a banquet and in one of the speeches he was called, for the first time publicly, "the Lawrence of Judea." In Hebrew he replied, "God give it to us to slay the enemies of the Jews, for the enemies of the Jews are the enemies of mankind."

In his enthusiasm to copy the exploits of his hero Gideon, who had routed the Midinites by the use of torches concealed in earthen pitchers and by the blowing of trumpets, Wingate asked the Jewish Agency to supply him with a large quantity of ram's horn trumpets, like those used in Jewish religious ceremonies. Instead, he received a shipment of brass bugles and the explanation that ram's horn trumpets were never manufactured in large quantities, and no rabbis could be found willing to give up the ones they had, even for whatever worthy military purpose the Englishman had in mind. Wingate was furious. Eventually he tried the brass bugles, but without the spectacular success that the original Gideon had had.

The Special Night Squads put an end to the periodic blowing up of the Mosul-Haifa pipeline and considerably reduced the incursions of Arab gangs from across the frontiers. But Wingate's unconventionality, his dedication to Zionism, and his arming of Jews—for whatever purpose—had made his name anathema with most of his superiors in the British Army. They especially resented his boast that the SNS were the beginning of a real Jewish Army.

Late in 1938, dismayed by the pro-Arab trend of British policy, Dr. Weizmann cabled Wingate to come to London at once, if he could get leave, to discuss a paper he had written on Zionist Policy and the Partition Plan. While in London he worked with Ben-Gurion and Weizmann on a new partition plan they intended to propose to the British. Also, he had an eminently unsuccessful conference with Lord Beaverbrook during which the newspaper publisher so annoyed him that when he began to say, "I have decided—"Wingate interrupted by

shouting, "It is not you but God who decides!" At a large dinner party to celebrate Winston Churchill's sixty-fourth birthday, he declaimed for a full ten minutes on what he thought of
British policy in Palestine. When he finally stopped, a female
guest sighed and said sarcastically, "Well, that's that!" Mrs.
Wingate, reporting the incident, said Churchill turned on the
woman slowly, like the gun-turret of a tank, and said, "Here
is a man who has seen and done and been amid great actions
and when he is telling us about them you had better be quiet."

Word reached Wingate in London that his superiors back
in Palestine were indignant over his intrusion into the political
field and he was cautioned to desist. To a friend in London he
said, "I have been ordered to shut my mouth, and I intend to
shut it, as noisily as I can."

When he returned to Palestine he found that the command
of the SNS had been taken away from him, that he was condemned to routine staff duty in an office, and that the headquarters camp at Ein Harod no longer existed. It was only a
matter of time, he knew, before the Special Night Squads would
be abolished entirely. Early in May 1939, he learned that for
his sins he was to be sent to England to serve in an antiaircraft
brigade.

About this time he received advance information of the White
Paper the British Government was on the point of issuing. It
would condemn the Jews to remain a minority people forever
in what they considered their own homeland, and would forbid
anything but a trickle of immigration. That night he called on
the Wilenskis. He made no reference to what he had learned
and stayed only a short time. As he was leaving, the Haganah
intelligence officer said, "Look, you forgot the package you
brought with you."

"That's for you," Wingate replied. "You'll be needing it,
tomorrow."

After he left, they found that the package contained four
bottles of whisky. The next day when the White Paper was
announced they understood.

Wingate's last request of his superiors was that he be permitted to pay a final visit to Galilee.

He said a sad good-bye to Ein Harod, the birthplace of

Gideon, and then, on the slopes of Mt. Tabor, he found a platoon of his old SNS men. There, looking down into the Valley of the Esdraelon that he loved so intensely, he made a speech to them, ending with these words in Hebrew: "I am sent away from you and the country I love. I suppose you know why. I am transferred because we are too great friends. They want to hurt me and you. I promise I will come back and if I cannot do it the regular way, I shall return as a refugee."

In Jerusalem at a farewell party Wingate was presented with a certificate of his enrollment in the golden book of the Jewish National Fund. At the end of his speech of thanks he raised his right hand and in Hebrew repeated the traditional Jewish oath: "If I forget thee, O Jerusalem, let my right hand forget her cunning. If I do not remember thee, let my tongue cleave to the roof of my mouth, if I prefer not Jerusalem above my chief joy."

A few days later he left for England.

It was some months before he learned the extent to which his superiors in the British Army had gone to punish him for his championship of a cause. The orders issued for his movement to Ethiopia via Cairo provided that he was not to go to Palestine, ever, for any reason whatsoever, either on duty or even on leave.

On March 24, 1944, in the hills of Burma, a Mitchell bomber with Major General Orde Wingate aboard crashed to earth and exploded. There were no survivors. By then the military genius of this man of destiny had been established. He had played a notable role in the defeat of the Italians in Ethiopia, and had been brilliant in his leadership of the Chindits in Burma during some of the blackest days of the war. But in Palestine he was still remembered as the Lawrence of Judea, or the modern Gideon, or simply as *Hayedid*, "The Friend."

During World War II, a group of soldiers in the Jewish Brigade who called themselves *Garin Wingate* (The Wingate kernal) decided to settle on the land in Palestine after hostilities were over. They chose a spot in Upper Galilee they called Ramat-Naphtali. In 1948, during the War of Independence,

Wingate's widow and son were in Israel on a visit at the precise time Ramat-Naphtali was under Arab attack. On the flyleaf of her husband's Bible Mrs. Wingate wrote this message:

> To the defenders of Ramat-Naphtali: Since Orde Wingate is with you in spirit, though he cannot lead you in the flesh, I send you the Bible he carried in all his campaigns and from which he drew the inspiration of his victories. May it be a covenant between you and him, in triumph or defeat, now and always.

It was dropped into the village from a low-flying plane. The settlers who retrieved it, successfully repelled the attack of their besiegers. Orde Wingate, whom Winston Churchill had called "a man of genius," was still with his adopted people—in spirit.

Chapter 10

*We had a spiritual urge to
Lead a full, free Jewish life.*

—DAVID BEN-GURION

ONE AUTUMN EVENING in 1940, when the blitz on Britain was at its height, Orde Wingate, knowing that he was soon to leave for Ethiopia, decided to make one last attempt to influence the fate of the people for whom he had developed such deep affection. He asked a friend, Dr. Ben Zion Kounine, a London physician, to drive him to Hampstead to call on David Ben-Gurion, who was temporarily living in England. Although an air raid on London was at its height, they found the chairman of the Jewish Agency sitting in his boardinghouse room, so absorbed in his study of Greek grammer that he was oblivious of the noise the planes and antiaircraft guns were making. Reluctantly he put down the book and agreed to enter the automobile so the conference could be held in strict privacy. For the next half hour, while the doctor drove around and around Hampstead Heath, Wingate subjected Ben-Gurion to a bombastic monologue on how he should resolve the Jewish Agency's current difficulties with the British Government, especially on what he should do to force British approval of the formation of a Jewish army.

Although Ben-Gurion respected Wingate's military brilliance and was grateful to him for organizing the Special Night Squads, he was suspicious of his bombast and his volatility. In background, experience, and viewpoint they were far apart—the thirty-seven-year-old son of a British Army officer and the fifty-four-year-old pioneer from Poland.

Since boyhood Ben-Gurion had had one ruling passion, the rebirth of Israel. When it would come to pass, thanks in large measure to his own persistent labors, he would acquire a new obsession: to help make Israel so strong that she would be able to fulfill the ancient prophecy of becoming "a light unto all all nations." His fanaticism was the measure of his greatness. As the years went by, his name would appear more and more frequently in lists of the ten or fifteen most colorful, or best known, or greatest leaders of the postwar era.

He was born one stormy day late in 1886 in Plonsk, a small factory city astride a river by the same name 38 miles north-west of Warsaw. He was the sixth child of Sheindal Green, a gentle woman still in her twenties. His father was Avigdor Green, an unlicensed lawyer who was known as one of the wisest of the 5,000 Jews in Plonsk. Yet Avigdor Green was a rebel. He wore a frock coat and striped trousers instead of the conventional long tunic, smoked cigarettes now and then, trimmed his beard and mustache in a most unconventional manner, had Gentile clients, and insisted that his children learn to speak Hebrew. While still a baby, David's head was so large that his mother consulted a physician, who told her, "Calm your fears. Your child is all right. But I can tell you this, he will some day be a great man. That is very clear from the shape and size of his skull." At a young age David startled his schoolmates by announcing, "One day I will be the leader of Israel!"

Lawyer Green was an ardent Zionist. His son, even before he could understand what they were talking about, was exposed to the speeches and debates of Zionist committee meetings in the Green home. He was ten when publication of *The Jewish State* accelerated Zionist activity in Plonsk, as elsewhere. Two years after Herzl formed the World Zionist Organization, David Green and other teen-agers formed a Zionist organization in Plonsk named after Ezra, the ancient scribe. Members took a solemn oath to speak only Hebrew to each other and to work to spread Hebrew culture. David made his first political speech before he was fifteen, his fiery oratory and the depth of his Zionist convictions causing a local rabbi to say, "Ten more like him and Israel will be redeemed." He joined Poalei Zion, a socialist-Zionist organization, at the time of the Kishinev pogrom. When the Uganda controversy broke out, he and his young friends all labeled themselves anti-Ugandists, arguing that Zionism meant something more profound than simply fleeing persecution.

One of David's closest boyhood friends was Shlomo Zemach, who disappeared one autumn night without his parents' consent but with 300 rubles of their money, and set off alone for Palestine. While he was gone, David went to Warsaw to study and became an active Zionist leader and socialist organizer, making speeches, directing strikes, and proselytizing simultaneously for the creation of a workers' society and the re-creation of Israel. When Shlomo came home on a visit, he told David and the other young men of Plonsk stories of Palestine that filled them with wonder. He told them of the competition between Jewish and Arab workers, of the slap he had received across the face in the winepress at Rishon-le-Zion, of Bedouin marauders, of camels and mosques, of the romance and the grimness of life in the Middle East. David announced to his father that when Shlomo returned, he was going with him. Half a century later, addressing a group of American editors, the man who once was David Green of Plonsk explained the reason for his going and the basis of his Zionism:

> "From about five years of age, I did not ever think that I was at home where I was, in Poland. I thought that this was going to be my home, Israel. Israel has a long history of four thousand years, and it is something that lives in the hearts of its people. I think it is not only a matter of persecution but of spiritual need. I am not sure all the one hundred and two people who came to your country on the *Mayflower* were refugees. They had an ideal of building a free country in a new land. In the same way many of us came here without persecution. We had a spiritual urge to live a free, full Jewish life."

In Palestine the two boys went first to Petah Tikvah, "the mother of Jewish settlements." Describing his reactions David wrote, "I was joyous. I was in the Land of Israel, in a Jewish village, and its name was the Gateway of Hope. I smelled the rich odor of corn. I heard the braying of donkeys and rustle of leaves in the orchards. Above were the clusters of stars, clear and bright against the deep color of the firmament. My heart overflowed with happiness."

For a year he sweated in Judea at eight piastres a day, hardly enough to pay for room and board. He wrote to his father that hunger was a frequent visitor. After a few months he contracted malaria. Next he worked in the wine cellars at Rishon-le-Zion. At a Zionist Workers' Conference in Jaffa, he became friendly with a serious-looking youth who had recently arrived from the Ukraine—Itzhak Shimshelevitch, who signed the hotel register with a pseudonym, Ben-Zvi, which he later adopted as his name. (In 1952 he would become the second President of Israel.)

From the settlements in Judea the two young men went to Sejera on the Galilee, which inspired David to write: "I follow the plow and see black clods of earth turning over and crumbling, while the oxen move slowly, gently and patiently, like helpful friends. Here there are opportunities to think and to plan and to dream. . . . No shopkeepers or speculators, no non-Jewish hirelings, no idlers living on the labor of others." At Sejera he became one of the founders of a Jewish watchmen's organization, Hashomer. It was the first attempt of Jews in Palestine to defend themselves. Then to Jerusalem, where he worked for the equivalent of $2.25 a week as assistant editor of a Hebrew weekly, *Ha'achdut* (The Unity) that had been started by his friend Ben-Zvi. He wrote under the pseudonym Ben-Gurion, which he soon took as his legal name. The Jewish population of Palestine then was about 100,000. The paper had a circulation of 250 copies.

In 1913, David Ben-Gurion went to Constantinople to learn Turkish and study law, accomplishments that would better equip him to become a leader of his people in Turkish-run Palestine. Moshe Shertok, who would become Ben-Gurion's first Minister of Foreign Affairs and replace him briefly as Prime Minister in 1953, was also a law student there.

When World War I broke out, Ben-Gurion happened to be back in Jerusalem on a holiday. He and Ben-Zvi were both arrested by the Turks and expelled from Palestine because of articles in *The Unity*. They went to Egypt, where they were arrested by the British for being enemy-aliens loyal to Turkey. Friends obtained their release and visas so they could go to the United States.

At a private social gathering in New York, Ben-Gurion, then twenty-nine, met Paula Munweiss, a twenty-three-year-old student nurse from Minsk, who according to her own description was "a plain, very serious-looking girl; a real Russian-student type." She had been in America only ten years but had become a typical New Yorker in many ways. She had never been a Zionist and had little interest in the Holy Land. Her idol was Emma Goldman, who had already served a prison term for inciting to riot. David and Paula fell in love almost at once and a few months later were married at City Hall, New York. The young Palestinian acquired a loyal helpmate and the most ardent supporter he would ever have. "I knew from the day I met him that he was a great man," she said. "I could tell that he was like one of the prophets out of the Bible." She never changed her mind. During their long married life she never referred to him, publicly or privately, as Mr. Ben-Gurion, or the Prime Minister, or B.G., or David. He was always, to her, plain Ben-Gurion.

When the Jewish Legion was organized in New York as a unit of the British Army (because the United States had not declared war on Turkey), Ben-Gurion and Ben-Zvi enlisted and went to the Middle East by way of Canada. The future Prime Minister was a corporal, the future President a lance corporal. They got as far as Eygpt, but never saw action.

Back in postwar Palestine, Ben-Gurion came under the influence of Berl Katznelson, a labor-socialist writer and newspaper editor, who resembled Albert Schweitzer in appearance and whom Ben-Gurion and others called "The Teacher." He was a firm believer in the equality of men, a profound student of the Bible, an ardent Zionist, and a convinced Socialist with a passion for justice. Once he was asked to summarize a three-day youth congress. His extemperaneous talk lasted six hours, with hardly a pause. (After Katznelson's death, Ben-Gurion delivered several six-hour speeches of his own.) Until his death in 1944, Katznelson was known as "the only man B. G. will listen to." Almost as close to him was Eliahu Golomb, who had fought alongside Jabotinsky to keep the Jewish Legion alive and, failing, began formation of the underground army called Haganah. In this he had the enthusiastic help of Ben-Gurion. About the time of the Paris Peace Conference, Ben-Gurion with Katznelson's guidance formed a new political party, Achdut Avoda (Unity of Labor) which he represented at a Zionist conference in London in 1920. There he clashed for the first time with Chaim Weizmann whom he accused of advocating caution, accepting restrictions on immigration, and failing to provide bold and fearless leadership.

In 1920, Ben-Gurion was one of the organizers of Histadrut, the General Federation of Israel Labor, which took on more functions than any other organization of its kind in the world. In order to create jobs in a country where capital hesitated to invest money, Histadrut went into business and before long was operating a network of construction companies, factories, transportation lines, marketing cooperatives, distribution centers and banks, as well as newspapers, schools, hospitals, clinics, convalescent homes, theaters, and a publishing house. In the early days, Ben-Gurion was secretary-general. When he began a campaign for enrollment of Arab members, he was bitterly attacked. "Imagine," opponents said, "a Jew organizing Arab workers to demand more pay from Jewish employers!"

Under the British Mandate the Jewish Agency was established to represent the Jews of Palestine as they struggled toward their independence. It was a state within a state, with its own cabinet (called the Jewish Agency Executive,) a budget, an unofficial army (Haganah), and an intelligence service. When Ben-Gurion was elected a member of the Executive, he announced he would serve without pay because he was already drawing a salary from Histadrut.

In the late 20's, Ben-Gurion's wavy black hair began to be streaked with white, and no wonder. Freedom from Turkey had brought no millennium to the Promised Land. There was a bloody pogrom in Jerusalem, a British White Paper restricting Jewish immigration, the Arosoroff assassination, and the Stavsky trial.

In the 1931 World Zionist Congress, Vladimir Jabotinsky and

his Revisionists were largely instrumental in defeating Weizmann for the presidency. Two years later the contest was between the forces led by Ben-Gurion (he was now head of a new, united labor front called Mapai) and Jabotinsky. The struggle was bitter, with Ben-Gurion finally obtaining control of the Congress. The short stocky labor leader, who now had a fringe of hair that was snow white, was finally in the seat of power. He was elected chairman of the Jewish Agency Executive, which amounted to becoming Prime Minister, except that it was a "shadow" government—the government of a country which did not yet exist, except in the dreams of men like Ben-Gurion.

The Peel Report, proposing the partition of Palestine into independent Jewish and Arab states, caused an even greater split in Jewish ranks than had the Uganda proposal. Ben-Gurion was for partition, Katznelson against it, as were the American Zionist leaders, Rabbis Stephen S. Wise and Abba Hillel Silver, as well as Mrs. Golda Meyerson (later Meir), whom Ben-Gurion would one day choose as his Foreign Minister, and many others. In the World Zionist Congress they made their speeches, most of them brilliant. Then the man with the halo of white hair arose and began to talk. He said the best mandatory government in the world was not comparable to having a government of their own. He predicted that when a Jewish State was finally declared, a million and a half immigrants would arrive in the first ten years. (He was not far wrong. Almost a million did arrive between 1948 and 1958.) He told the Congress, "This is the beginning of the redemption for which we have waited two thousand years." A resolution was adopted that saved face for everyone: the Congress leaders were instructed to get more details from the British.

When the idea of illegal immigration was advanced, Katznelson persuaded Ben-Gurion to approve the formation of a Haganah Committee for Illegal Immigration, Hamosad for short. It was to save as many Jewish lives as possible, while at the same time serving as a political weapon against the British. Early in 1939, the British called a conference between the Arabs and Jews of Palestine. It was not much of a success; the Arabs refused to sit in the same room with the Jews. But Ben-Gurion, in black morning coat, striped trousers and gray tie, warned the

British that the only way they could halt Jewish immigration would be with bayonets—and maybe not even that way.

The 1939 White Paper restricted Jewish immigration into Palestine to 15,000 a year for five years and promised the Arabs that Palestine eventually would be made into an independent Arab state. While the World Zionist Conference was in session in Geneva in the late summer of 1939, Germany and the Soviet Union announced their ten-year nonaggression pact. Everyone knew war was now inevitable. Ben-Gurion issued a statement that served as a slogan for his people for the next few years: "We will fight the White Paper as if there were no war, and the war as if there were no White Paper."

Back home in Palestine he told a meeting of Haganah leaders that World War I had brought the Balfour Declaration; World War II would bring the Jewish State. Eight months after the war's start, Ben-Gurion, now almost fifty-four, packed a few clothes and some of his favorite books and went off to London to try to help persuade the British to permit the formation of a Jewish army. He had to spend so much time in London air-raid shelters that he decided to teach himself to speak ancient Greek while he sat waiting for the all-clear. When asked why he chose Greek, he replied, "I want to read Thucydides on military strategy, in the original." He also wanted to know more about Plato, his favorite philosopher. In London he began to grow in intellectual stature, his interests becoming wider and wider, until before long he was able to discuss Greek philosophy with either a Greek or a philosopher, metaphysical problems with professional metaphysicians, and abstract ideas with men who had had much more formal education than he. During this London period he also came under the spell of Winston Churchill and learned from him qualities of leadership that would serve him in good stead in a few years when his own people would have their backs against a wall.

Ben-Gurion and Weizmann now interceded with the British Colonial Secretary for the right to form a Jewish army. They were told that if they wanted to help Britain in this hour of her distress they should go to New York and try to convince influential Americans of the gravity of the Nazi menace. Weizmann was busy with wartime chemical research, so Ben-Gurion put Plato in one pocket, his Greek dictionary in another, and headed across the ocean.

In America, Ben-Gurion decided that the time had arrived to speak boldly. Stunned by the Pearl Harbor attack, the United States was now in the war. The awful truth about gas chambers and crematoria was beginning to leak out. For Ben-Gurion the moment had arrived to "proclaim the Jewish State." And he did—in the face of opposition from Weizmann, Henrietta Szold, Dr. Judah Magnes, the president of Hebrew University, and others. The occasion was the 1942 emergency conference attended by six hundred Jewish leaders from all parts of the world. It convened at the Biltmore Hotel in New York. The demands Ben-Gurion enunciated there came to be known as the Biltmore Program: unlimited Jewish immigration, creation of a Jewish army, all Palestine to become a Jewish common-wealth. The delegates went home to explain to their followers and get their approval. Ben-Gurion went to Palestine to try to win support for the program there.

Three months after D-Day, Churchill told the British Parliament his government had decided to permit formation of a Jewish Brigade. It was a victory for Jabotinsky, now dead, and Ben-Gurion, very much alive.

After victory in Europe, Ben-Gurion made a tour of the extermination camps. "I saw," he said, "the pitiful relic of European Jewry, what is left of the six million, butchered before the gaze of the world, frigid, aloof and indifferent to the fate of a people that had been hounded and tormented for two thousand years of exile."

Then to New York, where in the apartment of Rudolf Sonne-born, a wealthy American businessman, he addressed a secret meeting of 19 prominent Jews who pledged themselves to under-write the arming of Haganah for the war that Ben-Gurion told them was inevitable, if a Jewish state was to be established. The Sonneborn Institute (the clandestine name for this clandestine group) bought more than a dozen ships for illegal immigration.

For Ben-Gurion and other Palestinian Jews, 1946 and 1947 were years of international political maneuvering, interminable hearings by international commissions, and finally passage of the U.N. partition resolution just 30 years to the month after

the Balfour Declaration. It was a signal for the worst Arab out-
breaks Palestine had ever known. The British announced they
would give up their mandate the night of May 14. The closer
that date approached, the more chaotic the situation inside
Palestine became. Ben-Gurion accused the British Administration of using "every possible device to frustrate and nullify the
U.N. decision." He accused London of encouraging the Arab
states to move against the Jews by sending them ever-increasing
supplies of arms. His Herculean task now was to prepare his
people for the coming hostilities. Meanwhile there were many
meetings of the shadow government over such questions as
what the new state should be called ("Israel" was Ben-Gurion's
suggestion), over emergency water supplies, secret food dumps,
passports, taxes, a postal service—a thousand problems, large
and small. The sixty-two-year-old Jewish Agency chairman was
concerned about them all, but most important were his meetings with Haganah leaders—Yigael Yadin, the archaeologist, who
was acting Chief of Staff because Yaacov Dostrovsky was too
ill even to come to his office; Yigel Alon, commander of the
Palmach, the Haganah striking force, and many others.

On May 14, 1948, in the Municipal Museum in Tel Aviv
shortly after 4 P.M., David Ben-Gurion, wearing a dark suit and
blue necktie, and standing directly under an immense picture
of Herzl, took seventeen minutes to read to 200 secretly invited
guests a proclamation that began, "The Land of Israel was the
birthplace of the Jewish people . . ." Some of the spectators
choked up with emotion, sensing that this was probably the
most important moment in almost two thousand years of Jewish
history, but the man with the halo of white hair read on with
strong voice. At exactly 4:37½ P.M. he finished, then banged his
gavel and said dramatically, "I hereby declare this meeting adjourned. The State of Israel has come into being."

But the situation was grave and he knew it. The Etzion Bloc
protecting the southerly approaches to Jerusalem had fallen.
The Holy City was encircled by Arabs. Haganah, with its
50,000 ill-equipped soldiers, was about to face the armies of
forty million Arabs. It had no tanks or flamethrowers; none of
the modern devices of war. And he, David Ben-Gurion, who
had been all his life a politician, not a military man, was going

to have to direct the battles. That evening he joined with four other labor members of Israel's provisional government in sending a cable to Dr. Weizmann, who was ill in New York, extending their greetings to the man "who has done more than any other for the creation of Israel."

At 5:20 the next morning, as Ben-Gurion was making a broadcast to the United States, Israel had her first air raid. It was an Egyptian plane. That same morning the country was invaded by the armies of Egypt, Lebanon, Syria, Transjordan, and Iraq. (They were later joined by Yemenite and Saudi Arabian troops.) For the next 27 days, until a cease-fire, Ben-Gurion concerned himself with little but war. Paula and his children saw him seldom. Often he slept on a cot at GHQ. For 50 years he had had a single all-consuming purpose—to help create a Jewish state. Now he had to live up to his name and try to be a modern David and help defeat the Arab Goliath that threatened that state. But he took time out for one more noble gesture. It was his own idea that the man he had so often opposed—Chaim Weizmann—be unanimously elected President of Israel. Especially gracious was the way he phrased it. "I doubt whether the presidency is necessary for Dr. Weizmann, but the presidency of Dr. Weizmann is a moral necessity for the life of Israel."

In June a truce was declared. The Israelis needed it because they were dangerously short of ammunition, the Arabs because they needed to take stock of why they were being defeated by a handful of underground soldiers, mostly boys and girls. During the truce a ship called the *Altalena* (after Jabotinsky's pen name), bought with money raised in America by supporters of the Revisionists, approached the shores of Israel loaded with arms and ammunition for Irgun. One of Ben-Gurion's first orders after independence had abolished private armies, but the Irgun commander, Menachem Beigin, had ignored it and now insisted that at least the lion's share of the *Altalena* cargo be distributed to his followers. (The landing of arms was strictly forbidden in the truce agreement.) As the ship was being unloaded by Irgun, Ben-Gurion called his cabinet into emergency session. He asked for and obtained approval—not unanimously given—of an order to use force if necessary against the *Altalena*.

A brief civil war was fought, during which the *Altalena* was sunk by Haganah fire. The dead and wounded numbered almost a hundred, among them Stavsky, who had been accused of the Arlosoroff murder on the Tel Aviv waterfront close to where he himself was now killed. In a report to the Provisional Government, Ben-Gurion said, "So praise the gun that sank the surrendered ship," a statement Irgun never forgave.

Hostilities with the Arabs recommenced in July. Ben-Gurion as commander in chief directed operations that led to the capture of Lydda airport, the towns of Lydda and Ramla, and Nazareth. Planes that had been flown across the Atlantic then took on armament in Czechoslovakia and bombed Cairo and Damascus. An Israeli warship shelled the Lebanese city of Tyre. After 10 days, another armistice came into effect.

When members of the Stern Group assassinated Count Folke Bernadotte in Jerusalem, Ben-Gurion issued an angry order for the arrest of all Stern members and confiscation of their arms, but the murderers were never caught.

After the return of Dr. Weizmann as President and his appointment of Ben-Gurion as Prime Minister, there was a brief period during which it was uncertain which would become the strong man of Israel. If Dr. Weizmann had been younger and in good health it might have been a more serious conflict, but without protest he became nothing more than a dignified elder statesman, while young Ben-Gurion (now almost sixty-two) continued to be the irrepressible, effervescent, and indefatigable maker of decisions. At one time, in addition to being Prime Minister and Minister of Defense, he was the head of 82 government departments and bureaus. In the first election his Mapai party won 46 seats of the 120 in the Knesset, twice the number any other party gained, yet still far short of a majority. In no subsequent election did Mapai ever gain a full majority, so Ben-Gurion throughout his career as Prime Minister had to make one political deal after another, involving concessions to minority parties that held the votes Mapai needed to form a coalition.

It is impossible to tell the next chapter in the story of Ben-Gurion without recounting the history of Israel during the first 14 years of her re-creation, just as it is impossible to write

the history of Israel in that period without making the man with
the fringe of white hair the central character. This youngest
state in the world, surrounded by military dictatorships, pseudo-
republics, and feudal monarchies, became a democracy in fact
as well as theory, with bitter political debates on almost any
subject brought up in the Knesset. Yet during those 14 years,
the personality of Ben-Gurion dominated the political life of
Israel. Even when he tried to retire from public life and went
to live in a pioneer settlement deep in the Negev Desert, he was
frequently consulted and finally persuaded to return to office.

The hero of the 1956 Sinai campaign was Chief of Staff
Moshe Dayan, whose military brilliance had much to do with
the success of the operation. Yet Ben-Gurion was commander
in chief. He was the one who decided on the necessity for the
operation. It was at his bedside—he had a severe case of flu at the
time—that all the strategy conferences were held; it was from
his home that all the orders flowed. When President Eisenhower
decided to put pressure on Israel to withdraw to pre-Sinai
frontiers, he addressed his appeals personally to Ben-Gurion,
and it was Ben-Gurion who took the political risk of finally
acceding to the pressure and ordering the withdrawal. Again
it was Ben-Gurion personally who approved the plan to kidnap
Adolf Eichmann and bring him to Israel for public trial. He
knew that each one of these decisions involved a tremendous
risk for the nation he had helped revive. Would world opinion
approve? A country of a mere two million citizens, surrounded
by enemies who insisted a state of war still existed, and with an
economy not yet viable, was in a precarious position. Every decision he made was a calculated risk, and it was not always easy
to win the majority approval he needed in a democratically
organized society, but he never moved without such majority
approval. In most cases, even those who were loud in their
criticism of the risk he took eventually conceded, publicly or
privately, that the gamble had been justified.

The only attempt ever made on the life of Ben-Gurion was
not by a political opponent but by a young man adjudged
mentally disturbed since childhood. It happened in the Knesset
in 1957, on the first anniversary of the Sinai campaign. Moshe
Dueg, a young immigrant from Syria, threw a bomb from the

balcony that whizzed past the head of the Prime Minister and fell on the floor near the table at which the cabinet sat. The explosion caused serious injury to Foreign Minister Golda Meir and Minister of Transport Moshe Carmel. Many small pieces of steel lodged themselves in the right arm and right leg of Ben-Gurion. All three recovered, but the bombing had one tragic repercussion. Since the death of Katznelson and Golomb, the man closest to Ben-Gurion on the personal level had been his military secretary, Lt. Colonel Nehemiah Argov, 28 years his junior, a handsome, intelligent young man whom Ben-Gurion considered an example of the sort of new-type Jew a free Israel could produce. Argov's devotion to his chief was so great that nothing else in life was of importance to him. He seldom let the Prime Minister out of his sight, but on the day of the bombing he had gone to Tel Aviv on official business. He apparently brooded over his own responsibility for what had happened. Four days later, alone in his apartment, he committed suicide with his service revolver. He had written a long letter to his chief and one addressed to "My Dear Friends" in which he asked that no eulogies be uttered at his funeral, because "I am not worthy to be mourned."

Hadassah doctors decided that Ben-Gurion was in too great a state of shock from the bombing to be told at once of the suicide. But the day after Argov's funeral, Chief of Staff Dayan was chosen to break the news to him. As he grasped the import of Dayan's words Ben-Gurion turned pale, sat upright in bed, demanded that the news be repeated, then lay down and turned his face to the wall. As Dayan tiptoed away, a low sobbing began to fill the hospital room. Two weeks later, with one foot still in bandages, Ben-Gurion appeared in the Knesset and delivered a short tribute to his deceased friend in which he said: "Nehemiah like myself was not perfect. There are no perfect men in the world. Even the Bible does not describe any perfect man, without fault or failing. . . . But Nehemiah was endowed with a rare and precious gift, the gift of great love. It was a divine fire that burned in him without pause, and by this fire he was consumed, in love and in suffering. Permit me to stand here alone, silent, for a brief moment, in respect to his memory." It was one time that the public had a glimpse into the heart and soul of this very-alone man, who generally appeared to the world so self-contained and self-sufficient.

With the creation of Israel, Ben-Gurion became involved in several controversial issues with leaders of American Jewry. On the question of double allegiance, he made a statement on behalf of the Cabinet as early as 1950: "To my mind the position is perfectly clear. The Jews of the United States, as a community and as individuals, have only one political attachment and that is to the United States of America. They owe no political allegiance to Israel."

At the same time he prophesied that America would become socially and culturally over the next few decades a unitary nation, like the old-established European countries, and that American Jews would become amalgamated into this society. Aware that probably only a small number of American Jews would ever take up permanent residence in Israel, he often pointed out that they at least needed to keep alive a knowledge of Hebrew and should be able to read the Bible in its original language. He also urged American Jews to make frequent visits to Israel and to send their children there for as many years of study as possible. In his opinion, only those who become residents of Israel are entitled to be called Zionists.

As he became more and more a world figure Ben-Gurion grew in intellectual stature, yet lost none of his basic simplicity and ingenuousness. Statesmen and serious writers who came from abroad to visit him were rewarded with a combination of straight, clear talk devoid of cant or oratorical nonsense, a fresh philosophical viewpoint, and a profound historical perspective. For others his unconventionality was refreshing. He called shaking hands a barbaric habit, without utilitarian purpose now that men no longer needed to prove to each other that they were not carrying daggers. Birthdays also seemed foolish to him. "Why do you not celebrate some day on which *you* did something notable?" He dressed as he pleased, generally in loose-fitting trousers, comfortable shoes, and an open-necked shirt. Once he arrived at a Histadrut Congress wearing striped trousers, a cutaway coat, silk hat, and gloves. He had hurried to the meeting from a reception for a new ambassador. As he took his place on the podium and loosened his tie, he said, "Comrades, please excuse my working clothes." He owned no automobile and complained that the large American car the government supplied him was too pretentious. He would have traveled everywhere by jeep, except that his doctor forbade it. He disliked receptions and cocktail parties. Whenever his *chef de protocol* forced him to attend one he would search out some one person he felt might contribute to his store of knowledge or wisdom, and take him off in a corner, ignoring all the other guests.

He had no use for flashy minds, considering mere brilliance not enough. He was equally impatient with small intellects and small talk. He disliked people who sprinkled their talk with clichés, and careless thinkers who ended sentences with expressions such as, "and so forth." He once said that insincerity annoyed him as much as a mosquito buzzing in the ear. Stupidity made him spread his hands out in a hopeless gesture and shake his head in despair. He disliked mediocrity and was bored by people who were primarily interested in money, food, houses, and automobiles. His favorite characters, living and dead, were always zealots; men and women who were searching after something. Although not a sabra himself (a native-born Israeli), he was often called the spokesman for the sabras. Even in his seventies he was closer to the thinking of young Israelis than many half his age. More and more he became noted for humility without self-effacement, meekness without weakness, shyness without fear. He had little sense of humor—yet he was able to smile at jokes about himself, such as the one about the delegation that was supposed to have attended him just before independence to ask if he would permit himself to be named King of Israel. He refused, so the story went, because he could not tolerate the thought of being King David *II*. The vigor of his personality was such that no one would ever have said, after a public gathering, "I think Ben-Gurion was there." For some it was a sign of his greatness that they could feel his presence the moment he entered a room, without either seeing him or hearing his voice. He always tried to act as a balance wheel. When others rejoiced, he expressed caution; when others were depressed by the turn of events, he encouraged them with his optitmism. Although a Socialist all his life, he was not doctrinaire in his political beliefs; often without hesitation he dropped a party principle when it be proved to be impractical.

His lack of interest in personal publicity always caused problems for his aides. He once said, "I would rather read an article *by* me than one *about* me." One day a photographer for a French magazine, looking out his hotel window in Israel, happened to see a figure on the beach standing on his head. The photograph he took with a telescopic lens showed the man to be Ben-Gurion. This led to the disclosure that the Prime Minister had been taking yoga exercises from Moshe Feldenkrais, personal pupil of the judo expert Jigoro Kano and founder of the Jujitsu Club of France. Feldenkrais had intrigued Ben-Gurion with some of his theories. "We all walk like badly made puppets, instead of like the kings of creation," he said. He also told Ben-Gurion, "The man we call a genius uses only five per cent of the human being's mental capacity." After five years of Feldenkrais' lessons, two or three times a week, Ben-Gurion was free of all physical troubles, was taking a brisk three- to five-mile walk a day, was standing on his head for as much as 20 minutes at a time, and in the opinion of his close associates was younger at seventy-six than he had been at sixty-six or perhaps even at fifty-six.

In his dealings with world-important people, Ben-Gurion's knowledge of the Bible kept him from ever suffering feelings of inferiority. He had a robust belief that Israel is something more than just a small group of people Hitler missed, trying to make a life for themselves on a desolate desert. His thinking was always ruled by the belief that his people—the Jews—have a historical destiny. For him the Bible was not only Israel's history book, but her Encyclopaedia Britannica, Baedaker's Guide, Blackstone's Commentaries, Bartlett's Familiar Quotations, the World Almanac, and the genealogy of every Jew in the world. For him the people of the Bible were more alive than some of his neighbors. He felt on more intimate terms with Joshua and Isaiah than with some of his cabinet members. One day a member of his own party came from Ben-Gurion's office shaking his head and saying, "I speak to him of yesterday and he talks about three thousand years ago. I speak of tomorrow and he discusses two thousand years from now. It's like trying to talk about the current meat shortage with Moses, or with some man who won't be born for another few thousand years." Some of his associates felt that he not only knew the Bible but was a figure directly out of it. His sense of the past was emotional as well as intellectual, patriotic as well as practical. He never ceased marveling that some of the cedars of Lebanon are as much as 5,000 years old, and several times said that "when peace comes" he would like somehow to obtain from Lebanon one of the ancient trees to plant somewhere in Israel.

Although a profound student of the Bible, he was not religious in the conventional sense, observing few of the Orthodox Jewish customs. He made a deep study of other religions, especially Buddhism. While a guest of Premier U Nu of Burma in 1961, he spent eight days in private retreat, studying and reflecting on Buddhism. He proved his intellectual as well as his physical courage by making many self-conducted excursions into remote fields of thought.

He was a three-dimensional man, living simultaneously in the past, the present, and the future. As an intellectual he had an almost compulsive instinct to escape into action, yet as a man of action he was always trying to escape into provinces of the spirit. He had a passionate belief in the limitless potentialities of man, and a sense of frantic urgency. In talking and writing of the future, he looked hundreds of years ahead and saw Asia and Africa as the new, dynamic centers of world civilization.

From Plato he learned that a philosopher is "a man perfect in wisdom, understanding, and knowledge, with the virtues of justice, truth, and humility, the love of good, the avoidance of power." In the seventh decade of his life he set out to become, as nearly as he would be able in the time left to him, a philosopher in the Platonic sense.

He was never lacking in enemies. At various times they included the British, the Arabs, vacillating Big Power politicians, anti-Zionists, assimilationists, skeptics, fainthearted friends, the Revisionists, the Communists, potential or actual Fascists, those who opposed a planned economy, those who fought him bitterly over his efforts to establish normal economic relations with Germany, those who wanted to make Israel a theocracy, those who were nettled by his criticism of the World Zionist Organization, those who misunderstood his desire to have some young American Jews settle in Israel, fanatics of various complexions, materialists, exploiters, and politicians who would have liked to be Prime Minister themselves.

One of his weaknesses as a government leader was his lack of diplomatic sense. Several times, with a single overly frank sentence, he upset plans that his own Foreign Office had been working on for months. He was also criticized at times for "playing politics," having a "messianic complex," and for giving in to pressure from Washington at critical moments in Israel's history.

One of his severest critics in the Knesset, after listing what he considered Ben-Gurion's gravest blunders, said, "But after all, only a great man can make great mistakes!"

Despite what his enemies at home and abroad might think, David Ben-Gurion, while still in office and while still a controversial political figure, had already won his place in the annals of his people. Few could doubt that future generations would call him one of the great Jews of all time, a synthesized product of three thousand years of history, perfectly in rhythm with the surging movements of his own time, a molder of events: a doer as well as a dreamer.

Chapter 11

Instead of being disarmed,
I'll do the disarming!

—RACHEL ZELTZER

RACHEL WAS KILLED as Israel was being born.
The Ministry of Defense has never officially determined who was the first Jewish soldier to die—in the eighteen centuries since the collapse of the Bar-Kochba Revolt—fighting on Israeli soil in defense of a recognized Israeli State. But the name of Rachel Zeltzer is on an official list as one of the first.

On May 14, 1948, as David Ben-Gurion in Tel Aviv was preparing to read the proclamation that would re-create the Jewish State, up in Jerusalem twenty young men and girls of the underground army called *Lechi* (the Stern Group) were preparing to storm an Arab-held monastery on the border between the Old City and the New. If they succeeded they intended to go on and try to breach the Jaffa Gate and thus open a way for the relief of the 1,700 Jews trapped inside the walled city. It was a reckless, almost suicidal venture, but the twenty were young and each had some special personal reason for gripping a gun so tightly and facing almost certain death so bravely.

Rachel's reason is a long story.

She was born on a farm in Bessarabia close to the frontier of Old Rumania, the daughter of a Russian refugee father and a Bessarabian mother. (She once described her mother to a friend

226

as "the most beautiful woman I ever saw in my life.") Shortly after Rachel's birth, Mrs. Ada Zeltzer left the farm with the child and moved to the capital of Bukovina, called Cernauți, Czernowitz, Tchernowitz, or Chernovtsy, depending on what language was being spoken. (Between the two World Wars, Bessarabia and Bukovina were both part of Rumania.) The mother came from a wealthy banking family and had studied both chemistry and bacteriology at the universities of Kiev and Odessa. She was also an expert weaver and knitter. She brought up Rachel in an atmosphere of culture and close contact with the arts, and devoted years of her life to seeing that her only child had the finest education possible in that part of the world.

Rumania in the thirties was being swept by a combination of Nazi poison and endemic Fascism. Rachel often came home from school crying because she had been the victim of some cruel piece of anti-Jewish discrimination.

In 1940, the Russians demanded both Bessarabia and Bukovina, and Rumania capitulated without resistance. A happier period began, now, for the Zeltzers. Anti-Semitism disappeared from Rachel's school and the Russians gave her mother an important position in a chemical laboratory. When Hitler attacked Russia, Ada Zeltzer, acting on a premonition, converted everything she owned into gold and turned it over to the local Jewish committee, with instructions that if anything happened to her, some way should be found to ship her daughter to Palestine, where she had a sister, Tcharna Rayss, who had gone there in 1934 and was a lecturer in botany at Hebrew University.

When the Nazis swept into Chernowitz, mother and daughter were at first merely herded into a ghetto, where, over and over again, Ada Zeltzer repeated to Rachel, and made Rachel repeat back to her, just what she was to do if "they take me away." After some months the Germans accused the mother of having aided the Russians and shipped her to a concentration camp. Thereupon the local committee tried to carry out the instructions about the child.

Rachel was fifteen when she began the longest and most unpleasant journey of her life. On September 15, 1942, with 106 other Jews she left Chernowitz by train. They were joined by 13 people from Bucharest, making 120 in all. Many were small children. It took them two days and two nights to reach the Rumanian port of Braila on the Danube River. There each was required to turn over 440,000 Rumanian lei (more than a thousand dollars) to a shipping firm, Turism-Roumania Company. For this total of over $120,000 they were given the use of a small boat, the *Viturol,* equipped with a motor and a sail. It had been built to carry a maximum of 50 passengers. By squeezing, jamming and shoving, the 120 got aboard. They also had to pay two and a half million lei (about $8,000) to obtain a permit to leave Rumania.

The *Viturol* started down the Danube toward the Black Sea on September 18, but almost immediately water started seeping through cracks and soon began flooding the engine room. The younger and stronger of the passengers, Rachel among them, took turns at the pumps. Finally they reached Sulina, the last river port before the open sea. One of their leaders went in to town and telegraphed the company in Bucharest demanding that the boat be put in seaworthy condition. For eight days they waited. With what money they had left they bought another pump and worked at trying to repair their damaged motor. Finally a representative of the shipping company arrived and by bribing port authorities obtained a certificate saying the boat was seaworthy. There was nothing to do now but attempt the voyage.

For two days they sailed at four knots. Although Rachel was only a child, she was so calm and so bright-minded that she was given many supervisory tasks. On the night of the third day the motor stopped, a high storm began to toss the ship, and heavy waves swept over the deck. Rachel spent the night trying to calm adults and children alike.

When morning came they found themselves within a quarter of a mile of some shoreland, so they dropped anchor. They had no idea whether they were off Bulgaria, occupied by the Nazis, or neutral Turkey. Rachel was the one who first spotted soldiers on the shore. Twenty of the refugees swam in, found that the soldiers were Turkish, obtained permission for all of them to land, and swam back with the good news. Then with ropes they towed the boat in as close to shore as possible. All the passengers were taken off safely, but before they could save any of their luggage the *Viturol* broke up in front of their eyes and sank. Rachel not only lost her luggage but she was in an especially unhappy plight because all she had on when she was forced to abandon ship was a thin pair of pajamas. But she consoled herself with the thought that she had not lost her watch. Inside the back was a picture of her mother, who, she presumed, by now was dead.

As soon as the sun set it began to rain. The Turkish soldiers had three tents, which they turned over to the refugees—three tents for 120 hungry, thirsty, frightened victims of shipwreck! The Turks were also generous in sharing their food, but it was almost nothing divided in 120 parts, so the refugees took turns watching for something edible to be washed ashore from the ship.

Two days later orders came for their transfer to a Turkish village. A month after that they were sent by train to Istanbul. There the majority was put on a ship for Cyprus, where they would have to spend the rest of the war in a British transit camp.

Meanwhile, back in Jerusalem Rachel's aunt, informed by Jewish authorities of what had happened, appealed to her friend Henrietta Szold and through Youth Aliyah obtained permission for the child to be admitted to Palestine.

Rachel arrived in Jerusalem one pitch-black night shortly before Chanukah. She knew no Hebrew but she spoke Russian, French, German and English, most of them fluently. In a few weeks in a Jewish school she learned enough Hebrew to pass examinations admitting her to secondary school. In 1945 she entered Hebrew University, after having completed four years of secondary school in two. One happy day that year Rachel's aunt received a letter from Chernowitz that her sister was free now and would try to make her way to Palestine. It took her many months, but finally she arrived. Daughter and sister both had difficulty recognizing her. There was only a trace left of the great beauty she had had when they last saw her. She was old now, and without spirit.

Ada Zeltzer found a small apartment for herself and her daughter and in it set up a loom, supporting the small family by selling her weaving to WIZO (Women's International Zionist Organization) shops. Gradually her interest in life began to re-

vive, thanks principally to the ever-growing beauty and brilliance of Rachel, whom she called "Bird of My Soul." The girl
was majoring in bacteriology, but by coincidence her botany
instructor was her own aunt, who never tired of telling what a
bright future the girl had, with such a mind.

Then came 1947, the partition vote in the United Nations,
and the Arab attacks on Jewish settlements all over Palestine.
Most students at the university volunteered for service in one or
another of the Jewish underground armies. Rachel and many of
her classmates in the College of Natural Sciences went into
Haganah. At first she was given routine field duties in the Jerusalem area, but as the Arab attacks grew in violence and the Jewish death toll mounted, she begged to be sent into action. On
December 25, 1947, she and 7 other girls and 49 men, all science
students, were sent as reinforcements to Kfar Etzion. They went
with a convoy of trucks and passenger cars taking food, fuel,
barbed wire and other supplies to the settlement.

Kfar Etzion was less than ten miles south of Jerusalem, just
off the main road to Hebron, City of the Patriarchs. This is the
hilly area Abraham, Isaac and Jacob once roamed with their
flocks, and which historians had long called the cradle of the
Hebrew nation. From her study of the Bible, Rachel knew that
in this very region the Maccabees had waged their desperate
revolt against the enemies of the Jews. For her the hills seemed
to be alive with history. But they were also inhabited, now, by
85,000 Arabs, mostly Moslems. The Arabs were attempting to
isolate Kfar Etzion and three smaller settlements, which together were called the Etzion Bloc, total population, 450, including women and children; total area, nine square miles.

The winter had already set in. From now on the area would
be plagued by fierce storms, heavy mists, and occasional snow.

Just two weeks before Rachel and her classmates arrived, a
convoy from Jerusalem bringing food and water to the four villages had been waylaid and ten of the drivers killed. Now there
were indications that the Arabs were planning an all-out attack
aimed at wiping out the entire bloc.

One of Rachel's first tasks was to help prepare the more than
200 women and children in the four villages for evacuation. On
January 7, more reinforcements came—all university students,

this time from the College of the Humanities—and the trucks that had brought them were used to take back to Jerusalem the women and children.

There was more room now at Kfar Etzion, but the settlers missed the laughter of their children. They spoke often of the "aching void."

The entire bloc began preparing for the attack they were certain would come soon. The students, girls as well as men, stood eight hours of guard duty in isolated posts on the perimeter of the bloc, then underwent four more hours of severe training. It was understood that from now on they would all sleep in their clothes, with their weapons always close at hand. A rigid blackout was imposed. Fuel for the electric generator was running low and had to be conserved for use in supplying current for the searchlights that helped prevent surprise attacks at night. Because the cisterns were running dry, no one was permitted to take more than one shower a week.

On the night of January 13, patrols reported that the road was completely blocked and the hills were filling up with concentrations of Arabs.

The attack on the Etzion villages began at dawn the next day. The defenders were aware that they were now completely isolated. Worse, there was such a scarcity of guns and ammunition that the men had to take turns with the rifles and shoot only when the attackers came dangerously close. Although Rachel was eager to take an active part in the battle, she was told that as long as there were so few rifles they had better be used by those with more experience. To a fellow student she said, "Well, at least I can serve as a sack of sand and maybe stop a few bullets!" The attack lasted most of the day. By the time the shooting died down, after dark, the bloc counted three of its men dead, many wounded. Kfar Etzion had a doctor, but because of inadequate equipment he was unable to operate even on those most gravely wounded. Rachel helped dress some of the wounds. It was her first experience with death and intense suffering. Instead of making her afraid, it stirred a deep anger—anger that people defending what was their own should have the life shot out of them this way, for no logical reason. It was estimated that more than a thousand Arabs had taken part in the attack. If they had not been so poorly organized and so ill equipped they could easily have overrun the bloc and massacred every one of the defenders.

The next day the Jerusalem radio was full of the Etzion victory. Along with congratulations came news that reinforcements were on the way: two squads of the field force, two of Palmach, Haganah's elite striking unit. They were coming well armed with Bren guns, grenades, rifles, and submachine guns. They were bringing 3,000 rounds of rifle ammunition for the bloc. Each man was carrying a heavy pack containing first-aid equipment, plasma, arms, and ammunition. On their first start the 35 men were picked out by Arab searchlights and had to return to Jerusalem. They set out again at 5 P.M. Friday. When they had not arrived at Kfar Etzion by midday Saturday, scouting parties went out looking for them. Saturday night, Jerusalem radio reported that the bodies of all 35 had been found by the British just three miles from the bloc. They had fought off seven waves of Arab attackers until their ammunition ran out. In death the hand of one of the 35 still clutched a rock.

The 35 bodies were brought in to Kfar Etzion on British half-tracks. As the British started to remove the canvas tarpaulins that covered each body, the girl students were told to go indoors. Rachel refused. Many of the 35 had been close personal friends of hers at the university. She had studied with them, sung pioneer songs with them, danced the hora with them, knew most of them by their first names. Among them were some of the most brilliant students in the university. They were her friends. Why must she go indoors? There was some whispering between the British soldiers and the bloc commander, who finally turned to Rachel and said, "Go indoors!" Later she learned why. One of the men told her that all the bodies had been mutilated. The men of the bloc wrapped each corpse in a white sheet. Then candles were lit and all night long the settlers took turns reciting Psalms over the 35.

The next day the British agreed to escort the families of the victims from Jerusalem to Kfar Etzion for the funeral. While the convoy was on the way, Rachel and the others dug a long mass grave. During the service, everyone strained to keep emotions under control. One of the dead was Danny Mass, who for months had been commander of the bloc until receiving a more important assignment in Jerusalem. Because there were not enough stretchers to carry the dead in the funeral procession, four were dropped from a low-flying plane. On the way through a forest of young pines to the mass grave each body was accompanied by friends and relatives. One woman with heroic self-control walked beside the stretcher of her son, supporting his head in her hands.

After the people from Jerusalem left, Rachel joined with the other students in filling in the grave.

Now the siege grew more intensive. Kfar Etzion was cut off so completely from Jerusalem that all food and fuel had to be dropped from planes. The defenders spent all their time when not on guard duty building stronger fortifications, manufacturing hand grenades, and planting bombs in the ground. But all the time, Rachel was obsessed by what had happened to the 35. They had been her friends. It was worse at night, when she would try to sleep. There was a phonograph but no one played anything but classical music any more. The older men gave lectures almost every night on serious subjects. Several times orders came from Jerusalem that the bloc must be held "at all costs." Everyone knew what that meant.

In February they built an airstrip so that small planes could land and take off. They celebrated when the first Auster used the strip, but a few days later one of the girl students, a close friend of Rachel's, went out onto the strip to speak to a pilot and was struck in the head by the whirling propeller. In one hour she was dead. That same day two Palmach men were making anti-vehicle mines in the carpenter shop when suddenly there was a fierce explosion. Out of the ruins of the building rescuers brought two bodies, one dead, one severely burned.

After a full month had gone by without a single convoy getting through to the bloc, it was decided late in March to try to send through the largest convoy ever assembled; 33 trucks carrying 120 tons of supplies; four armored buses filled with field troops; and 14 armored cars. The convoy would be escorted by more than a hundred Palmach soldiers, with an Auster flying overhead. The convoy would bring a vast quantity of arms and four radio transmitters. Preceding all the vehicles would be a roadblock buster to clear the way.

Despite elaborate preparations for a battle, not a single shot was fired at the convoy along the way. When the last vehicle entered Kfar Etzion, a shout of joy went up and a celebration began.

But it was a sad day for Rachel. All the students had been ordered back to Jerusalem. They were to travel in three of the armored cars. As the convoy was about to get underway the radio reported that the Supreme Arab Command had ordered the convoy destroyed on its way back. The Auster pilot carried out a reconnaissance and reported that six roadblocks had been put in place near Solomon's Pools and that Arab villagers by the hundreds were pouring out of the hills.

Rachel remembered every moment of what happened after they got started. The convoy left Kfar Etzion just before noon; first the scout car, then the roadblock buster, followed by armored cars with the students. The rear was brought up by a truck loaded with the wreckage of a Haganah plane that had crashed a few days earlier on the airstrip.

Four miles along the way they encountered their first roadblock. They forced their way through without much difficulty. Then five more. Arab snipers were aiming at the tires. One truck lost three of its four tires, but kept going on the steel rims. Near Solomon's Pools they encountered a seventh block made of immense boulders. As they were being removed by the crane, the roadblock buster toppled over onto its side in the ditch. This was a signal for an Arab mob to come from hiding and make an attack, screaming as they raced down the hills toward the road. Many tires were punctured by the hail of bullets and some of the trucks overturned.

The young convoy commander gave an order for all cars to turn around and return to Kfar Etzion. Many drivers were unable to obey because their vehicles were out of commission. Others, because the road was so cluttered with overturned trucks, were trapped where they were. The only vehicles able to be extricated were the command car, five armored cars, and five trucks, including the one carrying the plane.

The second in command decided that those who remained should take up a defensive position in an abandoned Arab building near the road, marked on his map as *Nebi Daniel* (the Prophet Daniel). The gate to the property was blown open and the men and girls crawled toward the house under murderous Arab fire. Rachel received a minor wound but kept going, dragging a Sten gun with her. She and about half the men and girls reached the house at 4 P.M. The armored cars were still cruising up and down the road, picking up stranded drivers.

One room of the house was converted into a first-aid station and there Rachel helped bind the wounds of at least a dozen men. Someone had dragged a radio transmitter into the house and over it an operator began sending an SOS. A survey of their armament showed that they had nine medium and light machine guns, one two-inch mortar, and a considerable number of rifles and Sten guns.

Nebi Daniel was a well-built Arab house with thick walls. A staircase led to an attic from which it was possible to get onto a flat roof. There some of the men established gun positions. The Arabs, obviously preparing for a siege of Nebi Daniel, had taken up positions on a ridge to the south and were setting up machine-gun posts in a building less than 200 yards away.

In answer to the SOS, Jerusalem headquarters said an appeal had been made to the highest British authorities. A short time later another message said the British had refused to intervene.

Haganah, Jerusalem, to Nebi Daniel: Burn any vehicles you cannot save and try to get back to Kfar Etzion.

Nebi Daniel to Jerusalem: Please send planes to cover the withdrawal.

Convoy Commander, Kfar Etzion, to Acting Commander, Nebi Daniel: Prepare to meet a night assault.

Rachel and her companions were worried most about the men in the overturned roadblock buster. Frequent attempts were made to rescue the crew trapped inside, but every vehicle that approached it was driven off by heavy fire.

Shortly after dark there was a thunderous explosion and then the road was lit up by the light of ugly red and yellow flames. An Arab had thrown a Molotov cocktail at the roadblock buster. After the explosion, fuel from the tanks began to burn. The entire crew was trapped inside except for three men who made a dash for it. When they reached Nebi Daniel they reported that the Palmachnik in charge, a man named Zerubavel, had ordered them to try to escape but had refused to leave himself, saying he couldn't abandon the wounded members of his crew.

As night set in, the Nebi Daniel situation grew desperate. The Arabs had closed in from all sides to within 200 yards of the house. It was impossible to carry out the order for withdrawal because of the great number of wounded who would have to be abandoned. Of the 180 in the building now, half were without arms. They sat on the dirt floor, dazed, hungry, tired, sure of death, but without any feeling of fear or regret. They felt they were in a situation similar to that of the 35.

Haganah, Jerusalem, to Nebi Daniel: Fortify your position, save your ammunition, and hold out until morning. Reinforcements cannot be sent yet, because the road from Jerusalem is so heavily mined.

One of Rachel's jobs during the night was to haul large stones up to the roof for use in building gun emplacements. Frequently Palmachniks risked death to go back to the main road to collect whatever had been left in the trucks. One man, although under heavy fire, disconnected two batteries to use in operating the radio transmitter. About midnight the Arabs started setting fire to the overturned vehicles. Shortly before 1 A.M. the besiegers came within 200 feet of Nebi Daniel and called out in Arabic, Hebrew and English for a surrender. Late in the night two Austers dropped ammunition and food, but the Arabs kept up such a heavy fire it was impossible to retrieve the bundles. In Jerusalem, although it was now Shabbat, the Chief Rabbi made a series of telephone calls—to the International Red Cross, to British military authorities, then to the High Commissioner. Finally the British agreed to go to the rescue of the Nebi Daniel garrison, but only if all arms were surrendered.

At 6:30 A.M. Jerusalem said a detachment of British troops was on its way. At 7 A.M. the Nebi Daniel radio began to fade because of battery trouble. At 7:30 A.M. the Arabs made an attack in force. By 8 A.M. the number of seriously wounded had reached 30. At 10 A.M. the Arabs on the north began advancing under cover of a smoke screen. At this moment one of Rachel's best friends, a science student, was hit by a bullet that came through a wooden door. He was dead by the time the girls reached him. The heat inside the building was now so intense that many of the men fainted. The wounded now numbered forty.

Nebi Daniel to Jerusalem: What's holding up the British?

Jerusalem to Nebi Daniel: The Arabs refuse to agree to an evacuation.

Finally at 2:20 P.M. a compromise was agreed on: three Arab leaders would accompany the British to make certain the British completely disarmed those in Nebi Daniel. While 14 British half-tracks were on their way, those in Nebi Daniel began destroying their arms. Machine guns were taken apart and vital pieces thrown down a well. The radio transmitter was smashed beyond repair.

At 4:45 P.M. the British arrived and the Arabs swarmed in from all sides, demanding the right to search for concealed weapons. The British ordered them away and did the searching themselves. Because there was such a scarcity of stretchers, the 13 dead defenders were rolled off their stretchers onto the ground so that the wounded could be transported.

Rachel and the other defenders of Nebi Daniel arrived in Jerusalem humiliated at having been disarmed in sight of the jeering Arab mob and bitter over the loss of so many of their comrades.

The wounded were taken to Hadassah Clinic, where doctors and nurses had been waiting up for them all night.

As Rachel left the half-track in which she had been riding, a Palmanchnick whispered a question to her.

Her face was grimy with a mixture of dirt and sweat, and her eyes were heavy from lack of sleep, but she smiled as she answered, "Yes, I've got a Sten gun under my clothes. They didn't disarm me, and they never will!"

Ada Zeltzer had been almost insane with worry. When she heard the knock she threw open the door of the apartment and flung her arms around her daughter, sobbing hysterically.

After food, a bath and a long sleep, Rachel told her mother she had a matter of business to attend to. At Haganah headquarters she said she wanted an immediate assignment to an action station. The commander argued with her. She'd had her share of action for a while. He'd find a quiet job for her. Her black eyes burned with indignation.

"What do you mean, a quiet job?"

The commander hesitated. "Haganah has decided that from now on no girls will be permitted to take part in actual combat."

"Then I resign from Haganah!" Rachel snapped back. Turning on her heel, she left the room.

Rachel was young and by nature a happy person, with an intense love of life. Whatever the experience, she always seemed to contribute to it more than anyone else, and to draw from it a greater feeling of joy than the other participants. Those who knew her remarked often about her great generosity. Her desire, now, to take an active part in the fight for the preservation of the state that was about to be proclaimed was not based on either hatred or a desire for revenge. Both those emotions were foreign to her character. She had never hated Arabs and still didn't, despite what had happened to the 35. What really motivated her was an overpowering urge to sacrifice everything she had to a cause she was sure was a just and noble one. She saw her side as the attacked rather than the attacker; as always outnumbered; as a modern David fighting a most powerful Goliath. She wanted to be in the center of action so she could give completely of herself. She stood ready to give even life, which she dearly loved, if fate decided it that way.

All this Rachel tried to explain when she applied that day for membership in Lechi, an offshoot of Irgun and the smallest of the underground forces. She told them why she had left Haganah and said she would join Lechi only if they gave her a battle post. As a clinching argument, she said, "Besides, I have my own gun!"

On the evening of May 13, over a walkie-talkie Rachel listened to the dying gasp of the Etzion Bloc. For two days and two nights she and many others in Jerusalem had been following the sufferings of the Etzion defenders as they tried to fight off a siege by the British-led, British-trained, British-equipped Arab Legion. One by one the villages of the bloc were overrun. At noon on May 12, Kfar Etzion reported 100 dead already. Artillery and mortar shells were tearing the fortifications to ribbons. As swarms of heavily-armed Arabs poured into the ruins of the village, 15 Haganah men came out with their hands above their heads. After disarming them, an Arab Legion officer lined them up so he could photograph them, in the humiliation of surrender. Just then an Arab with a submachine gun stepped forward and mowed down all 15. The last broadcast Rachel heard from Kfar Etzion was a very tired voice saying, "This is the end of the Etzion Bloc. Tonight we shall be no more." Only three men and a girl succeeded in getting out of Kfar Etzion alive.

From across the wall in the Old City, Rachel could hear church bells ringing to announce the glad news that Kfar Etzion had fallen. She gripped her Sten gun until her knuckles showed white.

Notre Dame de France was a monastery of the Assumptionist Fathers; a U-shaped, four-story stone building not far from Jaffa Gate, with its back directly up against the wall of the Old City. For nine years the monastery had been used by the British as a barracks for H. M. Forces, Jerusalem. But suddenly on May 14, 1948, they abandoned the building without turning it back, formally or informally, to its lawful owners, the French Church. Secretly informed in advance of the evacuation, more than 100 Arab soldiers swarmed in and took possession. With them they brought a sizable arsenal of rifles, machine guns and mortars, which they set up in the monastery, over the vehement protest of Abbé Pasquale St. Jean.

This was when Rachel and her 19 Lechi colleagues were ordered into action. It was just the sort of an engagement she wanted. Instead of bandaging wounds, she would be inflicting them. Instead of being disarmed, she would do the disarming. These things she said to some of her companions as they prepared for the assault on Notre Dame de France: 20 youngsters against at least a hundred trained, heavily armed Arab soldiers.

Although four of them were killed and most of the others received at least minor wounds, they took Notre Dame de France. Weeks later, Abbé Pasquale St. Jean described the attack to a group of visiting journalists. "They were just boys and girls," she said in wonderment. But they fought with such wild zeal that the Arabs fled, leaving many of their weapons behind.

Then Rachel and two of the Lechi men decided to see if Jaffa Gate could be breached. They got as far as the Hotel Fast, an Arab-German establishment. Rachel had a flag in her pocket. When they found that the hotel was deserted, she decided to hoist the blue and white Israeli flag to the top of the hotel flagpole. Just then there was the metalic rattle of gunfire and Rachel fell. When her two companions picked her up she was already dead.

For weeks after the funeral Ada Zeltzer seldom slept or ate. Finally her sister found a job for her in a military hospital, helping to take care of the wounded sons and daughters of other women. She worked long hours without complaint, caring for her patients with gentle devotion. But she never reconciled herself to what had happened.

One hundred days after the death of Rachel, Ada Zeltzer took poison. She was convinced that life, for her, no longer had any meaning.

Haganah, announcing her passing, called her "the mother of the sick and the wounded."

After the War of Independence, the remains of both Rachel and Ada were transferred to Mount Herzl, the resting place of distinguished Jews who had come from everywhere to help remake Israel.

Chapter 12

This is my land,
Where I belong!

—ZIVIA HABSHUSH

ZIVIA HABSHUSH and Israel are exactly the same age. They were both born between 4 and 5 P.M. on May 14, 1948. As David Ben-Gurion was reading the proclamation in the museum in Tel Aviv, a beautiful sixteen-year-old girl who had been a bride just nine months, was giving birth to her first child in San'a, capital city of the Mutawekelite Kingdom of Yemen, more than a thousand miles from Tel Aviv by plane, nearly two thousand by camel route.

It would take endless investigation and mathematical calculation in Israel and the hundred or more countries of the Dispersion to determine who was the first Jewish child born after the moment of Israel's rebirth, but Mr. and Mrs. Joseph Habshush like to think that Zivia was the one. They may be right. But what is beyond all denial is that Zivia is a perfect representative of the million Jews who during the first 10 years of the State took part in the greatest ingathering in Hebrew history. She is therefore the ideal subject for the final chapter of a book called *They Came From Everywhere.*

No one knows for certain, but the Yemenites themselves have always believed that their ancestors fled from Jerusalem after the destruction of Solomon's Temple. One tale is that 75,000 Jewish merchants, political leaders and military men, along

241

with their wives and children, crossed the Jordan and gradually worked their way through the hills, the valleys and the deserts of Arabia until they came to Yemen, and there finally settled down.

When Cyrus, King of Persia, sent word to them through Ezra the Scribe to come home and help rebuild the Temple, they refused, and to show how they felt about Ezra, they decreed that no child of theirs could ever again bear his name. After this they prospered and there was even a short period when a Jew was the King of Yemen. But in the seventh century, Moslem invaders swept in, the Jewish tribes were defeated in a great battle at Wa'th, and Yemen before long became a place of isolation and barbarism. The Jews, now second-class citizens, were persecuted, degraded and forced to dwell in a ghetto. Many believed that their adversity was punishment for not heeding the call of Ezra. In their misery their religion sustained them. They lived by the Book, which they could read in both Hebrew and Aramaic. They were lost to the world, but they kept in close communication with their God. In the Middle Ages there were Yemenite writers who composed scholarly commentaries on the Bible.

In the nineteenth century the spell of isolation was broken when a rabbi from Jerusalem went to Yemen searching for traces of the Lost Tribes. He found the Yemenite Jews oppressed by "a people which declares itself holy and pious, but which is very brutal, barbarous and hard-hearted." He found that the Jews of Yemen were forbidden to ride camels or horses and had to dismount from their donkeys if a Moslem passed; that the men could neither carry guns and daggers nor wear colored robes; that most were poor because of the protection money they had to pay Arab officials, and many were undernourished. Every orphan became the property of the state and was forced to convert to Islam. To prevent this, parents often married off their children when they became twelve or thirteen, so that if they became orphans they could pose as the heads of families. But despite all this they were clean, industrious and devout, and they had kept alive an almost mystic love of beauty, which showed in the women's needlework, in the filigree jewelry the men made, and in their poetry, their songs, and their dances.

Then in 1906, Imam Y'ahya came to power and issued a proclamation requiring every Jew to pay one-fifth of the value of all his property in taxes each year, and forbidding Jews to build houses higher than the houses of Moslems, so they could never "look down" on their neighbors. Also they must never annoy a Moslem on religious matters, display their own holy books outside the synagogues, raise their voices in prayer, or sound ram's horns. And henceforth they must always ride side-saddle.

Still the Jews of Yemen clung on, and still they found solace in religion and intellectual pursuits. Most of their Arab neighbors were illiterate, but the Jews, although they had few books, insisted that their own young learn to read and write. If a school was too poor to have more than one book, the teacher would sit in a semicircle, holding the book so everyone could see it. Thus, many Yemenite children learned to read sideways or upside down. To make new books they used sheepskins for paper, fruit juice for ink, and sharp-pointed pieces of wood as pens. Each square Hebrew letter was painstakingly drawn, as if it were an original painting.

Late in the nineteenth century these ancient Jews began to trickle out of Yemen, sometimes taking a whole year to reach Palestine. By the start of World War II, 36,000, more than a third the Yemenite Jewish population, had found their way to Palestine. They would go south, to the British-held port of Aden, and there wait for a ship to take them north again, through the Red Sea and the Suez Canal, to the land whence their ancestors had fled. In the early forties, the British refused to permit any more to leave for Palestine. But when those who had remained behind in Yemen heard in 1948 of the re-creation of Israel, they flooded into Aden. This time they were not going to be guilty of the mistake they had made when Ezra told them to come. Some arrived in Aden ill, even dying. Many had been robbed along the way of what few possessions they had been permitted to take, but still they clung fiercely to their precious religious scrolls which by stealth and bribery they had managed to retain. The British housed this stream of wandering Jews in an abandoned military camp, and the Joint Distribution Committee of American Jews cared for them while Operation Magic Carpet was being planned—the airborne evacuation of the Yemenites at Aden by a fleet of chartered American Skymasters.

Then suddenly the Imam of Yemen announced that any Jews who wished to could leave the country legally for Aden. The entire remaining Jewish population packed up and started south. Magic Carpet became a major operation in transmigration. Five or six planeloads left Aden every day on the eight-hour, nonstop flight. The planes could take 140 Yemenites at a time, because the average weight of an adult was only 86 pounds. Many had never seen a plane before, but they had no fear, for they knew the Book almost by heart and remembered the passage in Exodus that promised they would be brought to Israel on "eagles' wings"—and 50,000 of them were!

That brings the story back to Zivia—lovely, delicately chiseled, olive-skinned, finely featured Zivia, who would be a delight to paint or perfect as a model for a sculptor—Zivia, with the grace of a ballet dancer and the soft voice of a spring breeze blowing through pine trees—Zivia, who has the look of a cornered fawn in her immense brown eyes when something frightens her, but who smiles with heart-tearing sweetness when she is unafraid.

Her father, Joseph Habshush, was a cobbler in Yemen; his father before him a silversmith. As far as he knows, the family has been in San'a since they arrived from ancient Israel in King Solomon's day. He strokes his short black beard as he tells how Zivia was a year and a half old and still the only child when they were taken by truck from San'a to Aden, and then by plane to Israel. He had no fear on the plane, and neither did his wife, Naami. Zivia slept most of the way.

At first they were given a one-room house on the outskirts of Jerusalem, near where the fine new buildings of Hebrew University now stand, and an attempt was made to train him as a farmer. This phase of his new life he would rather not discuss. Farming is no occupation for a man who has been a cobbler, the son of a silversmith. Now he is a factory worker in Tel Aviv and that is more to his liking. Although so short a time ago he was living in what is generally considered the most primititve spot on earth, he is now engaged in making plastic parts for electric refrigerators. In his few years in the factory he has worked up to assistant foreman.

The new Habshush home is in a garden suburb of Tel Aviv, Kiryat Uno. The house is surrounded by greenery: trees, shrubs, a flower garden. There is a small veranda, a kitchen with a gas stove, a bathroom with a flush toilet and a shower, two bedrooms, and a living room that is also used for sleeping. There are electric lights in all the rooms. (In Yemen they had only kerosene lamps.) The house is substantially built, cool in summer, warm in winter.

Naami Habshush has given birth to nine other children in the last 12 years and is pregnant now with her eleventh. In Yemen, the infantile mortality rate was so great that eight of each ten children in the average family died at a young age. In Israel, Naami Habshush has not lost a child. In Yemen there were few educational opportunities for boys, none for girls. In Israel, a majority of the Habshush children are girls and six of them are already in school.

Of course it has taken a great deal of readjustment, the handsome young husband explains. In Yemen if you wanted something you raised it or you made it yourself. You raised wheat, ground your own flour, and made your own shoes from leather you had tanned yourself, after raising the animals that provided the hides. Here in Israel you learned to operate a machine in a factory, and at the end of the week they gave you money with which you bought everything you needed. It took a great deal of readjustment. Maybe life was better this way, because everything was produced by experts. Maybe not. Surely the food was better. Also, you worked fewer hours and enjoyed more—more "things." But when you worked in a factory they expected you to be there at a certain time and leave when everyone else left. This was the most difficult part. In San'a it was possible to close your cobbler's shop whenever you got the desire to go off and read the Torah in the synagogue. Here "learning" was made very difficult. Once he tried leaving the factory because he wanted to go to the synagogue to "learn" for an hour or two, but they told him politely that this was not done. He must wait until a whistle blew or a bell rang.

Zivia is short, by European standards, with delicate wrists, slim ankles, high cheekbones, and a skin coloration of the deep suntan shade that many American women spend a great deal of time and money trying to acquire. Her eyelashes are long, her hair jet black. She wears a pleated blue skirt, a white shirtwaist, cotton stockings, and pointed black shoes. She braids her hair and then lets the single braid hang down over her delicately formed adolescent breasts. If she were in Yemen she would be thinking of marriage by now, but in Israel she is still a young girl. On the wall of the living room there is a picture of her graduating class in the primary school in which she finished the eighth and final grade last year. Now she has completed one year of an all-girls' secondary school called Or Hayim (Light of Life). Some of the pupils have scholarships, but Zivia is proud that her father so far has been able to pay the full tuition for her. (There is no free secondary education yet in Israel.) She studies Hebrew, the Bible (which includes the geography and history of her country), mathematics, English, natural science, and for three hours a day, dressmaking. She is undecided whether to make a career as a dressmaker or kindergarten teacher. But one thing is certain: she is going to have a career. Her large dark eyes sparkle when she tells about it. Her father smiles as he listens to this very independent girl talk. It is a measure of the change that Israel has wrought in him that he has permitted her to go to secondary school, for by Yemenite tradition education is only for males. It is also significant that he is allowing her to make up her own mind about a career. The pupils in Zivia's school are divided between girls whose parents came from Europe and girls whose parents came from North Africa and Arabia. But there are no barriers between them and they play, study, dance the hora, and sing their Israeli songs happily together.

When Zivia is asked if she is happy in Israel she looks a little perplexed, then smiles shyly and says, "Happy? Of course I am happy. This is my land, where I belong."

It is a long way from Theodor Herzl to Zivia Habshush. It is even a long way from Rachel, who died that the State might live, to Zivia, who lives because the State did not die.

They Came From Everywhere has been a story of dreamers and doers; a story of the promise made and the promise denied; a story of blood, tears, hope deferred, and finally, victory secured. It really is the story of Zivia, who will always be exactly the age of the State; Zivia, who was brought back as a child to the land from which her ancestors fled because her parents believed that it was all written that way in the Book. But the Great Ingathering, of which she was a one-millionth part, would never have been possible without the dreaming and the doing of the other eleven, and of thousands like them.

Because of them, Israel lives.

Bibliography

These books are recommended for more details on the lives of the twelve herein portrayed.

CHAPTER 1.
Theodore Herzl, A. Bein, Jewish Publ. Society.
Theodor Herzl, I. Cohen, Yoseloff.
Diaries of Theodor Herzl, M. Lowenthal, Dial.
Altneuland, Herzl, Haifa Publs. Co.

CHAPTER 2.
Tongue of the Prophets, R. St. John, Doubleday.
Hebrew Revived, H. Lehrman, Midstream.

CHAPTER 3.
Rebel & Statesman, J. B. Schechtman, Yoseloff.
Fighter & Prophet, J. B. Schechtman, Yoseloff.

CHAPTER 4.
The Szolds of Lombard Street, A. Levin, Jewish Publ. Soc.
Woman of Valor, I. Fineman, Simon & Schuster.
Henrietta Szold, M. K. Freund, Reconstructionist.
H. Szold, Life & Letters, M. Lowenthal.

CHAPTER 5.
Trail & Error, Weizmann, Harper.
Chaim Weizmann, I. Berlin, Farrar.
Hollow Glory, S. Shihor, Yoseloff.

CHAPTER 6.
Guardians of Our Heritage, L. Jung, Bloch.
Banner of Jerusalem, J. Agus, Bloch.

CHAPTER 7.
The Return to the Soil, A. Bein, Zionist Org.
The Rothschilds, F. Morton, Atheneum.
The House of Rothschild, Count Corti, Gollancz.

CHAPTER 8.
A Village by the Jordan, J. Baratz, Harvill.
The Wild Goats of Ein Gedi, H. Weiner, Doubleday.
Sound the Great Trumpet, M. Z. Frank, Whittier.

CHAPTER 9.
Orde Wingate, C. Sykes, World.
Gideon Goes to War, L. Mosley, Scribner's.

CHAPTER 10.
Ben-Gurion, R. St. John, Doubleday.
The Establishment of a State, Sacher, British Book Center.

CHAPTER 11.
Siege in the Hills of Hebron, D. Knohl, Yoseloff.
The Edge of the Sword, N. Lorch, Putnam.
A Clash of Destinies, J. & D. Kimche, Praeger.

CHAPTER 12.
Israel Today, R. Gruber, Hill & Wang.

ALSO:
A Gallery of Zionist Profiles, L. Lipsky, Farrar, (containing sketches of many of the 12).

Acknowledgments

In addition to the authors and publishers whose books are listed in the Bibliography, thanks are extended to the following persons for helping in various ways in the preparation of these 12 stories:

Col. Chaim Ben-David, Prime Minister's Military Secretary
Baron Edmond de Rothschild, Paris and Geneva
Professor Tcharna Rayss, Hebrew University
Dr. A. Bein, Zionist Central Archives
Rabbi Alexander Safran, Geneva
Boris Guriel, curator, Weizmann Archives
Dola Ben Yehuda Wittman, New York
Moshe Shilo, director of Military Archives
Teddy Kollek, Director General, Prime Minister's Office
Eri Jabotinsky, Haifa
Joseph B. Schechtman, New York
Jerome J. Jacobson, Geneva
Rena Kishnir, Hadassah Hospital, Jerusalem
Dr. Reuben Hecht, Dagon, Haifa
Abraham Weinshall, Haifa
David Landor, director, Government Press Office
Malka Schulewitz, Hadassah, Jerusalem
Joshua Manoah, Degania
Jakov Palmoni, Degania
Schuma Lulav, Degania
Micha Kaufman, Military Archives
Stefa Wachtel, Hebrew University
Dr. Yaakov Weinshall, Tel Aviv
Jack Padwa, Tel Aviv
Rinna Samuel, Weizmann Institute
Dr. A. Frenkel, Government Press Office
Haim Zohar, Government Press Office
David Solomon, Government Press Office
Fritz Cohn, Government Press Office

Index